Baseball's First
Colored World Series

Baseball's First Colored World Series

The 1924 Meeting of the Hilldale Giants and Kansas City Monarchs

LARRY LESTER

McFarland & Company, Inc., Publishers

Jefferson, North Carolina

The present work is a reprint of the illustrated case bound edition of Baseball's First Colored World Series: The 1924 Meeting of the Hilldale Giants and Kansas City Monarchs, *first published in 2006 by McFarland.*

LIBRARY OF CONGRESS CATALOGUING-IN-PUBLICATION DATA

Lester, Larry.
Baseball's first colored world series : the 1924 meeting of
the Hilldale Giants and Kansas City Monarchs / Larry Lester.
p.   cm.
Includes index.

ISBN 978-0-7864-9557-3 (softcover : acid free paper) ∞
ISBN 978-0-7864-8736-3 (ebook)

1. Hilldale Club (Baseball team)   2. Kansas City Monarchs
(Baseball team)   3. Negro leagues—History.   4. Baseball—
United States—History.   I. Title.
GV875.H52L47 2014   796.357'6408996073—dc22   2006014351

BRITISH LIBRARY CATALOGUING DATA ARE AVAILABLE

On the cover: (top) 1924 Kansas City Monarchs (NoirTech Research);
(bottom) 1924 Hilldale Giants at Hilldale Park in Darby, PA
(Wm. Cash & Lloyd Thompson Collection, provided through the courtesy
of the African American Museum in Philadelphia)

Printed in the United States of America

*McFarland & Company, Inc., Publishers
Box 611, Jefferson, North Carolina 28640
www.mcfarlandpub.com*

"The Negro Leagues—Where baseball is as black as the Blues"
— Larry Lester

Acknowledgments

Several years ago, John Sanford, a scientist at the New York State Agricultural Experimentation Station in Geneva, developed the impeccable strawberry. The strawberry was a crossbreeding of two common varieties. It was disease resistant, large, regular in shape, not too hard or soft and supposed to be very tasty. Nevertheless, Sanford was unable to sell his perfect produce to the public. Why? The color of the berry's skin was black.

Despite the complexion of this publication, the people below assisted me in enjoying the fruits of my labor, through motivation, ideas, references, editing and a sincere commitment to tell the genuine story of the first colored World Series.

Writers: Ocania Chalk (McConnell, South Carolina) for his inspiration to write this story from a black man's perspective; Dick Clark (Ypsilanti, Michigan) for cross-checking the facts and figures throughout this manuscript; Bob Davids (Washington, D.C.) for his tutoring me in the art of research; John Holway (Alexandria, Virginia) for his inspiration to stay the task; and Jerry Malloy (Mundelein, Illinois) for his constant encouragement and attention to the minute details of this work.

Editors: Valcinia Lester, Christine Riccelli, Brenda Ward, Signe Shivers (Madison, Wisconsin), Marilyn Taylor (Ypsilanti, Michigan), Leslie Heaphy (Canton, Ohio), and Dick Clark (Ypsilanti, Michigan).

Researchers: Patsy Amory and Horace Peterson of the Black Archives of Mid-America (Kansas City, Missouri), Chuck Haddix of the Marr Sound Archives (Kansas City), Deborah Dandridge of the Kansas Collections, Spencer Research Center, Kansas University (Lawrence), Stan Arnold of the African American Museum (Philadelphia), Ernestine Strickland of Huston-Tillotson College (Austin, Texas), and Michael Thompson (Norman, Oklahoma).

Obituary research: Elizabeth Smith (Kansas City), Paul Debono (Cincinnati), Wayne Stivers (Evergreen, Colorado), Bob Bailey (Newton, Pennsylvania), John Russell (Boca Raton, Florida).

Former players and family members: Newt Allen, James "Cool Papa" Bell, Gene Benson, Chet and Tyna Brewer, Willard "Home Run" Brown, Alan "Lefty" Bryant, Joseph Craig, Jimmie Crutchfield, Saul Davis, Mrs. (John) Vera Drew, Frank Duncan, III, Wilmer Fields, George Giles, Willie Grace, Herman "Doc" Horn, Monte Irvin, Connie Johnson, Judy Johnson, Jim "Lefty" LaMarque, Walter "Buck" Leonard, Max Manning, John "Buck" O'Neil, Ted Page, Wilbur S. Rogan Jr., Alfred Surratt, Mrs. Clinton Thomas, Lloyd Thompson, Quincy Trouppe, Ted "Double Duty" Radcliffe, Normal "Tweed" Webb, Vernon Wells, Sr., and Jesse Williams.

Librarians from the Kansas City Public Library: Vivian A. Bell, Kelly Dugan, Velma Elion, Dianne Greene, Brenda Honeycutt, Theresa Pacheco, Keith Smith, Theora Stevenson, and Patricia Torres.

Other contributors: Luis Alvelo (Puerto Rico), Leo Ernstein, Melvyn McCalla (Darby, Pennsylvania), Luis Munoz (Allentown, Pennsylvania), Kazuo Samaya (Japan), David Skinner (Bisbee, Arizona), Sellie Truitt (Kansas City, Kansas), James Wiggins (Philadelphia) and the John Coates file.

Table of Contents

Preface

Many of us are afraid of the dark, the absence of light. To many it represents the unknown, the mysterious. To others, the darkness with its unknown treasures represents a challenge. I am one of several who found this challenge in confronting the darkness enveloping the Negro Leagues. In meeting that challenge I have attempted to recreate for history the leagues as they were — in spite of frustrating difficulties, including the loss of administrative and statistical records for the league and its players.

Many will agree that baseball has been a mirror image of our society's state of consciousness and; hence the label "Our National Pastime." America's acceptance of racial inferiority and its lengthy obedience in segregated and discriminatory practices toward African Americans have been well documented. Until 1947, for more than half a century, this country's collective consciousness could not find its way between baseball's white foul lines. For years, legions of black athletes labored in obscurity, awaiting baseball's triple crown of recognition, respect and redemption. They waited patiently and faithfully for the opportunity to showcase their skills, only to be refused entry into the white major leagues by a "gentlemen's agreement."

What baseball's gatekeepers failed to realize is that institutional racism cannot be validated by unanimous consent. A player's race as sole criterion for admission into any major league is, and always will be, inadequate. Indeed, some of yesterday's baseball executives acknowledge the extraordinary talents of these great black players whose slim hopes of integration were regularly prefaced by the dubious compliment: "If you were only white."

This hidden heritage of black ball players repeatedly has denied them their rightful stature in baseball history. References to black baseball have seldom gone beyond the media's saturation of the Jackie Robinson unveiling, along with a passing mention of Satchel Paige's pitching or Josh Gibson's hitting or Cool Papa Bell's speed. For baseball to recognize the white major leagues and ignore the contributions and accomplishments of Negro League players is like one hand clapping. At times, even today, baseball's black past can be seen with blinders on.

I am an advocate and activist for recognition of these "invisible men" into baseball's finest memorial, the Hall of Fame, and the acceptance of these forgotten athletes has been a sensitive subject for baseball fans everywhere. The oral history of these outstanding athletes had long been the only source for verification of their accomplishments. Searching for statistical support of their feats largely has been an exercise in frustration.

This exercise was vividly expressed by Robert Peterson in his classic book, *Only the Ball Was White*:

> Tracing the course of the organized Negro Leagues is rather like trying to follow a single black strand through a ton of spaghetti. The footing is unfirm and the strand has a tendency to break off in one's hand and slither back into the amorphous mass.

Many cynics have claimed that these records do not exist and players' credibility can never be established. These same critics contend African Americans were apathetic about their heritage and therefore did not record players' achievements and contributions to baseball. Such historical assassination of these fine athletes has inspired me to prove these critics wrong with facts and figures.

To that end, I have gathered box scores of every game played in the 1924 season from each league, the Negro National League and the Eastern Colored League. In addition, with interviews of former players, their families, former umpires and lifelong fans, I have gathered personal information about most participants of the 1924 season. Through these efforts I have compiled personal profiles and several statistical tables similar to those found in major league press guides, baseball encyclopedias and other baseball publications.

I am persuaded that the completeness of this project will shed some light in examining the representative quality of these players. I hope my ordeal will encourage the incorporation of more worthy black professionals into Cooperstown's National Baseball Hall of Fame and Museum, baseball encyclopedias, Topps, Fleer and Donruss baseball cards and other important baseball media. Optimistically, Casey Stengel's expression "You can look it up!" will someday apply to the records of Negro League players.

Sadly, this species of baseball player is vanishing faster than the American bald eagle — with no recourse. When I began writing this book, there were only two surviving members of the 1924 World Series: Judy Johnson, 90, living in a nursing home, and Clint Thomas, 93, partially blind and suffering from various old age ailments. Judy Johnson died in the final stages of this writing. Johnson, known for his intelligence and finesse as a player, wrote his lasting legacy in a June 26, 1989, letter to *Sports Illustrated*, praising a story about a reunion of former Negro Leaguers. In part, he expressed, "Negro league players of the earlier decade unfortunately were not recipients of enormous commercial residuals and bonuses. We played for something greater that could not be measured in dollars and cents. The secrets of our game were to enjoy and endure."

The players enjoyed the game, but their endurance was tested by the indignities of segregated public accommodations and common law racism. These black pioneers had tough skins and tender hearts, as joy and pain, pride and prejudice symbolized their baseball travels. Johnson adds, "Sometimes your heart may ache, but you can't let it get you down. There's always a better day coming. It was worth it. It taught you to be a man, a gentleman in every respect, how to treat your fellow man because a lot of things are said, and called to you. If you overlook it, why, you feel better the next day, and you get away from it." Major league baseball may have stripped players like Johnson of their human rights, but could not deny them their humanity.

My research has shown that the great Negro Leaguers were not the best *colored* ballplayers but simply the best ballplayers, black or white. They were often compared to their white counterparts, but never shared their celebrity status. As Satchel Paige once recalled, "Oh, we had men by the hundreds who could have made the big leagues, by the hundreds, not by the fours, twos or threes. They had a lot of Satchel Paiges out there — men who could throw the ball as hard as me. Ain't no maybe so about it."

History is slowly changing to recognize that not all our heroes were white. The saga of African Americans participating in baseball dates to the post–Civil War era, with the Philadelphia Pythians ball club. Our current history could lead many to believe black players were introduced to the game in 1947, the year of Jackie Robinson's debut. This blindness has caused a rich and exciting chapter of baseball history to vanish into history's black hole.

Do great moundsmen like Chet Brewer, Leon Day, "Bullet" Rogan, John Donaldson, Willie Foster, "Cannonball" Dick Redding, Nip Winters or "Smokey" Joe Williams sound familiar? Where in the record books can we find the great ebony sluggers like "Bingo" DeMoss, Pete Hill, "Biz" Mackey, "Turkey" Stearnes, Spottswood Poles or a Willie Wells? These great players were only an owner's "attitude" away from prime time. Sadly, their relative anonymity, even today, is a cruel joke on all of us.

When the legendary Leroy "Satchel" Paige accepted his Hall of Fame plaque in Cooperstown in 1971, he reported, "There were many Satchels and there were many Joshes." Yes, indeed there were! Would baseball be baseball without the contributions of the Black Barons' Willie Mays, or the Clowns' Hank Aaron, or the Elite Giants' Roy Campanella, or the Eagles' Monte Irvin and Larry Doby, or the Monarchs' Ernie Banks and Jackie Robinson? These men were products of the Negro Leagues and are now enshrined in baseball's finest memorial — the National Baseball Hall of Fame. These gifted players would have remained invisible, unappreciated and ignored had they played during baseball's socially retarded Jim Crow era. Their abilities, like other great black ball players, were only limited by the lack of opportunity — an opportunity denied to them because of skin color.

Other ebony stars were not great men in the ubiquitous sense in which we judge greatness. But history has never been reserved for just great men and great women. History is all about the people we know and cherish. Some of their stories and their contributions will be told here.

You will find these men of color represented in every segment of our American culture. Whatever their background, they shared one aspiration: to play in the big leagues. However, these aspiring men could only dream about the major leagues. While the dreamers are vanishing, their dreams live — on microfilmed newspapers, faded photographs and yellowed scorecards and programs. They live etched in the minds of baseball historians and true fans, who recognize talented ball players and teams regardless of skin color or social boundaries. A dream conceived in truth never dies.

Most Americans have grown past the negative folk tales, the racial stereotypes and a time when our beloved game of peanuts and Cracker Jacks issued tickets saying "By Invitation Only." The precious loss of this dark chapter of baseball history is not only about skin color. It's also about heroes and a way of life which is gone forever. A way of life whose legacy, sad as it may be, will be denied to a new breed of fans of all colors. My research at times brought heartfelt tears, as I would discover forgotten heroes of a past generation, invisible heroes of this generation, and new heroes for future generations to come.

Basically, the research was done before the Internet, e-mail and cell phones, between 1985 and 1990. I stopped researching because of a commitment to start and build the Negro Leagues Baseball Museum in Kansas City, Missouri.

I was inspired to write this story because of a 1924 Colored World Series photograph I found in Kansas City. I wanted to find out everything about each man pictured in the photograph and how this World Series came to fruition. I wanted to know every detail of the pennant race and who played the major and minor roles in the creation of this historic first.

I reviewed microfilmed copies of the *Kansas City Call, Kansas City Star, Kansas City Post-Journal*, the *Chicago Defender*, the *Chicago Whip, St. Louis Argus, St. Louis Post-Dispatch*, the *Birmingham Reporter, Memphis Commercial Appeal*, the *Cleveland Gazette, Indianapolis Recorder* and the *Washington Tribune*, among other newspapers, to track the travels of the Monarchs that season.

To cover the Hilldale Club, I researched the *Baltimore Afro-American*, the *New York Interstate-Tattler* and several Philadelphia newspapers, including the *Tribune*, the *Record* and the *Inquirer,* and others.

Trips to Indianapolis, St. Louis and Philadelphia were needed to fill in details. I spent five days in Philadelphia and Darby, Pennsylvania. I traveled each day by street car (or trolley) to Darby to interview relatives of Hilldale players in their homes and in restaurants and bars, where several photographs of the first World Series were proudly hung. I researched the Wm. Cash & Lloyd Thompson Collection at the African American Museum in Philadelphia and found the last two missing box scores, and at night I studied microfilm at Temple University. One night I stayed until the library closed at midnight. I tried to call a cab but was told by the janitorial staff that cabs did not come into that neighborhood after dark. So I tried to walk back to my hotel until a police cruiser pulled over and the officer escorted my poor black soul to the hotel.

All in all, my time machine journey into 1924 was extremely rewarding and set the stage for future research. I found the evidence of a story just waiting to be rediscovered. This challenged me to change my view toward hidden history. African Americans are not apathetic about recording their history. It's there, and it always has been, just waiting to be discovered. Discover greatness! Discover the greatness surrounding the creation of the first World Series in Black America.

No matter what your ethnic or racial roots are, the time has come to correct this vacuum in sports history. We must stop working with what is wrong and start working with what is right. No longer can we argue about who is right, but what is right. It is time for baseball to stop balking at inclusion of the Negro Leagues and its great black players into baseball's mainstream. It is time to let this hidden history enter America's game and get "off the bench." It is time to allow the forgotten African American player to step to the plate and take his swing. It is time for baseball to play ball — and play fair!

> "I remember standing alone at first base — the only black man on the field. I had to fight hard against loneliness, abuse, and the knowledge that any mistake I made would be magnified because I was the only black man out there. I had to fight hard to become just another guy." — Jackie Robinson

Note from the Author

The words "colored" or "Negro" are employed throughout *Baseball's First Colored World Series* because these were the terms that prevailed in common usage when events described in this text took place. Far from intending to make a political statement, I merely hope to recreate the spirit, attitude and sentiment of the period.

1

The Makings of the First Colored World Series

"Racism is so universal in this country, so widespread and deep-seated, that it is invisible because — it is so normal."
— Shirley Chisholm, congresswoman

Black baseball's trip down the Yellow Brick Road started in 1920, the first year of the Negro National League. It was the initial year of the Roaring Twenties, a decade of unbelievable excess, limitless possibilities and unprecedented social changes. The era was marked by prohibition of liquor, the resurgence of literature by black writers (now called the Harlem Renaissance by historians), increased technological ingenuity and the massive campaign by Marcus Garvey's Black Star Line to encourage colored folks to return to Africa.

Dramatic social changes were apparent in women's flapper fashions and clean-shaven men, promotions of black-faced white comedians, the introduction of motion pictures with sound and censorship, the revival of violence by white supremacist groups, and liberated women smoking cigarettes and seeking voting rights.

Additionally, the advancement of easy credit, an economic boom in ownership of new products (autos, phones and radios), increased union membership, and the crashing of stock prices on Wall Street were all phenomena of the period.

The 1920s were also known as the Golden Age of Sports. Babe Ruth smashed sixty round trippers (1927) and baby doctor Dr. Benjamin Spock won an Olympic gold medal in rowing (1924). The National Football League made its debut (1922) as running back Harold "Red" Grange ruled the gridiron. The creation of the Harlem Rens (1922) basketball team dominated the orange ball circuit. Major league baseball had its first radio broadcast (1921), with the Chicago American Giants becoming the first team to wear permanent uniform numbers (1928). Meanwhile the red, white and blue Harlem Globetrotters (1927) formed their magic circle to the sounds of "Sweet Georgia Brown." Faithfully the sport of boxing presented one of many future "great white hopes" in the mold of the Manassa Mauler, Jack Dempsey. In 1924, future Negro League officer DeHart Hubbard became the first African American to win an Olympic gold medal (in the long jump).

A significant sporting event that has been ignored through the years is the 1924 Colored World Series. In retrospect, the lifestyles, attitudes and expectations of Americans played a prominent role in its creation. Social and economic changes encompassed the formation of the series.

The year 1924 was when Congress made all people of Indian ancestry United States citizens. A year when Wyoming, the home of Yellowstone National Park, elected Nellie Taylor Ross, and Texas, with its celebrated bluebonnets, elected Miriam (Ma) Ferguson as this country's first women governors. A year when black congresswomen Shirley Chisholm and Patricia Roberts Harris along with jazzy blues singers (the Sassy) Sarah Vaughan and Dinah (the Queen) Washington were born. And a year when the gifted George Gershwin wrote his epic "Rhapsody in Blue." Lastly, it was a year when Rutgers scholar-athlete and black activist Paul Robeson starred in his first film, *Body and Soul*. Twenty years later Robeson would turn blue in the face in his attempts to pressure Commissioner Kenesaw Mountain Landis to end discrimination in major league baseball.

This was a time when a three-story house with hardwood floors sold for $13,000 to $20,000. When the Harlem-based Black Swan Records Company offered the latest soul sounds for 30 cents a copy and a boy's baseball uniform sold for $4.50. When a shiny black Ford touring sedan, complete with five blackwall tires, could be purchased for less than a grand. When tangerine, watermelon, powder blue and reseda were the popular summer colors for women's dresses. A time when phone numbers were composed of two-letter prefixes with four digits and postal codes were a single number. And it was a time when all telephones were black, all bank checks were green, and all bathtubs and baseballs were white.

This year pitted the champions from the Negro National League against the champions of the Eastern Colored League. It was the inaugural year of the Colored World Series, played between the Monarchs from Kansas City, Missouri, and the Hilldale Club from Darby, Pennsylvania.

As we approach the first championship series between two black leagues, the spawning of the series resulted in many pretenders to the Wizard's throne. Among the pretenders were giants Andrew "Rube" Foster and Edward Bolden, commissioners of the Negro National and Eastern Colored Leagues. Lacking the heart, the courage and the wisdom, each man, with rhetorical mirrors, tried to manipulate the trip to the Emerald City for his own financial and political advantage.

The Yellow Brick Road was first paved in May 1887, when the Negro Base Ball

League was formed with eight teams. The league lasted roughly a month, with games played by the Boston Resolutes, Philadelphia Pythians, New York Gorhams, Pittsburgh Keystones, the Baltimore Lord Baltimores and the Louisville Fall Citys. Two teams, the Washington Capitol City and the Cincinnati Browns, failed to open their season due to several rain cancellations.

Another attempt to organize a league was led by J.W. "Bud" Fowler in 1902. It was the 12-team Afro-American National Base Ball League, with five teams from Illinois, three teams from Indiana, two teams from Tennessee, and one each from Missouri and Kentucky. The league failed to get off the ground.

Rube Foster: Genius touched his soul, for a black league was his goal. As a genius, Foster had answers to questions before they were asked. He had the vision to see the unforeseeable. In 1920, he, along with other team owners, created the Negro National League, the first all black league to survive a full season (NoirTech Research).

The next detour came in 1906, when the International League of Independent Baseball Clubs, which had four black and two white teams, struggled through part of a season characterized by shifting and collapsing franchises. Four years later, Beauregard Moseley, an attorney and secretary of Chicago's Leland Giants, attempted to form a National Negro Baseball League of America, but the association folded before a single game was played.

The fizzled league, with a $300 membership fee, was originally composed of teams from Birmingham, Alabama; Memphis, Tennessee; Louisville, Kentucky; West Baden and Indianapolis, Indiana; Oklahoma City, Oklahoma; Kansas City, Kansas; and Chicago, Illinois. At the time, a structured plan appeared promising. But Moseley failed to consider a missing ingredient — the support of white booking agents and their wealthy investors.

In November of 1913, several Chicago businessmen filed articles of incorporation to establish the Negro Colored Baseball League. The league was to consist of teams from Chicago, New York, Philadelphia, Detroit, Baltimore, Cleveland and St. Louis. Tom C. McNamee of Pierre, South Dakota, led the effort, along with Walter M. Farmer, who would later team with Rube Foster to create the Negro National League in 1920. There were no league games reportedly played in 1914.

Emerging from this era was the Negro National League, also known as the Western Circuit, with a similar geographical makeup. Initially known as the National Association of Colored Professional Base Ball Clubs, the new organization marked the latest attempt, since the Emancipation Pro-

J.L. Wilkinson: Innovation and creativity were attributes of the Negro National League's only white owner. Future Hall of Fame writer Wendell Smith wrote, "There is no owner in the country — white or Negro — who has operated more honestly, sincerely or painstakingly" (NoirTech Research).

clamation, by free men of color to create and perform in their own viable league. The league consisted of two teams from Chicago, one each from Indianapolis, Kansas City, St. Louis, Detroit, and Dayton, plus the traveling Cuban Stars.

On February 13, 1920, in Kansas City, Missouri at the YMCA at 19th and Paseo, the first meeting was held. Located in Kansas City's jazz district, the YMCA was funded by noted Jewish philanthropist Julius Rosenwald. Rosenwald had provided $25,000 seed money for the $100,000 brick structure, with the balance coming from cooperative fund-raising efforts from black and white community groups.

The Negro National League was the brainchild of Andrew "Rube" Foster, who years earlier had created the Chicago American Giants ball club. His players were well paid and traveled stylishly in private Pullman coaches. Despite the first-class service, Foster would often lose players in their search for higher pay. He would complain about players "contract jumping"—leaving for another team despite any verbal agreement, contract or moral obligations. Rube felt a structured league would remedy this predicament and envisioned a black league with black owners.

As expected, Foster was elected acting president of the new league. Ironically, he was nominated for league president by Tenny Blount, who years later would try to impeach Foster for the mishandling of league funds. Rounding out the executive staff of this frontier league were J. Leslie Wilkinson as secretary and C.I. Taylor as treasurer. Wilkinson, as the only white owner in the league, endured some criticism. Historically, many white owners had employed carnival methods to promote the game and enticed players to perform circus-like baseball acts to entertain fans. Wilkinson's ability to book games in Association Park, home of the Kansas City Blues, and his ownership experience with the multi-ethnic All Nations Club, coupled with a sound baseball team built from the 25th Infantry Regiment (that didn't do vaudeville) proved to be too enticing for the other owners to ignore. The team representatives were: Foster for the Chicago American Giants, Joe Green for the Chicago Giants, John Matthews for the Dayton Marcos, John Tenny Blount for the Detroit Stars, Charles Ishum Taylor for the Indianapolis ABCs, Wilkinson for the Kansas City Monarchs, W.A. Kelly and Lorenzo S. Cobb for the St. Louis Giants and Foster representing Agustin Molina's Cuban Stars.

The original league constitution also included associated membership with the Hilldale Club from Darby, Pennsylvania, the Atlantic City Bacharach Giants and the Cuban Stars from the East. The associated members paid an inflated good-faith deposit of $1,000, twice the amount paid by the charter teams. To everyone's surprise, at the end of the meeting Foster revealed he had incorporation papers from six states: Illinois, Maryland, Michigan, New York, Ohio and Pennsylvania.

Each team paid a $500 entry fee binding them to the league's constitution. Prominent newspaper reporters Dave Wyatt from the *Chicago Whip*, Elwood C. Knox from *The* (Indianapolis) *Freeman*, Charles Marshall of the *Indianapolis*

STATE OF ILLINOIS

OFFICE OF
THE SECRETARY OF STATE

To all to whom these Presents Shall Come, Greeting:

Whereas, a STATEMENT OF INCORPORATION, duly signed, acknowledged and verified under oath, has been filed in the Office of the Secretary of State, on the _18th_ day of _November_ A.D. 19 _24_ for the organization of the

THE NEGRO NATIONAL LEAGUE OF PROFESSIONAL BASEBALL CLUBS

under and in accordance with the provisions of "AN ACT IN RELATION TO CORPORATIONS FOR PECUNIARY PROFIT" approved June 28, 1919, and in force July 1, 1919, and all acts amendatory thereof, a copy of which statement is hereto attached.

Now Therefore, I, LOUIS L. EMMERSON, Secretary of State of the State of Illinois, by virtue of the powers and duties vested in me by law, do hereby certify that the said

THE NEGRO NATIONAL LEAGUE OF PROFESSIONAL BASEBALL CLUBS

is a legally organized Corporation under the laws of this State.

In Testimony Whereof, I hereto set my hand and cause to be affixed the Great Seal of the State of Illinois. Done at the City of Springfield this _18th_ day of _November_ A.D. 19 _24_ and of the Independence of the United States the one hundred and _49th._

SEAL

LOUIS L. EMMERSON

Incorporation Papers: On November 18, 1924, the Negro National League was incorporated as The Negro National League of Professional Baseball Clubs. One hundred shares of capital stock worth $2,500 were issued, with 40 shares going to Willie Foster, 20 shares apiece to Rube Foster and J.L. Wilkinson, 15 shares to Russell Thompson and five shares to Walter M. Farmer (NoirTech Research).

Box......**1779**.. No.......**124748**

Articles of Incorporation

of

......THE. NEGRO. NATIONAL. LEAGUE. OF
PROFESSIONAL BASEBALL CLUBS

....

.............CHICAGO..............

Capital Stock, - - $.....**2500.00**.......

Duration.........**fifty**...........years

FILED

NOV 1 8 1924

Louis L. Emmerson
SECY. OF STATE

(19762-5M+24) 9-

(16237—10M—6—24)

(THIS STATEMENT MUST BE FILED IN DUPLICATE)

PAID

NOV 18 1924

$ 20⁰⁰ ___

7 ⁵⁰ **F.T.**

STATE OF ILLINOIS,

Cook _____ County, } ss.

To LOUIS L. EMMERSON, Secretary of State:

We, the undersigned, adult citizens of the United States, at least one of whom is a citizen of Illinois,

NAME	NUMBER	STREET	ADDRESS	CITY	STATE
Willie Foster	3342-44 Indiana Ave., Chicago, Illinois.				
Russell Thompson	3342-44 Indiana Ave., Chicago, Illinois.				
Walter M. Farmer	184 W. Washington St., Chicago, Illinois.				

propose to form a corporation under an Act of the General Assembly of the State of Illinois, entitled, "An Act in relation to corporations for pecuniary profit," approved June 28, 1919, in force July 1, 1919; and all Acts amendatory thereof: and, for the purpose of such organization, we hereby state as follows, to-wit: OK

1. The name of such corporation is THE NEGRO NATIONAL LEAGUE OF PROFESSIONAL
BASEBALL CLUBS

2. The object for which it is formed is

Section 1. This organization has for its objects, the organizing, equiping and maintaining Baseball Clubs, composed of Colored Professional baseball players, sufficient to constitute and form a Circuit for the playing of championship games among the clubs belonging to THE NEGRO NATIONAL LEAGUE OF PROFESSIONAL BASEBALL CLUBS.

Its further object shall be to protect and promote the mutual interests of Colored professional baseball clubs belonging to THE NEGRO NATIONAL LEAGUE OF PROFESSIONAL BASEBALL CLUBS as well as Colored Professional Baseball Players.
Section 2. To establish and regulate professional baseball championship games under the supervision of the the Board of Control of THE NEGRO NATIONAL LEAGUE OF PROFESSIONAL BASEBALL CLUBS.

Section 3. To maintain and own by purchase, gift or otherwise, amusement parks or buildings for the carrying out of the objects and purposes of THE NEGRO NATIONAL LEAGUE OF PROFESSIONAL BASEBALL CLUBS.

3. The duration of the corporation is   Fifty (50) years   Years

4. The location of the principal office is 3342-44 Indiana   Avenue

City of Chicago _____, County of ____ Cook and _____ State of Illinois.

5. The total authorized capital stock is { Preferred $_____ } and _____ shares of
{ Common $2500.00 }

{ Preferred }
{ Common } without par value.

6. The amount of each share having a par value is $25.00

7. The number of shares having a par value is One hundred (100)

8. The number of shares of no par value is

9.   The name and address of the subscribers to the capital stock, and the amount subscribed and paid in by each, are as follows:

NAME	ADDRESS				NUMBER OF SHARES	AMOUNT SUB-SCRIBED	AMOUNT PAID IN
	NUMBER	STREET	CITY	STATE			
Willie Foster	3342	Indiana Ave.,			40	$1000.00	$1000.00
		Chicago, Ill.					
Russell Thompson	3342	Indiana Ave.,					
		Chicago, Ill.			15	$ 375.	$ 375.00
Walter M. Farmer	184 W.	Washington St.,					
		Chicago, Ill.			5	125.	125.00
Andrew R. Foster	3342	Indiana Ave.,					
		Chicago, Ill.			20	500.	500.00
J.L. Wilkinson	4118	Agness St.,					
		Kansas City, Mo.			20	500.	500.00

10.

Amount of capital stock which it is proposed to issue at once:

   (a) On shares having no par value _____ Preferred $_____ / Common $_____

   (b) On shares having a par value of $25.00 _____ Preferred $_____ / Common $2500.00

12. Amount of capital stock actually paid in:

   (a) On shares having no par value _____ Preferred $_____ / Common $_____

   (b) On shares having a par value of $25.00 _____ Preferred $_____ / Common $2500.00

13. Amount of capital stock paid in cash is _____ $2500.00

14. Capital stock paid in property, appraised as follows: _____ $_____

15. The location and a general description of such property is as follows: _____

_____

_____

_____

16. The management of the corporation shall be vested in ___5___ directors.

17. The name and address of the first board of directors, at least one of whom is a resident of Illinois, and the respective term for which elected are as follows:

NAME	ADDRESS				TERM FOR WHICH ELECTED
	NUMBER	STREET	CITY	STATE	
Willie Foster	3342	Indiana Ave.,	Chicago,	Ill.	One (1) year
Russell Thompson	3342	Indiana Ave.,	Chicago,	Ill.	One (1) year
Andrew R. Foster	3342	Indiana Ave.,	Chicago,	Ill.	One (1) year
Walter M. Farmer	184	W. Washington St.,	Chicago,	Ill.	One (1) year
J.L. Wilkinson	4118	Agness St.,	Kansas City,	Mo.	One (1) year

18. Subject to the conditions and limitations prescribed by "The General Corporation Act" of Illinois, this corporation shall have the following powers, rights and privileges:

To have succession by its corporate name for the period limited in its certificate of incorporation, or any amendment thereof:

To sue and be sued in its corporate name;

To have and use a common seal and alter the same at pleasure;

To have a capital stock of such an amount, and divided into shares with a par value, or without a par value, and to divide such capital stock into such classes, with such preferences, rights, values and interests as may be provided in the article of incorporation, or any amendment thereof;

To acquire, and to own, possess and enjoy so much real and personal property as may be necessary for the transaction of the business of such corporation, and to lease, mortgage, pledge, sell, convey or transfer the same; and to acquire and to own real property, improved or unimproved, for the purpose of providing homes for its employes or aiding its employes to acquire and own homes and to improve, lease, mortgage, contract to sell, convey the same, and to loan money to its employes for such purpose upon such terms as may be agreed upon;

To own, purchase or otherwise acquire, whether in exchange for the issuance of its own stock, bonds or other obligations or otherwise, and to hold, vote, pledge, or dispose of the stocks, bonds, and other evidences of indebtedness of any corporation, domestic or foreign.

To borrow money at such rate of interest as the corporation may determine without regard to or restrictions under any usury law of this State and to mortgage or pledge its property, both real and personal, to secure the payment thereof;

To elect officers, appoint agents, define their duties and fix their compensation;

To lease, exchange or sell all of the corporate assets with the consent of two-thirds of all of the outstanding capital stock of the corporation at any annual meeting or at any special meeting called for that purpose;

To make by-laws not inconsistent with the laws of this State for the administration of the business and interests of such corporation;

To conduct business in this State, or other states, the District of Columbia, the territories, possessions, and dependencies of the United States and in foreign countries and to have one or more offices out of this State, and to hold, purchase, mortgage, and convey real and personal property outside of this State necessary and requisite to carry out the object of the corporation;

In time of war to transact any lawful business in aid of the United States in the prosecution of war, to make donations to associations and organizations aiding in war activities and to loan money to the State or Federal government for war purposes;

To cease doing business and to surrender its charter;

To have and to exercise all the powers necessary and convenient to carry into effect the purpose for which such corporation is formed.

19. An estimate of the per cent. of tangible property of the corporation to be used in Illinois for the following year is _____100%_____

20. An estimate of the per cent. of the business of the corporation which will be transacted at or from places of business in Illinois for the following year is _____100%_____

21. Give the location of the principal places of business of the corporation for the following year and an estimate of the amount of business which will be transacted through each.

_____ Chicago, Illinois; no estimate _____

Willie Foster
Russell Thompson
Walter M. Farmer

Incorporators.

OATH AND ACKNOWLEDGMENT

STATE OF ILLINOIS,

COOK _____ County, } ss.

I, **Aug. L. Williams** _____ a Notary Public in and for the County and State aforesaid, do hereby certify that on the _____ **8th** _____ day of _____ **November** _____ A. D. 19 **24** , personally appeared before me **Willie Foster, Russell Thompson and Walter M. Farmer** _____

to me personally known to be the same persons who executed the foregoing and severally acknowledged that they executed the same for the purposes therein set forth, and being duly sworn hereby declared on oath that the foregoing statements made, subscribed and verified by them are true in substance and in fact.

In Witness Whereof, I have hereunto set my hand and seal the day and year above written.

Aug L. Williams

(Seal)   Notary Public.

CORPORATION FOR PECUNIARY PROFIT.

Fees payable in advance.

Statement of Incorporation of

THE NEGRO NATIONAL LEAGUE OF PROFESSIONAL BASEBALL CLUBS.

FILED

NOV 18 1924

Louis L. Emmerson
SECY. OF STATE

INCORPORATION FEES.

Initial fee of 1/20 of one per cent. on the authorized capital stock, with a minimum fee of $20.00, also franchise fee as required by Section 129 of the General Corporation Act.

*NOTE—In paragraph 10 you should set out a brief description of the rights and preferences of the holders of preferred stock, or any other provision or the regulation of the business and the conduct of the affairs of the corporation, in case of a building corporation you will also give in, the same space a specific and definite description of the site of such building. Before you delay read carefully each paragraph in the statement of the statement compare every recital in the before interpolating the data required. Before ment of the and so forth, whether or other balances with other and other recital relating to the same matter.

Ledger, and Cary B. Lewis from *The Chicago Defender* assisted the renowned Kansas attorney Elisha Scott in drawing up the new "Baseball bill of rights." Foster emphasized that Scott and the writers in attendance would handle the allocation of players to balance the talent within the league.

A 1916 graduate of Washburn Law School, the eloquent Scott was known for his courtroom wit and dramatic performances. One story that went the rounds of the local legal profession may be apocryphal. After Elisha Scott had exhausted all legal procedures for commutation of a client who had been sentenced to be electrocuted, the doomed client asked, "Mr. Scott, do you have any further advice?" Scott replied, "Yes, just don't sit down in that chair."

Elisha Scott: He wrote the Negro National League's solid constitution. The graduate of Washburn Law School was known for his charismatic courtroom wit and dramatization. Years later, his sons, John and Charles Scott, Sr., joined forces with future Supreme Court Justice Thurgood Marshall in the landmark case *Brown v. Board of Education*, involving integration of public schools (NoirTech Research).

Thankfully, Scott didn't lose many cases. In one of his first major cases, he won a desegregation case against the Board of Education of Weir City, Kansas, and later he presented a similar case of Victoria Thurman against the school board of Coffeyville, Kansas, to admit colored students. Among those to testify was George Sweatt, a teacher at Roosevelt Junior High and Kansas City Monarch outfielder. Accordingly, Scott won the case, but Sweatt lost his job.

One of Scott's most noteworthy clients was the ever-controversial Jack Johnson. He successfully defended the heavyweight champion before the Department of Justice for the District of Columbia on misdemeanor charges. A capital case involved application by the First National Bank of the historic black town of Boley, Oklahoma. He defeated the government's Department of Currency, causing the feds to grant, for the first time, a charter to a colored corporation for a national bank.

Thirty-four years later, in the family's tradition, Scott's sons, John J. and Charles Sheldon, Sr. represented the Linda Brown family of Topeka, Kansas, in the landmark Supreme Court case *Brown v. Board of Education*, involving integration of the public schools.

With the foundation laid by attorney Scott and Foster's administrative genius, black clubs enjoyed a decade of prosperity as some clubs acquired their own parks, traveled by stately Pullman coaches and drew comparatively high salaries for black workers. To the great satisfaction of many black businesses, local black papers, like the *Broad Ax*, *Chicago Whip* and *The Chicago Defender*, boasted of the new league outdrawing the Cubs and the White Sox. Foster had become the Wizard of the Western Circuit.

On March 2, 1920, in Atlanta, Georgia, Rube proposed a Southern League. The plan was for the league to work in conjunction with the white Southern League, with games scheduled in towns where Southern League teams played. Foster aspired to use their facilities while the white teams were on the road. Distinguished southern leaders represented at the meeting included: W.M. Brooke and Monroe D. Young of Knoxville, Tennessee; Mal Carl and Henry Brinson of Chattanooga, Tennessee; J.W. White and Marshall Garrett of Nashville, Tennessee; Dr. O.M. Thompson and J.R. Kennedy of Greenville, South Carolina; F.M. Purdue and L.L. Barber of Birmingham, Alabama; Henry Hannon of Montgomery, Alabama; Dan Brown of Pensacola, Florida; Godfrey Williams of Jacksonville, Florida; Fred Caulfield of New Orleans, Louisiana; and L.R. Lautier of Atlanta, Georgia.

A jubilant Lautier expressed: "We expect the league to be a financial success. And that *The Chicago Defender* would be a big factor in making it a go."* But the white Southern League teams refused to lease their stadium facilities to the black teams. The credibility of the new league was a day-to-day struggle.

The Southern League only completed one solid season, with the Knoxville

*Chicago Defender, March 6, 1920.

Oscar Charleston: Perhaps the league's top player, he was traded by Rube Foster to the Indianapolis ABCs to help create a more competitive balance of talent throughout the league. Other players involved in the musical chairs of skills included Pete Hill, Bruce Petway, Ed Wesley, Dick Whitworth, Jimmie Lyons, Walter Ball and John Beckwith (Courtesy of Kimshi Productions).

Giants beating out the Montgomery Gray Sox for the league championship. Afterwards the league mostly consisted of semipro teams playing local clubs for survival.

Back in the Midwest, resisting the urge to field a dominant team, Foster sought to stabilize the league, with the assistance of Elisha Scott. In an unusual display of cooperation among the owners, players were shifted between clubs to maintain a competitive balance of talent. As league president, Foster showed his true color by sending his premier player, Oscar Charleston, and a submarine pitcher, Dizzy Dismukes, to the revamped Indianapolis ABCs. The Chicago Giants received over-the-hill pitcher Walter Ball and power hitter John Beckwith. The

Detroit Stars got veteran Pete Hill, Bruce Petway, Ed Wesley, Dick Whitworth and Jimmie Lyons, while the Monarchs got former All-Nations pitchers Jose Mendez and John Donaldson.

For enduring personal sacrifices and hardships in formulating the league, Foster was hailed by writer Dave Wyatt as the "King of Baseball." In an April 1920 article for *The Defender*, Wyatt bragged:

> Foster broke up one of the greatest playing machines of all time. And citing the necessity of organization, he decided to advance a few strides farther in the game of sacrifice. When the idea of a foundation for a Colored Baseball League was conceived its sponsors at once hearkened to the popular demand for a circuit as evenly balanced in playing strength as was possible. It was seen that success could only be attained by the distribution of players so that each club in the circuit could at least acquire one, two or three players of such established prestige that it would at once arouse the interest of the public to a point where there could be no possible doubt of a complete evolution of antiquated ideas into a full realization of modern methods of baseball government.

Capitalizing on their successful meetings, the Western Circuit, which was originally scheduled to start on April Fool's Day in 1921, debuted a year earlier. On May 2, a long-lived dream became reality in Indianapolis, Indiana, only 82 days after the league constitution was written. Before 8,000 fans, C.I. Taylor's ABCs won the first league game. The alphabet team, behind the pitching of Ed Rile's seven-hitter, defeated 20-year barnstorming veteran Walter Ball and his Chicago Giants, 4–2.* Big-time black baseball had finally arrived upon the national scene.

Despite his benevolent reputation, Foster was a constant subject of controversy and criticism. In 1923, *The Chicago Defender* published an anonymous letter from a disgruntled ball player stating that Foster was taking more than his fair share of the gate receipts and at times paying his players less than the contractual rate. The anonymous writer also suggested the powerhouse American Giants did not play up to their full potential because of clubhouse dissension over low wages. The player further claimed this disharmony caused the team to lose its first league championship since its inception.

Unknown to the accuser, Foster had earlier in the season made arrangements with the black-owned Binga State Bank, founded by Jesse Binga, formerly a barber and Pullman porter, to bankroll his team. On May 4, he sent his captain, Bingo DeMoss, a letter announcing bonuses for the staff:

> Dear Mr. DeMoss:
> I wish that you would have the following men to call by the Binga State Bank, where they will find bank books made out to their credit: Elwood DeMoss, John Beckwith, James Brown, Leroy Grant, James Lyons, Robert L. Williams, Cristobal Torrienti, Floyd Gardner, Edward Rile, Louis Woodfolk and Richard Whitworth.

**Chicago Defender, May 15, 1920.*

Several of the men on our club deserve something not from present or past actions, but as long as they are good enough to be identified and retain the reputation as members of the American Giants baseball club, I feel that they are due some consideration.

This money that they will find to their credit at the bank is given gratis and will not be charged.

Yours Respectfully,

A.R. Foster

Additionally, other players were given unidentified sums of cash. Included in this group were three regular players who played less than twenty league games—one a sore-arm pitcher and two outfielders.

In review of the salary schedule of the 1923 American Giants roster, the lowest-paid player was at $175 a month. And in most cases, over the course of the season, each player had received bonuses of at least $1,100 and up to $3,000.

The average monthly salary of a black ballplayer in the early 1920s was $175 a month, from $75 for rookies to $375 for stars, with $1 to $1.50 a day for meal money. Meanwhile, major league white players typically received from $300 to $2,000 a month salary and about $15 a day for meals. Baseball wages compared to wages of about $80 a month for meat packing employees and $115 a month for government mail carriers for the period. In comparison, the federal government reports that the average income in 1924 was $1,266 per household or $105.50 per month.

Offering a substantial income for the period and with five years of somewhat consistent play, the league would be incorporated on November 18, 1924, and renamed the Negro National League of Professional Baseball Clubs with a total authorized common stock of $2,500. Each share of stock was worth $25. The original board of directors and stock-holders included Walter M. Farmer with five shares, Russell Thompson with 15 shares, and Andrew Foster and J.L. Wilkinson with 20 shares apiece. The politically astute Rube Foster named his 20-year-old brother, Willie Foster, as the majority stockholder of the corporation with 40 shares. Moreover, shareholders Willie Foster and Thompson listed 3342 Indiana Avenue as their address, in the same apartment complex as Rube.

Earlier, in 1923, against Rube's wishes, Willie had started his professional career with Bubbles Lewis' Memphis Red Sox. Initially, Rube had discouraged his younger brother from entering the sporting profession, citing extensive travel and inconsistent paydays as deterrents. Despite Rube's advice, Willie split his first two seasons with the Red Sox and Giants, and in his third pro season he shared time with the Giants and the Birmingham Black Barons. When Rube suffered a nervous breakdown in 1926, Willie came to the Chicago team, permanently, to oversee the kingdom's operations.

With the Negro National League firmly established with a solid constitution, the owners' primary concern was competition from another league. A competing league could entice players to abandon Rube's ship for higher pay. Probably the most important feature of the new constitution was Article 3, describing the league's policy on team jumpers:

> No player which has played with a club in either league for a season or part of a season shall be employed or permitted to play with a club in the same or other league during the season immediately following without a proper release from the club last employing him.

This ruling came in handy for the Cuban Stars of the Western League and prevented their star outfielder, Estaban Montalvo, from being retained by the Lincoln Giants of the Eastern League. Montalvo had asked for a $25 raise at the beginning of the 1926 season. Manager Agustin Molina refused to accede to his demand and Montalvo elected to remain idle throughout the 1926 season. At the close of the season, the secretary of the team failed to list Montalvo's name among the list of players under contract and the Lincoln team immediately grabbed him. This caused a protest from the Western League and from Commissioner Keenan of the Eastern League.

At this time, Keenan announced that he would keep Montalvo out of the lineup. He did this with the expectation that the Westerners would send for him. But as time went on and no offer came from the West, the Lincoln owner became restless and decided to put Montalvo back into his lineup since the other club made no effort to secure his services.

Keenan was one of the founders of the Eastern Colored League in 1922 with his club as a member since its inception. Although he was secretary and treasurer, his associations with the other commissioners had been anything but cordial over the past three years. When his team started having survival problems, Nat Strong, the other New York commissioner, blocked his attempts to get new players.

Keenan and Strong were rival managers in New York City and each fought for territorial bragging rights. Being a part owner of Dexter Park in Brooklyn and booking agent for Farmer's Oval and several other parks in the Metropolitan district, Strong had an advantage over his rival, and his influence was used with the other commissioners against the Lincoln Giants owner.

Strong was even successful in having president Isaac Nutter change a decision he made earlier in the season declaring that the Lincoln Giants had a legal right to Montalvo's services. Nutter eventually decided to return Montalvo to his Western club, the Cuban Stars.

For reasons unknown, on September 21, 1925, revisions to the NNL charter were filed, increasing the number of directors from five to nine. They added Steve Pierce (Detroit), Joe Rush (Birmingham), R.S. Lewis (Memphis), Richard Kent, and Dr. G.B. Keys (St. Louis), Warner Jewell (Indianapolis), and Agustin Molina (Havana), removing Willie Foster, Thompson and Farmer and retaining Rube

Foster (Chicago) and J.L. Wilkinson (Kansas City) as directors. The proposal was accepted on December 5 with the league now being represented by each team owner.

Going from the office to the dugout, Foster was still upset with his ace, Richard Whitworth, a sinker ball pitcher, for signing with Hilldale. Whitworth, along with third baseman Bill Francis and outfielder Jess Barbour, had signed with Bolden's club in November 1919, before the initial meeting in February 1920 to form the new league. Foster accused Bolden of retroactive player tampering. Bolden countered that the bylaws of the league constitution against transfer of players was not effective until the 1920 season. Foster had also sent Bolden an itemized statement for $188.47, for unpaid advance money to Whitworth. Bolden refused to pay the charges, responding:

The Fans Want It: Cartoonist J.M. Howe begs Rube Foster and Ed Bolden to put aside their legitimate differences to give the fans what they want, a World Series between the top teams from each league (courtesy of *Chicago Defender*).

Was not the aforementioned player led to believe that the indebtedness that he had subjected himself to, by accepting advance salary would be taken care of by you, released our club of any obligation.

After the 1922 season, Ed Bolden's team, the Hilldale Club, withdrew its membership from the Negro National Baseball League. Bolden noted that two of the league teams had refused to make the long, expensive trip to Darby (outside of Philadelphia) and league officials had not included the Hilldale team and other associate members in the league standings.

When Bolden withdrew his team, he demanded the return of his $1,000 good-faith deposit. The bylaws of the league constitution specifically stated that the deposit would be forfeited if a team withdrew. Bolden was furious when he discovered he could not receive his deposit and claimed some team owners had never made deposits. Bolden felt Foster had taken advantage of him, but Foster countered with a claim that Bolden had induced players to join his eastern team and the $1,000 was an advance payment for their contract releases.

Just before the Christmas holidays, on December 14, 1922, Bolden submitted a letter of resignation to the league's board, citing that the amendment for forfeiture of deposits was made when no associated members were present. In part, Bolden expressed,

> The hitch came when President Foster accepted the resignation but chose to juggle the funds, by refusing to return the $1,000 deposit of good faith belonging to the Hilldale Club, basing his ruling on an amendment that had been made to the constitution at a meeting that was not attended by a representative of the Hilldale Club and no copy of said amendment had been exhibited to the officials of the Philadelphia Club prior to the tendering of their resignation.
>
> ... As an associate member, we did not figure in the league standings, received only two attractions from the West, yet complied with all the requirements of the organization and owe nothing.
>
> We are far from satisfied with the manner in which our money has been withheld and unless the association speedily rescind their ruling, the officials are due for a legal shake down that will "rattle" the bones in the closet and someone will get much more publicity than they desire.

Strong had been introduced to baseball at the early age of sixteen as manager of the Manhattan-based Bushwicks Baseball Club. Under his guidance the Bushwicks became one the most talented white clubs outside of the major leagues. Bolden, once an opponent of Strong's monopolizing techniques, now sought alliance with his former adversary.

In January 1923, Rube Foster responded to the news media with his version, blaming Eastern bookie Nat Strong for influencing Bolden to resign.

A year earlier, Bolden had resigned from the league but changed his mind when the Eastern League did not materialize under Nat Strong's guidance.

On December 16, 1922, Ed Bolden and Nat Strong formed the Mutual Association of Eastern Colored Baseball Clubs, better known as the Eastern Colored League. Bolden was elected chairman and James Keenan secretary-treasurer of the six-team league. The league consisted of Bolden's Hilldale Club, Nat Strong's Brooklyn Royal Giants, Thomas Jackson's Atlantic City Bacharach Giants, Keenan's New York Lincoln Giants, Alex Pompez's Havana Cuban Stars, and Charles Spedden's Baltimore Black Sox.

Ed Bolden — A shrewd, cunning "Philadelphia lawyer," he was adept at exploiting baseball's legal technicalities, as founder of the Mutual Association of Eastern Colored Baseball Clubs. As owner of the Hilldale club, he was the chief adversary to the founding father Rube Foster with both having the game's best interest at heart (From the Wm. Cash & Lloyd Thompson Collection, provided through the courtesy of the African American Museum in Philadelphia).

Foster was not impressed that four of the six eastern club owners were white Americans (only Hilldale and Cuban Stars were black-owned). Historically, many white owners had employed carnival methods to promote the game and enticed players to perform circus-baseball acts to entertain fans. The most prominent of these owners was Nat Strong. Strong was owner or part-owner of several eastern powerhouse teams, the Brooklyn Royal Giants, the Philadelphia Giants, the Cuban Stars, the Cuban Giants and the renowned white semipro team, the Bushwicks. Foster feared that Strong, a powerful New York booking agent, would economically exploit black baseball and eventually control all of black baseball. His

Olivia Taylor: She became the first female owner in black baseball when her husband, C.I., died in February 1922. Her Indianapolis ABC's were decimated by the raids from teams in the Eastern Colored League, forcing her from the league in June 1924 (NoirTech Research).

fears were confirmed when black-owned franchises like the Richmond Giants and Harrisburg Giants split from the original body of the league because of their non-affiliation with power broker Strong. On January 13, the Chicago *Defender* questioned the alliance, writing "colored baseball in the East has gone back a decade when Nat Strong offered ball clubs $100 flat [fee] and two 15-cents meals for a Sunday game."

Some of Foster's fears were manifested on opening day of the 1924 season, when Strong refused to play the league's weak team, the Harrisburg Giants. Later in May, his Royal Giants, a traveling club without a home park, refused to play Keenan's Lincoln Giants. Financier Strong only wanted to play teams that attracted large crowds. By unanimous vote from team owners, with Alex Pompez of the Cuban Stars voting by proxy, the Royal Giants were removed from the Eastern circuit. Eventually, because of Strong's influence in scheduling games with major league cities and their parks, the league's top power broker was reluctantly reinstated. Still, his team played only 41 league games, while the champion Hilldale Giants played 69 games that season.

The lack of a consistent schedule also plagued the Western League simply because most teams did not own parks. Teams from Chicago, St. Louis, Kansas City and Detroit usually booked games while the local white major or minor league teams were on the road. With the exception of the traveling Cuban Stars, the teams would rent minor and major league parks when available. In addition, intercity, intrastate and interracial rivalries often generated far greater revenue than regular league games. When given a choice between a league game and an exhibition game, teams usually chose the latter. The exhibition games, with the attraction of rivalries and local interest — especially interracial competition — produced larger, better paying crowds. Many team owners insisted that these types of games determined whether they would be able to survive into the next season.

However, Foster's greatest concern with Strong was his position on "contract jumping." Contract jumping, known today as free agency baseball, caused undesirable raiding wars by both leagues. Bolden eventually attracted marquee Western players like Biz Mackey from the Indianapolis ABCs, Clint Thomas and Frank Warfield from the Detroit Stars, and George Carr and Rube Currie from the Kansas City Monarchs to join his Hilldale team. The eastern league teams were located in areas with significantly larger black populations than the midwestern and southern teams. This enabled the league to offer higher salaries to influence stars of the Western circuit, the Negro National League, to make the transition to the Eastern league.

Mrs. Olivia Taylor, who inherited the Indianapolis ABCs when her husband died in February 1922, was victimized by the raiding. In 1924, her Indianapolis team was decimated by assault from the Eastern League teams. The lack of players made it impossible for her team to finish the season. They had lost one of the league's stars, outfielder Oscar Charleston, a future Hall-of-Famer. Also leaving the ABCs were slugger Crush Holloway and submarine pitcher, William "Dizzy" Dismukes, who had pitched no-hitters in 1912 and 1915. Although, the ABC's were paid comparably well, they were attracted by the glamour and promise of eastern city baseball.

According to figures from Mrs. Taylor's payroll ledger in 1923, Oscar Charleston was the highest paid Hoosier, at $325 a month, followed by:

"Dizzy" Dismukes (P) at $200
George Shively (OF) at $200
Henry Blackman (3b) at $180
Gerard Williams (SS) at $175
Wilson C. Day (2b) at $175
Fred "Tex" Burnett (C) at $160
Crush Holloway (OF) at $150
Namon Washington (utility) at $150
Darltie Cooper (P) at $150
Charles Corbett at $145
Omer Newsome at $135 per month.

The players often took advantage of the soft-hearted Olivia by requesting numerous cash advances. This caused the club to bathe in red ink. When the 1924 season started, many players sought the free agent market for financial security. Player dissension, team management and an unwillingness of other owners to accept a female owner forced Mrs. Taylor to dissolve her team. The team had an outstanding debt of $1,556.56 for operating expenses and Mrs. Taylor had a personal debt of $620.25 owed to Rube Foster. These debts plus an unpaid room and board bill of $275.25 to a Chicago hotel made it impossible for her to continue operating. The ABCs uniforms were held in lieu of payment by league officials.

In June, Taylor's Indianapolis club was succeeded by the Memphis Red Sox (who reluctantly inherited the ABCs record of three wins and 19 losses) to complete the season. Because Mrs. Taylor's husband, Charles, had been instrumental in the formation of the league in 1920, the disbandment of the ABCs caused great concern among the Western League owners.

Withstanding the distraction of the once-solid ABCs leaving the league, neither Bolden nor Foster were willing to compromise their position on player jumping, making the likelihood of a World Series between the two leagues remote. Media pressure from such writers as Ollie Womack of the powerful syndicated Associated Negro Press, Frank "Fay" Young of *The Chicago Defender*, Wendell Smith of the *Pittsburgh Courier* and A.D. Williams of the *Indianapolis Ledger* (former business manager for the Indy ABCs) bombarded the media with numerous editorials, calling for an end to the standoff.

The September 6, 1924, *Chicago Defender* printed an undated letter from J.L. Wilkinson's business manager and secretary Quincy J. Gilmore, pleading:

> There has been considerable agitation on the part of the base-ball fans throughout the country for a series of games to determine the Negro championship of the world between the winners of the pennant in the National Negro Baseball League and the Eastern league.
>
> It seems that there has been a general hesitancy on the part of the management of the two prospective winners to issue a challenge for such a series. There seems to be a disagreement between the owners of both leagues which I hope for the benefit of the game and the fans in general, will not interfere with such an event.
>
> On behalf of the Kansas City Monarchs, winners of the 1923 pennant, and the prospective winner of the 1924 pennant of the National Negro League, I herby issue a challenge to the winner of the Eastern League pennant for a series of games to determine the Negro world's championship.
>
> This series to be arranged by a commission representing both leagues and to be carried out under the same plans as the world's series between the National and American leagues.
>
> Respectfully, Q. J. Gilmore, Secretary.

On August 14, Womack, from Kansas City, Missouri, sent a letter to the *Pittsburgh Courier* optimistically anticipating the first colored world series.

The 1923 Champions of the Negro National League, and apparently sure repeaters for the current season, have shown themselves to be the real Monarchs of Negro baseball in the west, which is by no means a small achievement, knowing as we do the class of ball that is and has been played by the American Giants, Detroit Stars, and other strong teams in years past and present — recalling the defeat of the Bacharach Giants, the cream of the east two years ago.

The fans of Kansas City, who should share equally the credit of success of the sterling athletes under the able guidance of Joe Mendez, because of their loyal support — are demanding a reward for their pets in the form of a championship series at the end of the season with the

Judge Landis: In an historical twist, the egotistical monarch of segregated baseball was asked by Foster and Bolden to arbitrate the indecisions surrounding formation of the first colored World Series (NoirTech Research).

champions of the Eastern League. This popular demand is by no means unreasonable, but instead is very logical. There must be some great objective to which the players may aspire or they as well as the fans will lose some of the interest which makes them play to win.

The National and American Leagues (white) are wonderful organizations, and their entertainment is of the highest type. Why? Because of the reward they receive when they win. For instance, they have received $3,500 or better — and the honor of being World Champions.

So why should these Negro athletes, who are pioneers in their line, not be allowed to enjoy the same advantages and distinctions as others do? How would the following news item sound in late September? "The World Series Between the Hilldale Eastern League Champions and the Kansas City Monarchs, National League Champions," consisting of the first five out of nine games to decide. And how would this article sound in October? — "The Monarchs of Kansas City, Mo., are the World Champions Negro Baseball club, having defeated the Champion Hilldale club of the East in five out of nine games played, total attendance being 150,000. Total receipts, over $100,000; players' share over $2,000 each, 'so much' to losing owners, so much to winners, and so on.

At any rate one can see that this would mean hundreds or thousands to all considered, besides the first-class entertainment the fans would receive as their reward for their loyalty to their local teams.

Fans! Let's pull for a World Series this fall with the Eastern League champions.

Ironically, it was Judge Kenesaw Mountain Landis, major league baseball's commissioner, who was asked to arbitrate this personal feud. Landis, born in Milville, Ohio, grew up in Logansport, Indiana. After failing an algebra course he dropped out of high school. He later taught himself dictation to secure a job as a courtroom reporter. He earned his diploma in night school and later received his law degree from the Union Law School of Chicago. A social illiterate, the tobacco-chewing, inarticulate, foul-mouthed but shrewd Landis never went to college.

In 1905, he had been appointed a federal judge in Illinois by President Theodore Roosevelt. Later Landis became nationally known for forcing millionaire John D. Rockefeller to testify in the much publicized case against his Standard Oil Company. Landis issued an unprecedented fine of over $29 million. Rockefeller never paid the fine because he won the case on appeal.

The ultraconservative Judge Landis also had exposure to baseball. In 1914, he had presided over the monopoly suit against the major leagues brought by the newly formed Federal League. After several years of appeals and months of deliberation, the case was settled out of court.

With damage to the image of America's national pastime brought on by the infamous Black Sox Scandal in the 1919 World Series, Landis was pressured to accept a job as baseball commissioner. His no-nonsense approach to matters made him an ideal candidate. His salary rose from $7,500 as a judge to $50,000 as baseball commissioner.

As commissioner, Landis was often portrayed as an egotistical monarch with authoritative influence. He was often accused of a restricted outlook on America's game, particularly in matters of race relations. He had long been a proponent of segregated baseball, issuing a decree in 1921 to prevent white major league teams from competing against any barnstorming teams during the season. Landis had stated quite firmly that he was "agin it." Players rallied in support of the Bambino, threatening to form a union. Regardless, Ruth and Bob Meusel continued to play against teams—predominantly black teams like Oscar Charleston's Colored All-Stars in the Southern California League during spring 1922 — and Landis eventually suspended the New York Yankees' bad boys Ruth and Meusel (the second leading hitter on the team) and Wild Bill Piercy (a third-string pitcher), for 39 days, or until May 20 of the 1922 season, for not adhering to his dictum. Piercy would start the season with the Boston Red Sox.*

Now the omnipotent Landis, in an unofficial capacity, was being asked by Bolden and Foster to arbitrate the remaining indecisions surrounding the first Colored World Series. Judge Landis agreed to draft an agreement similar to ones

---

*J.G. Taylor Spink, *Judge Landis and 25 Years of Baseball*. New York: Thomas Y. Crowell, 1947.

by the American and National Leagues. In substance, the agreement would decide all questions related to future drafts, contracts, players, salaries, postseason games and any protest filed by teams. In response to Landis' acceptance of the appointment, Rube Foster sent a telegram on September 2, 1924, to the *Pittsburgh Courier*, stating in part:

> Delighted at opportunity for peace.... Judge Landis will arbitrate each complexing situation, decide its merits, and draft an agreement between the leagues and pledge to accept whatever his decision will be, or will agree on lines agreeable through compromise between the leagues....
>
> Judge Landis sees no reason why peace should not be restored, for the good of the

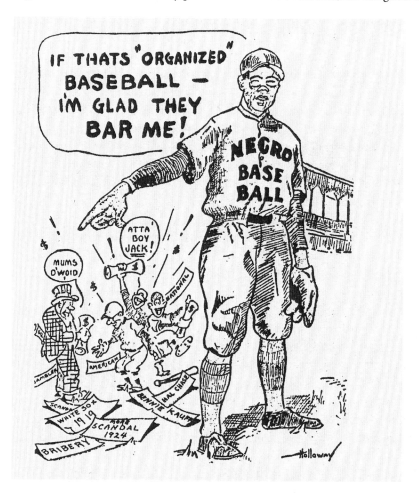

They Bar Me: In the aftermath of the Black Sox Scandal of 1919, when Prince Hal Chase had enticed players of the Chicago White Sox to throw the World Series, another scandal erupts! Commissioner Landis bans New York Giants outfielder Jimmy O'Connell and coach Cozy Dolan from the World Series after they admit they tried to bribe Philadelphia Phillies shortstop Heinie Sand to limit his fielding range during the 1924 playoffs (courtesy of *Pittsburgh Courier*).

game, and sees no reason why the winners in Negro baseball World's Series should not meet winners in regular World's Series if the public demands same.

Western fans want to see Hilldale and Kansas City meet this year. The Western League is willing to let the East keep contract jumpers now held providing some agreement of protection to both leagues can be signed for the future. Landis is willing to draw up agreements the same as protects the National and American Leagues.

The World Series participants appeared to be the Kansas City Monarchs, who would clinch the pennant on September 13, against Foster's Giants, and Bolden's Hilldale club, who had clinched the pennant on August 28.

The compromise agreement by outside arbitrator Landis was a major step in reconciling the differences between Foster and Bolden. The two leagues coming under the same umbrella of regulations meant the club owners had the right to develop men and to keep them under contract during the entire year. It also prevented the players from borrowing money on the strength of their contacts and then jumping to another league.

An amendment to Landis' constitution by the Negro National League stated additional rules:

1. To allow all players who have jumped contracts to remain in the Eastern League.

2. To respect and draw an agreement to respect contracts between players and clubs.

3. That each league who has contract jumpers to see that the money each player owes an owner is paid to that owner.

On September 6, 1924, Edward Bolden responded to the Landis decisions in an open letter to the *Pittsburgh Courier* and the *Philadelphia Tribune*, stating in part:

If the proposed World Series between colored clubs of the East and West does not materialize in 1924, you may put it down that it will not be due to any obstacle placed in the way by me....

The player question, however, was not the seat of the trouble between the Hilldale Club and the Negro National League, but the fact that our deposit of good faith to the amount of One Thousand Dollars had been retained by the Western body, since we resigned from the Western League in 1922....

This matter, of course did not set well with our organization and hitherto we were not in any mood to compromise. However, the matter, when compared to public opinion, is very trivial and I personally am far removed from standing in the way of popular sentiment. If any club in the Eastern Circuit has an axe to grind it is ours.

You may put it down that I am waiting on the actions of our Commission and the advance from the West. The East will concede to the wishes of the fans.

With neither Bolden nor Foster willing to tarnish their excellent baseball image with the fans and the media, they were overcome with a spasm of pride and proceeded to organize this gala event. Like diamonds, these invisible, colorless men emitting shades of crystalline carbon introduced a flashy brand of baseball, between the white foul lines, never seen before by a rainbow coalition of fans. They will shine brightly and brilliantly as any precious gem of talent ever born, as the first colored World Series was about to begin.

2

The Race for the 1924 World Series Championship

The six clubs of the Eastern Colored League finished the 1923 season with the Hilldale Club winning the championship. In 1924, the league was increased to an eight-club circuit by admitting the Harrisburg Giants of Harrisburg, Pennsylvania, owned by C.W. Strothers, and the Washington Potomacs of Washington, D.C., owned by George W. Robinson.

1924 Kansas City Monarchs. The Monarchs hit .313 — tops of any baseball team during the decade. Bullet Rogan hit over .400, while Heavy Johnson, Newt Joseph, Dobie Moore and Hurley McNair hit over .350. Standing from left to right: George Sweatt, Plunk Drake, Deke Mothell, Bill McCall, Frank Duncan, Lem Hawkins, Cliff Bell, Moore, William Bell, Jose Mendez, Rogan, Newt Allen, Yellowhorse Morris, Johnson and Joseph (NoirTech Research).

1924 Hilldale Giants at Hilldale Park in Darby, PA. Back row, from left: Scrip Lee, Phil Cockrell, Biz Mackey, Nip Winters, George Carr, Zip Campbell, Ed Bolden (suit), Wade Hampton, Wilbur Pritchett, Judy Johnson, Red Ryan (sweater) and Louis Santop. Front row, from left to right: Clint Thomas, Rube Currie, Cliff Carter, Tom Allen, batboy, (first name unknown) Lambert (sweater), Frank Warfield, Otto Briggs, Joe Lewis and Paul Stephens. This team stole more than 100 bases during the season. (From the Wm. Cash & Lloyd Thompson Collection, provided through the courtesy of the African American Museum in Philadelphia)

The league was governed by a commission with one representative from each club and headed by Edward Bolden, a prime factor in attaining organization among the colored professional baseball clubs. As it was found impractical to play a closed league schedule, or confine the league teams to playing each other, a moderate schedule was decided upon and all clubs were at liberty to schedule other games between league games. The Philadelphia Hilldale Club repeated its performance of 1923 and captured its second straight championship. The Eastern Colored League proved to be a successful financial project, with the prominent Lincoln Giants of New York, the Baltimore Black Sox of Baltimore and the Hilldale Club furnishing the meal ticket to the weaker clubs. The league standings for 1924 follow.

Eastern Colored League Standings

	TG	W	L	PCT.	GBL
Hilldale Club	70	47	23	.681	
Baltimore Black Sox	51	32	19	.627	5½
Lincoln Giants	57	32	25	.561	8½
Bacharach Giants	59	30	29	.508	11½
Harrisburg Giants	54	26	28	.481	13
Brooklyn Royal Giants	42	16	26	.381	17
Cuban Stars (East)	48	17	31	.354	20
Washington Potomacs	58	21	37	.362	20½

Won-Lost Records Against ECL Clubs

Bacharach Giants	6–4	.600
Baltimore Black Sox	7–3	.700
Cuban Stars East	8–1	.888
Harrisburg Giants	7–3	.700
Lincoln Giants	6–6	.500
Brooklyn Royal Giants	7–2	.777
Washington Potomacs	6–4	.600

In anticipation of a winning season, John Howe, a writer for the *Philadelphia Tribune*, rapped:

Hilldale — Alphabetically Speaking
H — stands for Home runs, we don't care how many
I — stands for It, it's the pennant we mean
L — stands for Liquor, but we don't want any
L — stands for Luck too, the best ever seen
D — stands for Dollars, we hope they come pouring
A — stands for Action, we give it you know
L — stands for Ladies, the kind we're adoring
E — stands for Everything good, so let's go!

The Hilldales were steady throughout the season, never losing more than two games in row. They started the season with a bang when the tireless Nip Winters won the first three games. Their toughest league opponent was the Lincoln Giants, splitting the series at five games each. And they beat the league's runner-up Black Sox seven out of ten games and won six of ten from the tough Bacharach Giants. They won fourteen team series, sweeping six of them. Their longest winning streak was five games in late August, beating the Cuban Stars and Brooklyn Royal Giants twice and the Harrisburg Giants once, clinching their second pennant in the process.

The batting leaders for the Hilldale Club were Judy Johnson and Biz Mackey, with averages of .342 and .332 and slugging percentages of .510 and .464. Louis Santop finished second to Clint Thomas for the team home run crown (he hit eight). Hilldale had four batters with averages over .300, all under .350. Frank Warfield was the leader in stolen bases with 22 steals. Pitcher Nip Winters led the league in wins with 20 and had the lowest ERA on the club with 2.16. His 21 complete games were tops in the league. Overall the Hilldale staff pitched 51 complete games out of 70, much higher than most pitching staffs around the league. The complete 1924 Hilldale roster with season statistics follows.

Hilldale Giants, Eastern Colored League
Ed Bolden, Manager, 47–23 Record

B/T	Age	Hilldale Batting (games at position)	G	AB	R	H	2B	3B	HR	RBI	W	SB	AVG.	SLUG.
R L	30	Allen, Tom (1b28)	28	66	5	13	2	1	0	3	3	1	.197	.258
L R	33	Briggs, Otto (rf56, cf2)	58	228	38	65	12	2	0	14	**31**	11	.285	.355
R R	?	Campbell, Zip (p1)	1	1	0	0	0	0	0	0	0	0	.000	.000
S R	29	Carr, George (1b31, lf12, rf11, cf1)	54	180	36	53	13	4	1	26	8	13	.294	.428
R R	26	Cockrell, Phil (p15, lf3, rf1, rp2)	21	47	8	11	0	1	0	5	2	3	.234	.277
R R	25	Currie, Rube (p10, rp1)	12	19	2	5	0	0	0	3	1	0	.263	.263
R R	34	Johnson, George (cf64)	64	224	32	56	13	2	3	28	23	4	.250	.366
R R	24	Johnson, Judy (3b62, ss9)	70	263	**51**	**90**	**22**	5	4	**48**	20	10	.342	**.510**
R R	25	Lee, Scrip (p4, 3b1, ph2, pr2, rp4)	13	17	2	6	0	0	0	3	2	1	.353	.353
R R	29	Lewis, Joe (c23, ph4)	27	84	15	28	11	1	0	9	7	3	.333	.488
S R	27	Mackey, Biz (ss33, 1b24, 3b9, c5)	70	**280**	50	93	19	3	4	41	14	8	.332	.464
L L	23	Pritchett, Wilbur (p1)	1	1	0	0	0	0	0	0	0	0	.000	.000
R R	27	Ryan, Red (p25, ph1, pr1, rp1)	28	77	6	12	1	0	0	3	3	3	.156	.169
L R	35	Santop, Louis (c46, ph3)	49	181	28	62	10	2	5	29	9	4	.343	.503
R R	24	Stephens, Jake (ss28)	28	104	11	19	4	1	1	6	6	4	.183	.269
R R	27	Thomas, Clint (lf60, cf11, 2b2, 3b1)	70	273	46	77	15	**7**	**8**	**48**	18	14	.282	.476
R R	26	Warfield, Frank (2b67, 3b2, ss2)	70	272	49	85	14	1	2	36	18	**22**	.313	.393
L L	25	Winters, Nip (p29, ph4, rp1)	34	87	11	25	4	1	4	12	2	3	.287	.494
				2403	390	700	140	31	32	314	167	104	.291	.415
		Home Games		1400	229	410	92	20	19	182	81	72	.293	.428
		Away Games		908	153	274	47	11	13	125	83	32	.302	.421
		Neutral Sites		95	8	16	1	0	0	7	3	0	.168	.179

B/T	Age	Hilldale Pitching	G	GS	IP	H	R	ER	BB	K	W	L	ERA	C/G	S/O
R R	28	Campbell, Bill	1	1	3	5	4	2	1	2	0	0	6.00	0	0
R R	26	Cockrell, Phil	16	15	115⅔	100	59	51	32	49	10	1	3.97	9	0
R R	26	Currie, Rube	11	6	56⅓	71	39	34	12	19	1	6	5.43	3	0
L L	25	Lee, Scrip	8	2	38⅔	35	18	16	5	12	2	4	3.72	2	0
L L	23	Pritchett, Wilbur	1	0			0	0	1	0	0	0	0.00	0	0
R R	26	Ryan, Red	26	22	199	201	79	68	29	87	14	7	3.08	16	2
L L	25	Winters, Nip	29	24	**208**	170	76	64	55	**114**	**20**	5	**2.77**	**21**	2
				70	621⅓	583	275	235	135	283	47	23	3.40	51	4

Note: RBIs, walks, stolen bases, base on balls, earned runs and strikeouts are understated. The newspapers did not report these stats for each game. Bold type is for team leader.

Coming into the 1924 season, the Dayton club of the Negro National League was no longer in operation, and Green's Chicago Giants had disbanded. Although the ABCs started the '24 season, they were unable to continue due to financial problems complicated by the death of their owner, Charles I. Taylor, in 1922. The Memphis Red Sox took their place, while the Birmingham Black Barons and the Cleveland Browns joined the league. Meanwhile, the St. Louis Giants had become the St. Louis Stars.

The Monarchs ruled the season with majestic authority. They jump-started the season with 14 consecutive wins, sweeping the St. Louis Stars in two, the American Giants in four, the Detroit Stars in two and the ABCs in four before taking two more from St. Louis. Their streak was stopped by Fred Bell. The Monarchs averaged nine runs per game during the streak, with Bullet Rogan capturing four wins, Plunk Drake and Jose Mendez winning three each, Cliff Bell winning two and Yellowhorse Morris and William Bell with one apiece.

The Monarchs marched on. By the middle of June, they embarked on another 14-game winning streak. This time the bounties were the Birmingham Black Barons (four), Detroit Stars (four), Cuban Stars (four) and two more wins over Foster's American Giants. Once again Bullet Rogan led the way with four victories, while Morris and William Bell picked up three wins each, and Drake and Cliff Bell each scored two wins. In August they put together a streak of eight games, conquering the Black Barons and the Memphis Red Sox four times each.

As the Monarchs drove to their first World Series title they were not without a weakness. Of the 22 losses, the American Giants' pitching duo of Luis Padrone, a lefty with junk, and George Harney, a right-handed spitballer, won three games each. While the American Giants gave the Monarchs their only serious competition, they lost the season series to the Monarchs, 12–14. The incumbent Monarchs could not be denied their throne, sweeping a record nine-team series.

In fact the Monarchs scored 551 runs in 77 games, an average of more than seven runs per game. They scored a season high of 20 runs against the Detroit Stars and reached the 19 and 15 marks twice. In all, the powerhouse Monarchs scored in double figures 20 times, a fourth of their games.

Negro National League Standings

	TG	W	L	PCT.	GBL
Kansas City Monarchs	77	55	22	.714	—
Chicago American Giants	73	49	24	.671	4
Detroit Stars	64	37	27	.578	11½
St. Louis Stars	76	40	36	.526	14½
Birmingham Black Barons	69	32	37	.464	19
Memphis Red Sox*	66	29	37	.439	20½
Cuban Stars (West)	49	16	33	.327	25
Cleveland Browns	49	15	34	.306	26

*Succeeded Indianapolis ABCs, who started season.

Won-Lost Records Against NNL Clubs

Birmingham Black Barons	11–1	.917
Chicago American Giants	14–12	.538
Cleveland Browns	3–1	.750
Cuban Stars West	4–0	1.000
Detroit Stars	9–3	.750
Indianapolis ABC's	4–0	1.000
Memphis Red Sox	4–0	1.000
St. Louis Stars	6–5	.545

Bullet Rogan paced the Monarch pitching staff with 16 wins. Batting leaders were Rogan with a .413 average and .652 slugging percentage. The Monarchs had, incredibly, five hitters who batted over the .300 mark, all over the .350 plateau. The team batting average was .313, the highest mark of any professional team, black or white, during the Roaring Twenties. The team home run crown was won by Hurley McNair with eight, followed by Rogan, Dobie Moore and Heavy Johnson with five each.

The Monarchs averaged more than seven runs a game and presented a robust offensive attack. They also had a strong bench with George Sweatt and Dink Mothell, both capable of playing many positions and hitting well against all types of pitchers. Their only weakness in the batting lineup was their young catcher Frank Duncan, who exhibited a mature ability to call the signals despite his age. The Monarchs had exceptionally great talent at the infield corners with Newt Joseph at the hot corner and Lem Hawkins at first. Up the middle, they were solid with Dobie Moore and Newt Allen despite the usually high number of errors made during the season because of unmanicured infields. Their pitching rotation was adequate with Bullet Rogan, William Bell and Plunk Drake holding opponents to less than five runs a game, but the team lacked a quality left-handed pitcher and a solid closer. They picked up lefty Bill McCall late in the season to remedy this problem.

Hilldale had excellent pitching led by lefty Nip Winters, along with Phil Cockrell and Red Ryan. And Scrip Lee and Rube Currie were spot starters and relievers. A well-rounded staff—with Winters' devastating sinking curveball, Ryan's forkball and Cockrell's spitter, along with submarine deliveries from Lee — they could keep batters off balance for weeks. The Hilldale pitching corps held their opponents to an unusually low total of less than four runs per game. And their infield was normally error-free when Jake Stephens was in the lineup at short. But due to injuries to Country Jake throughout the season, Biz Mackey and Judy Johnson had to fill in at shortstop. Meanwhile, first baseman Tom Allen and second sacker Frank Warfield were the best in fielding their positions. And the outfield of George Johnson, Otto Briggs and Clint Thomas was sometimes called "The Beast of the East" by the press for their devouring appetite for outfield flies. Any ball hit with a hump in it got gobbled up by this demonic outfield.

The Hilldale Club also possessed exceptional speed on the basepaths. The fastest team in black baseball was led by Frank Warfield, with 35 stolen bases against all comers, followed closely by George Carr (34), Clint Thomas (32), Otto Briggs (32) and part-timer Jake Stephens (21). Pitching and speed were the trademarks on this fine Hilldale team. The previous year, the *Washington Tribune* had dubbed Hilldale as "unquestionably the best in the East and quite possibly the country."

While Hilldale had great pitching and blinding speed, the Monarchs boasted of players who loved to hit that white apple. The Monarchs would meet the Hilldale Giants from Darby, Pennsylvania, for the first Colored World Series. Both teams had won their respective league titles in 1923, but would be meeting for the world title. This World Series would feature great pitching against great hitting. Once again, the baseball adage "Does good pitching stop good hitting?" would be put to the test.

The complete 1924 Kansas City roster with season statistics follows.

Kansas City Monarchs, Negro National League
Jose Mendez, Manager, 55–22 Record

B/T	Age	Kansas City Batting (games at position)	G	AB	R	H	2B	3B	HR	RBI	W	SB	AVG.	SLUG.
S R	23	Allen, Newt (2b75, ss1)	75	302	52	83	10	3	2	32	41	3	.275	.348
R R	35	Bartlett, Homer (Rp1)	1	2	0	0	0	0	0	0	0	0	.000	.000
R R	28	Bell, Cliff (p5. rp2)	7	17	1	2	0	0	0	2	1	1	.118	.118
R R	27	Bell, William (p15, rf5, lf2)	22	57	3	9	1	0	0	2	0	0	.158	.175
L L	32	Donaldson, John (cf2)	2	5	1	1	0	0	0	0	0	0	.200	.200
R R	29	Drake, Plunk (p19, lf1, rp7)	27	59	5	16	3	1	1	6	2	1	.271	.407
R R	23	Duncan, Frank (c70)	70	247	51	66	10	3	0	37	35	0	.267	.332
R R	32	Green, Willie (3b1)	1	5	0	2	0	0	0	1	0	0	.400	.400
L L	29	Hawkins, Lem (1b63)	63	272	58	76	7	6	0	27	25	2	.279	.349
R R	30	Hill, Fred (lf2, rf1)	2	7	1	1	1	0	0	0	0	0	.143	.286
R R	28	Johnson, Heavy (lf54, rf15, cf1, 1b2)	72	272	60	101	19	7	5	62	25	2	.371	.548
R R	24	Joseph, Newt (3b73)	73	279	60	101	21	6	4	60	21	2	.362	.523
R R	?	Manese, Ed (2b1, rf1)	1	4	2	0	0	0	0	0	0	0	.000	.000
R R	?	Marshall, Jack (p3, rf1)	4	10	0	2	1	0	0	2	2	0	.200	.300
L L	?	McCall, Bill (p3)	3	6	3	2	0	0	0	0	0	0	.333	.333
S L	35	McNair, Hurley (rf49, cf18, lf4, ss1, rp1)	72	275	65	97	10	6	8	55	25	5	.353	.520
R R	37	Mendez, Jose (p2, cf2, ph1, rp11)	16	23	6	5	2	0	1	1	3	0	.217	.435
R R	28	Moore, Dobie (ss77)	77	309	68	111	22	11	5	53	23	3	.359	.550
L L	28	Morris, Yellowhorse (p9, cf1, rf9, pr1)	19	39	8	8	0	2	0	3	4	0	.205	.308
S R	27	Mothell, Dink (cf35,1b13,c11,rf7,3b5,lf5,p1,2b1)	70	243	50	69	11	7	0	37	34	2	.284	.387
R R	31	Rogan, Bullet (p22, cf9, rf6, lf5, ph5, rp2, 2b1)	50	155	32	64	10	6	5	44	13	4	.413	.652
R R	30	Sweatt, George (lf15, cf13, ph5, 2b1, 1b1 rf1)	34	118	25	32	5	2	3	16	9	1	.271	.424
R R	25	Williams, Henry (rf1)	1	4	0	0	0	0	0	0	0	0	.000	.000
				2710	551	848	133	60	34	438	266	32	.313	.444
		Home Games		1373	314	447	57	41	8	234	142	11	.326	.444
		Away Games		1266	233	391	75	18	26	200	120	20	.309	.458
		Neutral Sites		71	4	10	1	1	0	4	4	1	.141	.183

B/T	Age	Kansas City Pitching	G	GS	IP	H	RS	ER	BB	K	W	L	ERA	C/G	S/O
R R	35	Bartlett, Homer	1	1	5	4	1	1	3	0	0	0	1.80	0	0
R R	27	Bell, Cliff	8	8	43	35	16	14	11	7	4	1	2.93	3	1
R R	27	Bell, William	17	14	118⅔	117	55	50	28	41	10	2	3.79	8	0
R R	29	Drake, Plunk	26	19	148	146	81	**64**	57	59	11	**8**	3.89	10	0
R R	?	Marshall, Jack	3	3	15⅔	15	11	6	8	5	0	1	3.45	0	0
L L	?	McCall, Bill	3	1	15⅔	13	6	6	6	8	2	0	3.24	1	0
S L	35	McNair, Hurley	1	0	2	1	0	0	0	2	0	0	0.00	0	0
R R	**36**	Mendez, Jose	13	2	44	38	19	15	5	31	4	1	3.07	0	0
R R	28	Morris, Yellowhorse	18	9	87⅓	72	46	39	28	24	6	4	4.02	4	2
S R	27	Mothell, Dink	1	1	9	10	3	3	0	0	1	0	3.00	1	0
R R	31	Rogan, Bullet	23	22	**176**	**154**	**85**	71	**57**	**101**	**16**	5	3.63	**18**	1
				77	**664⅓**	**605**	**323**	**269**	**203**	**278**	**55**	**22**	**3.64**	**45**	**4**

Note: RBIs, walks, stolen bases, base on balls, earned runs and strikeouts are understated. The newspapers did not report these stats for each game. Bold type is for team leader.

Projected Starting Nines for the World Series

With Hilldale's splendid fielding shortstop Jake Stephens out with a sprained ankle, the Giants will have to juggle their lineup. Taking Stephens' place at short will be third sacker Judy Johnson. Biz Mackey, normally a catcher, will move to the hot corner replacing Johnson. The old vet Lou Santop will take Mackey's backstop position.

Having no injuries to report, the Monarchs remain solid at each position. With the Monarchs' versatile, hard-hitting George Sweatt coming off the bench, he may play a key role throughout the series.

MONARCHS   HILLDALE

Staff Aces

Bullet Rogan   Nip Winters

	G	IP	H	R	BB	K	W	L	ERA
Rogan	23	176	154	85	57	101	16	5	2.71
Winters	29	208	170	76	55	114	21	5	2.16

The toughest call of all of the matchups. Without a doubt, Nip Winters is the superior of the two pitchers. His no-hitter this season and his mound demeanor sets him apart from all other hurlers. Although a fine hitter for a pitcher, he is no match for Rogan in the batter's box. Rogan is an everyday player who led the Monarchs in batting, along with the most wins on the mound. The series may be decided on which one of these men rise to the challenge. *Advantage: Even*

Catchers

Frank Duncan   Louis Santop

	G	AB	R	H	D	T	HR	AVG.	SLUG.
Duncan	70	247	51	66	10	3	0	.267	.332
Santop	49	181	28	62	10	2	5	.343	.503

The young Frank Duncan is a rising star, while Louis "Big Bertha" Santop is a falling meteor. "Top" has power at the plate and is considered an average receiver. He was considered one of the premier catchers in his prime, but his best days are behind him. While Duncan is a pitcher's dream behind home plate, he is a punchless hitter, therefore pushing the nod to ole Santop. *Advantage: Hilldale*

First Basemen

Lem Hawkins   Tom Allen

	G	AB	R	H	D	T	HR	AVG.	SLUG.
Hawkins	63	272	58	76	7	6	0	.279	.349
T. Allen	28	66	5	13	2	1	0	.197	.258

Lem Hawkins is an all-star first sacker. He is dependable in the field and a consistent contact hitter who seldom strikes out. Tommy Allen is also an excellent fielder but lacks any sort of threat with the bat. Thus, a clear edge to the Hawk. *Advantage: Kansas City*

Second Basemen

Newt Allen							Frank Warfield	
	G	AB	R	H	D	T	HR	AVG.	SLUG.
N. Allen	75	302	52	83	10	3	2	.275	.348
Warfield	70	272	49	85	14	1	2	.313	.393

Another tough call. Newt Allen is the premier second baseman in the National League, while Captain Warfield holds the title in the Eastern League. Both men possess the fiery spirit to instill their teams in moments of crisis. Real battlers and supercompetitors in the clutch, each man is a leader by example. Take your blindfolded pick of either all-star and you won't go wrong. *Advantage: Even*

Third Basemen

Newt Joseph							Biz Mackey	
	G	AB	R	H	D	T	HR	AVG.	SLUG.
Joseph	73	279	60	101	21	6	4	.362	.523
Mackey	70	280	50	93	19	3	4	.332	.464

Although strikeout prone Joseph had an excellent season at bat, no hitter on Hilldale is more feared than the Big Mac. Joseph has a definite edge at fielding because Mackey is playing out of position and his concentration at the plate may be diluted. But when the chips are down my money is on Mackey. This tough call could prove pivotal in the series. *Advantage: Hilldale*

Shortstops

Dobie Moore							Judy Johnson	
	G	AB	R	H	D	T	HR	AVG.	SLUG.
Moore	77	309	68	111	22	11	5	.359	.550
J. Johnson	70	263	51	90	22	5	4	.342	.510

The toughest out on the Monarchs, Dobie Moore can match hit-for-hit with one of the Eastern Colored League's best in Judy Johnson. Unfortunately, the erratic Dobie doesn't have the "D" that the smooth-fielding Judy shows in the field. The quicker Johnson can cover more territory and had fewer fielding errors during the season than Moore. Johnson is equally adept as Moore in clutch situations. *Advantage: Hilldale*

Left Fielders

Heavy Johnson								Clint Thomas	
	G	AB	R	H	D	T	HR	AVG.	SLUG.
O. Johnson	72	272	60	101	19	7	5	.371	.548
Thomas	70	273	46	77	15	7	8	.282	.476

Power versus speed! Oscar "Heavy" Johnson can hit the ball as far as anyone in the game. Clint Thomas gets his homers by hitting to the outfield gaps. Johnson is an outstanding fielder, but no one in baseball covers as much ground as Thomas. Each man is an integral part of his team's offense. An outstanding performance by either athlete can tilt the victory in his favor. Roll the dice for an edge. *Advantage: Even*

Center Fielders

Dink Mothell								George Johnson	
	G	AB	R	H	D	T	HR	AVG.	SLUG.
Mothell	70	243	50	69	11	7	0	.284	.387
G. Johnson	64	224	32	56	13	2	3	.250	.366

The man of many positions is Dink Mothell, a dependable substitute at any position. He will probably share the center field position with Bullet Rogan and George Sweatt during the World Series. Although George Johnson had a subpar season, he is the superior of the two men in overall ability because of his potential batting power and speed in the outfield. *Advantage: Hilldale*

Right Fielders

Hurley McNair								Otto Briggs	
	G	AB	R	H	D	T	HR	AVG.	SLUG.
McNair	72	275	65	97	10	6	8	.353	.520
Briggs	58	228	38	65	12	2	0	.285	.355

The toy cannon is Hurley McNair. He can take a pitcher deep on any given count. Equally adept in the field, McNair is known to have the better arm of the two men. An excellent outfielder, speedy Briggs is one of the best leadoff hitters around, but no one can pound the horsehide like McNair. *Advantage: Kansas City*

3

Scouting Reports

Brief biographical sketches of prominent participants in the Colored World Series are provided for introductory purposes.

Kansas City's
"Blue Ribbon Performer"

NEWT ALLEN
(Newton Henry Allen, Sr.)
Height 5'8", weight 170, bats switch, throws right

Nicknames: Newt, Colt, Little Napoleon, Ashes.
Born: May 19, 1901, Austin, Texas.
Died: June 9, 1988, Cincinnati, Ohio.
World Series Age: 23.
Career: 1922–44, 1947: 2b, ss, manager, All Nations, Kansas City Monarchs, St. Louis Stars, Homestead Grays, Indianapolis Clowns, Detroit Wolves, Chicago American Giants.
Personal: Allen is married with two sons and a daughter. Allen resembles the marathon monarch butterfly; he doesn't weigh very much, but displays amazing strength and endurance in his baseball travels. He is, pound for pound, the best baseball package ever assembled.

An extremely dangerous switch hitter, the line-drive hitter is known to hit in clutch situations. He is also a skilled bunter and seldom strikes out, making him the ideal No. 2 hitter, capable of moving the runners up. Allen possesses great enthusiasm for the game, evident by his aggressive running on the basepaths. He is never afraid to break up a double play. Allen has a reputation for his quick temper.

	G	AB	R	H	D	T	HR	AVG.	SLUG.
World Series	10	40	8	11	7	0	0	.275	.450

Currently the premier second baseman in the Negro National League, he possesses great range in the field, making plays around the keystone bag an art form. Allen floats like a butterfly on double plays. Somewhat superstitious, sometimes he plays with a flower stem between his teeth for good luck. Allen studies hitters by recording data in his diary.

1924 Season: This is Allen's first season as a regular, and he is still learning the game. He beat out regular George Sweatt for the second base slot. Allen had five games with three or more hits. He has been a steady performer for the Monarchs throughout the year.

Scouting Reports: Former teammate Chet Brewer once said of Allen: "Newt was a real slick second baseman, he could catch the ball and throw it without looking. Newt used to catch the ball, throw it up under his left arm; it was just a strike to first base. He was something! Got that ball out of his glove quicker than anybody you ever saw."

How did Allen compare to eight-time Gold Glove winners the Pirates' Bill Mazeroski and the Royals' Frank White? According to Buck O'Neil, who joined the Monarchs in 1938: "He was one of the best I've ever seen. I'd compare him with Frank White, except Newt's arm might have been a little stronger. He had soft hands and great range. The three best players I ever saw at the position were Newt, Frank and Bill Mazeroski."

Newt Allen: During the season, Newt is considered the cat's meow of second basemen around the league. He possesses great range in the field, making plays around the keystone bag an art form. He is a cat burglar in the field, stealing fans' breath as they gasp at his sensational skills. With catlike quickness, Allen seemed to move before the ball was even hit. Other times, he appeared to throw the pellet before it settled in his glove. John McGraw of the New York Giants claimed, "Allen is one of the finest infielders, white or colored, in organized baseball" (NoirTech Research).

"Boy, that Newt was a heck of a second baseman," said Saul Davis, former infielder of the Chicago American Giants.

"A good ballplayer — man, he could make that double play!" said Quincy Trouppe, former Negro Leaguer catcher. "Anything hit to either side of him, he got it. But making the double play, nobody was better. A good hitter, too! Hit some shots, a line-drive hitter."

"Newt Allen was so good that I've see him field a bunt and throw to first base without even looking," said Leo Ernstein, a Monarch fan.

John McGraw of the New York Giants once said, "Allen is one of the finest infielders, white or colored, in organized baseball."

"Newt Allen was a fair hitter, had trouble with the curve ball," said former Monarch first baseman, George Giles. "But he could field, a human vacuum sweeper. Him and Willie Wells could make more double plays than anybody in the world. They could make double plays backwards."

J.L. Wilkinson's son, Richard said: "Newt has Hall of Fame credentials, because he could do everything around second base. He was one of the best I have ever seen in making the double play."

Hilldale's
"Blue Light Special"

TOM ALLEN
(Toussaint L'Ouverture Allen, Sr.)

Height 5'9", weight 180, bats right, throws left

Nicknames: Tom, T.A.
Born: June 7, 1894, Atlanta, Georgia.
Died: March 3, 1960, Philadelphia, Pennsylvania.
World Series Age: 30.
Career: 1914–28: 1b, Havana Red Sox, Hilldale, Wilmington Potomacs, Newark Stars, Mohawk Giants, Philadelphia Tigers.
Personal: Allen was named after the architect of the fight for independence in Haiti. He is rated as an above-average fielder. With his extremely large hands, he has no equal for scooping low throws out of the dirt from infielders. But he is considered an Alka-Seltzer hitter — plop, plop, fizz, fizz. As a runner, slower than a school bus but faster than second class mail. Allen is considered a hard worker, a lunch-pail type player. He was a member of the 349th Field Artillery Unit in World War I.
1924 Season: Allen was used mostly as a backup first baseman. He can also play the outfield. He only had two games with two hits. Allen lacks power at bat but makes up for it with hustle in the field and a solid gold glove.

	G	AB	R	H	D	T	HR	AVG.	SLUG.
World Series	6	19	3	3	1	0	0	.158	.211

Kansas City's "Cherry Cola"

CLIFF BELL
(Clifford W. Bell)

Height 5'10", weight 180,
bats right, throws right

Nicknames: Cliff, Cherry, Cee Bell.
Born: July 2, 1896, Kilgore, Texas.
Died: April 13, 1952, Los Angeles, California.
World Series Age: 28.
Career: 1921–32: p, Kansas City Monarchs, Memphis Red Sox, Cleveland Cubs, Nashville Elite Giants.
Personal: Married to the former Myrtle McKnight. Cee Bell is a quiet man, seldom speaking to teammates. Bell's best pitch is a screwball. He possesses supreme control. Although described as a tough competitor, he lacks staying power. Normally used as a middle reliever. Bell has an excellent mental approach to the game, he never wants to lose. He always carries a gun for protection.
1924 Season: Early, Bell pitched three complete games in three starts, giving up only three runs. His three wins included a shutout. His shutout was only one of three shutouts for the staff. Bell later suffered a sore arm, making only four other appearances. He compiled a 2.70 RPG in Detroit's tough, miniature Mack Park.

Cliff Bell: Before suffering a sore arm, Bell pitched three complete games in three starts, giving up only three runs (NoirTech Research).

	G	IP	H	R	BB	K	W	L	ERA
World Series	2	9⅓	6	6	3	4	0	1	4.82

Kansas City's "Blue Collar Pitcher"

WILLIAM BELL
(William Bell, Sr.)

Height 5'9", weight 180, bats right, throws right

Nicknames: Bill, W Bell.
Born: August 31, 1897, Galveston, Texas.
Died: March 16, 1969, El Campo, Texas.
World Series Age: 27.
Career: 1923–48: p, manager, Kansas City Monarchs, Detroit Wolves, Homestead Grays, Pittsburgh Crawfords, Newark Dodgers, Newark Eagles, New York Black Yankees.
Personal: William Bell is married to a schoolteacher. He enjoys the scholarly works of Greek philosophers like Plato and Aristotle, with Socrates

William Bell: With the exception of Bullet Rogan, the best pitcher in the league. He won 10 games in a row in 1924 with his arsenal of four pitches and excellent control (NoirTech Research).

being his favorite. He is a member of a Masonic lodge. During the winter, he provides customers with coal and chopped wood.

Bell is the workhorse of the Monarch pitching staff. The total game dominator, he possesses a hellacious curve ball and has a better than average fastball. He is considered a technician on the mound. With his pinpoint control, he can paint the corners. Normally a notorious slow starter, Bell, once he gets lathered up, is tough to beat.

Bell retired to El Campo, Texas, in 1948. He devotes his life to helping black youngsters through Little League baseball. He died in a car accident, when his Cadillac lost control en route to a Houston airport to pick up relatives.

1924 Season: His pitching record at home was six wins and one loss, with five complete games. Bell won 10 games in a row before losing on August 30 to the Chicago American Giants. He had eight complete games in 14 starts. Of his ten wins, Bell beat the Birmingham Black Barons and the Chicago American Giants three times each. His excellent control allowed him to give up less than a hit per inning.

	G	IP	H	R	BB	K	W	L	ERA
World Series	3	24	29	13	13	6	1	0	3.38

Scouting Reports: "A fine gentleman and a scholar," said three-time 30-game winner and former teammate Chet Brewer.

"William Bell pitched a lot like a major league pitcher, had good control, would mix up his pitches and would just outsmart you at the plate," acknowledged former Crawfords outfielder Jimmie Crutchfield.

"Bell had about three or four different pitches," claimed Leo Ernstein, traveling Monarch fan.

"He would keep the great Mule Suttles at bay with a slow floating curveball that would just barely nick the outside corner of the plate. Suttles was just like putty in Bell's hands."

Hilldale's "Silver Bullet"

OTTO BRIGGS
(Otto Briggs)

Height 5'8", weight 175, bats left, throws right

Nicknames: Mirror.
Born: April 7, 1891, King's Mountain, North Carolina.
Died: October 28, 1943, Philadelphia, Pennsylvania.
World Series Age: 33.
Career: 1914–41: of, manager, West Baden (IN) Sprudels, Indianapolis ABCs, Dayton Marcos, Hilldale, Quaker Giants, Bacharach Giants, Santop's Broncos, Louisville Giants, Detroit Giants.
Personal: Briggs is quick as a wink, fast as a blink. He has turbo acceleration. Briggs' speed allows him to catch up with anything in his airspace. A

Otto Briggs: Perhaps the finest leadoff hitter in the league, blessed with speed and an ability to score somehow, someway. The slap hitter is also an outstanding fielder (From the Wm. Cash & Lloyd Thompson Collection, provided through the courtesy of the African American Museum in Philadelphia).

smooth performer and a dependable player, Briggs is a consistent performer in the outfield, a mainstay in Hilldale's right field. He has a reputation as an iron man because of his gold glove and silver bat.

Briggs is the prototype leadoff hitter. He works out of a deep crouch. Always an aggressive runner, he gets on base and somehow scores. Briggs is known for working the pitcher for a walk or two. With his trademark baggy pants, he is famous for getting nicked by a pitched ball. His hitting style is flares to all fields, making for a high on-base average. When Briggs gets on base, pitchers get busy.

Briggs is known for his odorous cigars and foghorn voice. He served with the 368th Infantry, Company E, 92nd Division that was stationed in Paris, France. He contracted malaria in Paris. He coaches a boys' and men's basketball team in the off-season and also coaches the Tribune Girls, who won eleven straight national championships. That team featured tennis pro Ora Washington (who won an unprecedented eight American Tennis Association championships) and swimming star Inez (Pat) Patterson.

He is married to the former Beatrice Perry, daughter of Christopher Perry, Jr., founder of the *Philadelphia Tribune* and co-founder of the first colored Catholic Church in Philadelphia. After retirement from baseball, he worked as the circulation manager for the *Tribune*. In the winter of 1941, he was diagnosed as having tuberculosis, spending his last days at the Castle Point Sanitarium in New York.
1924 Season: Briggs makes his home in King's Mountain, North Carolina. He was out the first half of August with a sore knee. His injury forced first baseman Carr to his outfield position and third sacker Mackey to first base. Briggs batted .387 for August upon return to the lineup. He had five games with three or more hits. Briggs batted over .300 at home but had no homers.

	G	AB	R	H	D	T	HR	AVG.	SLUG.
World Series	10	44	5	10	3	0	0	.227	.295

Scouting Reports: "Briggs is death to a fly ball hit in his territory and full of spirit on the ball field," noted in the *Philadelphia Tribune*. "His energetic play helped the morale of the club during the torrid [1925] pennant chase."

Former outfielder Gene Benson said: "He was a manager of the Bacharach Giants when I came on the team, in 1934. I heard he was one of the great outfielders in the Negro Leagues. And a good hitter. As a manager, he had a hot temper. But he was a knowledgeable man, he knew baseball. Overall, a good manager."

"Otto Briggs was an exceptionally good lead off man," said Dick Powell, former owner and business manager of the Baltimore Elite Giants. "He was what they would describe today as a hard-nose ball player. Briggs was a slap hitter, didn't hit for any real, great power. And also that was a period in that all the players used padding. He was the type of guy that would like the ball to hit him in certain situations, in order to get on base. And then he would look forward to stealing second. Otto was that kind of ballplayer. Briggs was like Rickey Henderson but lacked Rickey's power. In a crisis situation, Briggs would get on base, by hook or crook."

Hilldale's "Buster Brown"

GEORGE CARR
(George Henry Carr)

Height 6'2", weight 225, bats switch, throws right

Nickname: Tank.
Born: September 2, 1894, Atlanta, Georgia.
Died: January 14, 1948, McPherson, Kansas.
World Series Age: 29.
Career: 1912–1934: 1b, 3b, of, c, Los Angeles White Sox, Kansas City Monarchs, Hilldale, Bacharach Giants, Philadelphia Stars, Lincoln Giants, Washington Pilots, Baltimore Black Sox.

George Carr: The former Monarch is a versatile player with a good stick who can play several positions (NoirTech Research).

Personal: Carr is an underrated player who usually hits for a high average. He likes to wear his baseball cap to one side while sporting a painted smirk on his face. As strong as a bulldozer, Tank also has good speed. He is known as a free-swinger, prone to strike out, because of his vulnerability to off-speed pitches. Carr has a reputation as a moody player. At times, he will not play to his full potential.

In the field, Carr is an excellent first baseman. He has a desire for alcoholic refreshments. In the off-season, Carr drives a cab for the Panama Cab Company and also works part-time for a moving company. Carr has been known to sleep for long periods. Wears glasses when not on the field.

1924 Season: Carr played mostly first base and left field. He hit an incredible .571 against the Harrisburg Giants while slugging them for a 1.000 percentage. He also banged the Cuban Stars with a .434 average. He really enjoyed the friendly confines of Hilldale Park, batting .330 at home, but hit only .250 on the road.

	G	AB	R	H	D	T	HR	AVG.	SLUG.
World Series	8	18	1	6	0	0	0	.333	.333

Scouting Reports: He had a propensity for consuming large quantities of alcohol. Teammate Clint Thomas said, "On payday, every time you saw Carr he had a fish sandwich in one hand and a pint of liquor in the other."

"George Carr was a big fellow, a good first baseman," said Dick Powell, former owner and business manager of the Baltimore Elite Giants. "He could hit the ball far, but was slow afoot. Typical of the period, they would put slow fellows like Carr at first. But he was a good hitter and a dangerous hitter. He played a good game at first base, but he wasn't a fancy Dan, but he played a steady game at first."

Carr talked about the time he won a horse. "Yep, I won a horse with a hit. That was at the Olive Street Park (Association Park). It was in the ninth inning of a hard fought game. We were on the short end of a 2–1 score. There were two outs and the tying run was on second. Just before I went to bat a fan yelled to me that he'd bet his horse against a five-dollar bill that I couldn't get a hit. I yelled back that his bet was called.

"Well, sir, I never wanted to hit a ball in my life as much as I wanted to hit then, but the pitcher kept cutting the corners on me and the umpire yelled 'Strike Two.'

"I said a short prayer. The next ball came down the middle. I let go and the ball streaked over the fence and on down 19th Street, somewhere. After the game this man who had made the bet with me came leading a big bay horse up by the bridle. 'He's yours,' he said and thanked me for hitting the ball. Later, J.L. Wilkinson, who owned the team, purchased the horse from me and paid me in Liberty Bonds."

**Hilldale's
"Purple Panther"**

PHIL COCKRELL
(Philip Williams)

Height 5'9", weight 180, bats right, throws right

Nicknames: Fish, Georgia Rose, aka Phil Cockerell.
Born: June 26, 1898, Augusta, Georgia.
Died: March 31, 1951, Philadelphia, Pennsylvania.
World Series Age: 26.
Career: 1913–46: p, of, Havana Red Sox, Lincoln Giants, Hilldale, Darby Daisies, Bacharach Giants, Philadelphia Stars; umpire, NNL.
Personal: Phil is married to Addie. For unknown reasons, Williams started his pro career under the name of Cockerell, later changing to Cockrell. He is known as a talented all-around athlete. Cockrell is known around the league as the Director of Aquatic Activities, because of his quality spitter. He is definitely a sprinkler with 100 percent probability of immeasurable precipitation. He

also has an excellent fastball and good control. Cockrell is the third man in the pitching rotation behind Winters and Ryan.

Before the season, Cockrell was credited with two no-hitters: on September 5, 1921, defeating the Detroit Stars, 4–0, and against the tough Chicago American Giants on August 8, 1922, with Hilldale winning 5–0.

Cockrell is a fairly good hitting pitcher. He has good speed on the basepaths and is considered the cleverest baserunner in the league. He is often used as a pinch runner or as a defensive replacement in late innings.

In 1951, Cockrell was killed while walking home from his bartending job one morning. The assailant mistakenly believed Cockrell to be his wife's boyfriend and fatally stabbed him.

Phil Cockrell: Likes to throw the wet one. A pitcher with a decent fastball and very good control, Cockrell was undefeated at home in 1924. He has thrown two no-hitters (NoirTech Research).

1924 Season: Cockrell is undefeated at home with a 9–0 record, which included nine complete games in eleven decisions. He had a 3–0 record against the Cuban Stars and compiled three complete games in three starts against them. He won his last five starts, all complete games, coming into the series.

	G	IP	H	R	BB	K	W	L	ERA
World Series	2	9⅔	10	10	4	5	0	1	5.58

Scouting Reports: "Cockrell was a great pitcher," said Hilldale's diminutive shortstop Jake Stephens, "but you hated to play behind him because he threw that grease ball and you would get a hold of the grease sometimes, and just couldn't throw it true."

"Phil Cockrell with his spitball was some pitcher," said Dick Powell, former owner and business manager of the Baltimore Elite Giants. "Doc Sykes and Cockrell were both outstanding spitball pitchers."

"I remember once when Ambrose Reid refused to let Cockrell get away with a calcimine job and hit one of Phil's slippery slants behind the left field fence," said scorekeeper Lloyd Thompson. "But Cockrell's choicest saliva slants gave him many a win for the [Hilldale] Daisies Club."

Thompson added: "Phil was one of the lost art spitball hurlers, small of stature as pitchers go, however was a master of the profession, combining great skill with a strong right arm. Phil's spitter routine on every pitch was often just fake motions to baffle the batter. Cockrell was also a dangerous hitter."

Hilldale's "Red Snapper"

RUBE CURRIE
(Reuben Currie)

Height 6'4", weight 195, bats right, throws right

Nicknames: Rube, Sprout, King Kurrie.
Born: October 10, 1898, Kansas City, Missouri.
Died: June 15, 1966, Chicago, Illinois.
World Series Age: 25.
Career: 1916–32: p, Kansas City Tigers, Chicago Union Giants, Kansas City Monarchs, Hilldale, Chicago American Giants, Detroit Stars, Cleveland Red Sox, Baltimore Black Sox.
Personal: Currie is married with no children. He is known around the league as a control pitcher with a test-tube curveball. He has a high-powered slider plus an above average cut fastball. Currie is considered one of the best pitchers in the game because of his studious nature. He is also a tough-luck finesse pitcher because his team

Rube Currie: Another former Monarch taken in the raid by Eastern teams, Currie has one of the best curveballs ever. Injured earlier in the '24 season, he is still trying to recoup his form (Courtesy of Kimshi Productions).

often failed to score runs for him. Currie has silky smooth delivery and sporadic spurts of emotions. He attended Lincoln High School in Kansas City with Monarchs Frank Duncan and Newt Allen.

1924 Season: Currie joins the team after spending the previous season with the Monarchs. He pitched excellent ball during the winter for the champion Santa Clara team of the Cuban league. In the first game, he injured his pitching shoulder while sliding into first base, attempting to beat out a sacrifice bunt. Currie never fully regained pitching form. He pitched in a few semipro games in an attempt to get back into shape. He did not pitch a complete game until September against the semipro Lit Brothers of Philly. He pitched a shutout, giving up five hits. Currie had a subpar season for a normally superb pitcher.

	G	IP	H	R	BB	K	W	L	ERA
World Series	3	16⅓	12	3	2	3	1	1	0.55**

Scouting Reports: "A student of the game, taught me the finer points of the game," said former teammate, Chet Brewer. "He taught me how to set up hitters and make them swing at my best pitch. Truly an outstanding pitcher."

"That son-of-a-gun had a great curve ball," said former teammate Saul Davis, second baseman for the Chicago American Giants. "He was a honey of a player."

"Currie had a variety of curveballs, but not much of a change-up," said Leo Ernstein, a Monarch fan. "But he would always cross up Cristobal Torrienti. Torrienti had power to the opposite field, and Currie always pitched him inside all the time."

Umpire Billy Donaldson spoke highly of Currie: "King Currie was a curveball artist and a victor in many a close contest, but was the jinx moundsman of this staff. It seemed as though the boys would never hit behind or field their best when he was on the mound."

Kansas City's "Black & Blue Bruiser"

Plunk Drake
(William P. Drake)

Height 6'0", weight 210, bats right, throws right

Nicknames: Bill, Plunk.
Born: June 8, 1895, Sedalia, Missouri.
Died: October 30, 1977, St. Louis, Missouri.
World Series Age: 29.
Career: 1914–30: p, manager, Brown's Tennessee Rats, St. Louis Giants, St. Louis Stars, Kansas City Monarchs, Indianapolis ABCs, Detroit Stars, Memphis Red Sox, Tulsa Black Oilers.
Personal: Plunk was known for his habit of throwing at batters. He called his

high-and-tight pitches "chin music," and he could play an entire symphony for the opposing team. Drake is a tough competitor who keeps batters loose in the box. He is a finesse pitcher who nibbles at the corners. Sometimes Drake has control problems, intentionally and unintentionally. His best pitch is the roundhouse curveball, which he loved to throw on full counts. Along with the curve, he has a variety of trick pitches, including an emery ball and a hesitation wind-up. Drake is rumored to sometimes add a little "do-it to-it" fluid to the baseball. He competes like a madman.

Drakes claims he taught the legendary Satchel Paige his hesitation pitch. He is renowned for his quick pickoff move. Some players called it a balk, while others say it is a superb maneuver. Drake is a good hitting pitcher.

Superstitious, Drake would always shine his baseball shoes before each game for good luck. He is known as a comical storyteller with a boisterous laugh who keeps his teammates loose on the bench. The team's perennial poker player also owns a chicken farm in Sedalia, Missouri.

Plunk Drake: They didn't call him Plunk for nothing. The professor of chin music at times uses an emery ball to go along with his hesitation wind-up. Drake also has an excellent pickoff move (NoirTech Research).

1924 Season: A fine hitting pitcher (.271), Drake homered against the St. Louis Stars in September to help his cause. He was bombed by his hometown St. Louis Stars for 16 runs in 18 innings. However, Drake did pitch five complete games in seven starts against arch-nemesis the Chicago American Giants, winning three games while losing four.

	G	IP	H	R	BB	K	W	L	ERA
World Series	4	13⅔	14	8	5	5	0	1	3.95 **

Scouting Reports: All-around athlete and educator George Sweatt said, "He liked to throw at people. He'd throw three balls—one at your foot, one at your head, one behind you. Then he'd pitch. You didn't know what he was going to do, he was so crazy."

Even Drake half-heartedly agreed: "I guess I was just too chesty."

Former Chicago American Giant infielder Saul Davis said: "That Plunk Drake was a mean pitcher. He could cut that ball in a minute, knock you down, too. He just didn't care."

Former Negro League umpire Billy Donaldson said: "Big Plunk Drake was right there with the goods throughout the season and pitched many wins by close scores. I would consider him a very brainy pitcher."

Frank Duncan: One of the top defensive catchers in the league. The charismatic catcher is known to showboat behind the plate when he is framing pitches or talking to batters. The hitters must really concentrate in the batter's box when Dunk starts his chatter (NoirTech Research).

Kansas City's "Browning Automatic"

FRANK DUNCAN
(Frank Lee Duncan, Jr.)

Height 6'0", weight 170, bats right, throws right

Nicknames: Dunk, Bat Boy.
Born: February 14, 1901, Kansas City, Missouri.
Died: December 4, 1973, Kansas City, Missouri.
World Series Age: 23.
Career: 1920–48: c, of, manager, umpire, Chicago Giants, Kansas City Monarchs, New York Black Yankees, Pittsburgh Crawfords, Homestead Grays, New York Cubans, Chicago American Giants.
Personal: Duncan is young but the top defensive catcher in the league. He is a tough catcher to steal on. Duncan is blessed with a rifle-accurate arm and a quick release. He can explode from the crouch position to throw out potential base stealers in a flash. Duncan often likes to showboat for the fans by turning flips on pop-ups behind the plate or diving for big-breaking curveballs out of the strike zone.

He is known as a fastball catcher, which can be a positive or negative attribute. Duncan is called a superb technician by his pitching staff because he possesses excellent recall of batters' weaknesses. The down-'n'-dirty defender is known for his manicured fingernails.

As a hitter, Duncan is a line drive place hitter. He is tough in the clutch, but lacks power. He is an excellent fastball hitter, while breaking stuff gives him fits. Duncan has reputation as a nice guy off the field and a tough-as-toenails player on the field. He runs the bases with reckless abandon.

The former Navy man with three sons has a magnetic personality. Duncan has been married three times—Nelle Wormley, Bertha Bennett and finally Julia Lee, known as the "Princess of the Boogie-Woogie." Lee sang for big band master Bennie Moten, along with legendary jazz queens Clara Smith and Bessie Smith. Duncan drove the bus for the team and for Moten's band and a cab in the off-season. He and his son, pitcher Frank Duncan, III, became the first father and son battery to play on the same professional team during a 1941 exhibition game. **1924 Season:** Duncan became the full-time catcher when Henry "Wildcat" Williams went on the injured reserve list with a broken hand early in the season. He had a nine game hitting streak but no homers to show for his efforts. Duncan started out hitting a .321 average in the first 15 games before slumping after Memorial Day. He hit over .300 against the Birmingham Black Barons and the Indianapolis ABCs.

	G	AB	R	H	D	T	HR	AVG.	SLUG.
World Series	10	36	2	5	1	0	0	.139	.167

Scouting Reports: Monarch second baseman Newt Allen bragged: "Duncan was a great receiver and thrower—one of the best. We both went to Lincoln High School three years. Frank was a very fine fellow, a good manager, a very, very likable fellow, even among other ball clubs and a wonderful catcher. We roomed together for 16 years. We spent all those nights on the seats of the bus. And we got to love one another, all of us. That's the reason we had a good ball club."

"I can't say enough about him," Dizzy Dean said. "I sure got a kick out of Duncan [in the 1934 exhibition series]. One time when Duncan catches me, he has a glove that makes the ball pop, and it makes my pitch sound like a rifle shot and Duncan keeps telling them hitters, 'Boy, don't get near that plate. Don't let that ball hit you or it'll kill you.'"

"You couldn't fool around with him none with men on bases," recalled Willard (Home Run) Brown. "He could hit better with men on base, because he'd choke up and be right on that plate. He was a good clutch hitter. He was a line-drive hitter, and when he went up there with men on bases, he hit a whole lot of doubles."

"Frank was one of the greatest receivers and throwers I ever saw behind the bat and he was always full of vim, vigor and fight 'em," said T.Y. Baird, co-owner of the Monarchs.

"A hard worker behind the plate, the best catcher I ever seen," said former Chicago American Giant Saul Davis. "A sweetheart of a catcher. He had better catching skills than the great Josh Gibson."

"In our baseball, our manager had to be the one to go in and see if we could eat," said John "Buck" O'Neil, former Monarch manager and teammate. "He also went in to see if we could sleep. Frank could 'talk-that-talk' and he had to be able to. Because if Frank didn't, we were not going to get in and out of some of the spots we were in."

O'Neil added: "When I lost Frank I lost one of my best friends. Baseball lost one of its best managers. He was one of the best catchers we ever saw. I couldn't say he was better than Josh Gibson or Biz Mackey or [Bill] Dickey or [Roy] Campanella, but I think he had the best throwing arm in baseball."

Speedster "Cool Papa" Bell boasted: "To this day Frank was one of the greatest catchers ever. He could throw. You had to get a bigger lead on the pitcher with Frank behind the plate. If you didn't, you might as well turn right around and go back to first. Nobody could hardly beat him throwing."

"Frank was one we were kickin' on to get in the Hall of Fame," said Hall of Famer Satchel Paige. "Campanella got a break, I got a break, but nobody was a better catcher than Frank outside of Josh. It was like clockwork pitchin' to that man. I guess I could throw harder than anybody. I musta thrown hard because nobody ever hit me hard. But Frank was the man who keep me going. When I wanted to quit in 1938 [because of a bad arm], Frank kept tellin' me, keep at it, keep at it, keep at it. If it hadn't been for him, I never would have gone to Cleveland."

Richard Wilkinson, son of J.L., recalled: "He was a good manager, but Frank loved everybody and he wanted everybody to love him. This was actually impossible, because a lot of players took advantage of this. Despite all of this, he was a knowledgeable baseball man."

Frank Duncan, III, who pitched for the Baltimore Elite Giants from 1944 to 1946, recalls of his father's gamesmanship: "I don't think I've ever seen a better defensive catcher. Nowhere! Black leagues, major leagues, nowhere else. There was one thing he did that I have never seen another catcher do. And that's when a runner would try to steal third base and a right-handed hitter came up to bat. Very seldom would you see a potential base stealer try to steal third with a left-handed batter up. The catcher would then have a clear shot at getting him out. Always steal with a right-hander up there. But something my Dad used to do, either he knew or had an assumption that the guy was going to third base. He would tell the umpire to back up a little. He would never let a hitter hear him say this. He would usually say to the umpire just before the hitter came up to the plate, 'The man is going to third now, but I gotta have some room. I don't throw over the top of a right-handed hitter's head. Nor do I step out in front to throw — I take one step back and throw behind him. And I haven't missed one yet!'"

Son Frank added: "Remember Charlie Dressen [former American and

National League manager for 16 years]? Well, Charlie told me one time that while playing against my father in Cuba one winter, he had never seen a catcher compare with father anywhere, defensively."

Former battery mate William Bell claimed: "Dunk was an excellent catcher. Every owner wanted him. He played in nearly as many places as Hamlet: the Philippines, Japan, Hawaii, Cuba, South American and North America."

Kansas City's "Prison Gray"

LEM HAWKINS
(Lemuel Hawkins)

Height 5'10", weight 165, bats left, throws left

Nicknames: Hawk, Lem, Hawkshaw, alias Leonard.
Born: October 2, 1895, Macon, Georgia.
Died: August 10, 1934, Chicago, Illinois.
World Series Age: 29.
Career: 1919–29: 1b, of, manager, Los Angeles White Sox, Kansas City Monarchs, Chicago Giants, Chicago American Giants, Shreveport Black Sports, Dallas Black Giants, Booker T's.
Personal: Hawkins has a reputation as a ladies' man. He is known for his "skirt alerts" to notify teammates of passing females. As a player, he is a very good first baseman and spirited base runner. He is also a dependable hitter and protects

Lem Hawkins: The league's top fielding first sacker, the emotional leader of the Monarchs is a top-flight lead-off hitter, much like his Hilldale counterpart Otto Briggs (NoirTech Research).

the strike zone, making him an excellent leadoff hitter. Hawkins is a contact hitter, but lacks power. He has a refuse-to-lose attitude. Hawk is an emotional player, and sometimes cries after a tough loss.

Hawkins is also known as a big-time spender. He turned to crime after his baseball career. In May 1931 he was cleared of murder charges in the death of Lon Campbell (for reasons of self-defense) in an incident involving a card game. Later that year, Hawkins was convicted of driving a getaway car in the robbery of A.M.E. Zion Church, resulting in two years in Leavenworth (Kansas) State Prison. He was also wanted for questioning regarding a holdup of Bordman Investment Company. While attempting to rob a beer truck in a Chicago alley, he was accidentally shot in the left ear by his accomplice, and the bullet pierced his brain.

1924 Season: Hawkins is captain. The *Chicago Defender* rates him the league's best first sacker. In July, Hawkins was suspended for fighting and fined $25. He started with a 16-game hitting streak, batting .371. Hawk built a 13-game hitting streak during June. He has no homers. Hawkins loves to hit against the Indianapolis ABCs and the Memphis Red Sox, hitting .466 and .444 respectively.

	G	AB	R	H	D	T	HR	AVG.	SLUG.
World Series	9	31	4	6	1	0	0	.194	.226

Scouting Reports: "Hall, Swinton, Morgan, Collins [Lem] Hawkins, Goliath, [Dobie] Moore, Fagan, Jackson and Sweatt, all these guys did their bit and then some," said acclaimed 25th Infantry Captain John H. Nankiwell. "They are the men that made the 25th Infantry Baseball Team the champions of the Hawaiian Islands."

Hilldale's
"Plain Brown Rapper"

GEORGE JOHNSON
(George Washington Johnson, Jr.)
Height 6'1", weight 180, bats right, throws right

Nicknames: Dibo, Junior.
Born: April 20, 1890, San Marcos, Texas.
Died: August 13, 1940, Philadelphia, Pennsylvania.
World Series Age: 34.
Career: 1909–31: of, Fort Worth Wonders, Kansas City (KS) Giants, Brooklyn Royal Giants, Hilldale, Lincoln Giants, Philadelphia Tigers, Philadelphia Giants, Bacharach Giants.
Personal: Dibo is married and is a steady-heady ballplayer with a strong throwing arm. Johnson is known for his ability to cover center field. His tremendous speed allows him to haul in drives to the gap, and stretch his doubles to triples. Johnson has power at the plate. If he gets a pitch in his zone, he can drive it as

far as anyone in the game. He is a serial killer of curveballs. He and Judy Johnson are known as the Band-Aid boys, Johnson & Johnson, who give first-aid support to their pitchers. In 1924, he became the first ballplayer on record seeking to organize a players' union.

1924 Season: Dibo suffered one of his worst seasons, batting only .250. He is a streaky hitter, hot and cold. He almost hit for the cycle, with a double, home run and single against the Brooklyn Royal Giants in the third game of the season. Some of his streaks include a four-game series against the Lincoln Giants in June, when Johnson batted .437 (7 for 16). In July, he batted .666 in four games (8 for 12) and in the last six games of the season batted .400 (8 for 20) with three doubles.

George Johnson: A hot-and-cold hitter who hits curveballs as well as fastballs. The speedy centerfielder with the brawny arm can cover the outfield from foul pole to foul pole (From the Wm. Cash & Lloyd Thompson Collection, provided through the courtesy of the African American Museum in Philadelphia).

	G	AB	R	H	D	T	HR	AVG.	SLUG.
World Series	10	38	3	9	2	2	0	.237	.395

Scouting Report: "George covers more ground in the center pasture of Hilldale Park than a wig does on a bald man's head," wrote the *Philadelphia Tribune* (1925).

Kansas City's "Black Power"

HEAVY JOHNSON
(Oscar Johnson)
Height 5'11", weight 235, bats left, throws right

Nickname: Heavy.
Born: April 20, 1895, Atchison, Kansas.

Died: January 12, 1964, Cincinnati, Ohio.
World Series Age: 28.
Career: 1922–33: of, c, 2b, Kansas City Monarchs, Baltimore Black Sox, Harrisburg Giants, Cleveland Tigers, Memphis Red Sox, Dayton Marcos.
Personal: Married Juanita Powell of Atchison, Kansas, in July 1923. Johnson is known to put on a little extra weight during the off-season. He is as heavy as a Chevy. Oscar is known for leaning "heavy" on the horsehide. He is labeled as one of the nasty boys—moody and temperamental.

Johnson is a strength hitter and considered one of the league's most dangerous power hitters. Don't hang a curve ball because he is recognized for his cloud-kissing home runs.

Despite his size, Johnson is an average outfielder with average range. He is a remarkably fast runner for his bulk. He can occasionally play catcher. **1924 Season:** Johnson had four games with four hits. He hit three doubles against the Indianapolis ABCs in a game. He also batted .588 in the four-game series vs. the ABCs in May, going 10 for 17. Johnson later batted .529 in four-game series vs. the Birmingham Black Barons in July, going 9 for 17. On August 9, he was beaned by the Black Barons' pitcher Poindexter and carried off the field. Upon his return to action, he hit a torrid .460 in August. Heavy slugged for over .400 against the Black Barons, Cleveland Browns and the Memphis Red Sox. Known for his consistency, Johnson unloaded for a .373 average at home and .370 on the road. Heavy was steady.

Oscar "Heavy" Johnson: Heavy as a Chevy, but runs like a Corvette. One of the most feared batters in the Monarch lineup, and with good reason. Mister Johnson hit over .400 against three teams in 1924 (NoirTech Research).

	G	AB	R	H	D	T	HR	AVG.	SLUG.
World Series	9	27	2	7	3	0	0	.259	.370

Scouting Reports: "Heavy Johnson hit a home run off the Yankee Carl Mays, and Mays was a high price pitcher," said Leo Ernstein, a Monarch super fan. "Mays was making something like $20,000 a year, a submarine pitcher. He hit that ball about 400 feet. He hit the ball over the scoreboard at Association Park, that was on 20th and Olive Street."

When reminiscing about the 25th Infantry team, Captain John H. Nankivell recalled: "First of all, there comes to mind Rogan, whose masterful pitching carried the regimental team to victory in many a tight game, but then there was Oscar [Heavy] Johnson, who made the record breaking hit and home run in the last half of the ninth inning against the Olympic Club of California."

"I remember one time he was sleeping on the bench and they woke him up to go in and pinch-hit," said a laughing pitcher Plunk Drake. "He reached down and got a fungo bat and went out there and hit a home run."

**Hilldale's
"Blue Chip Prospect"**

JUDY JOHNSON
(William Julius Johnson)
Height 5'11", weight 155, bats right, throws right

Nicknames: Judy, Papa, Jing.
Born: October 26, 1899, Snow Hill, Maryland.
Died: June 15, 1989, Wilmington, Delaware.
World Series Age: 24.
Career: 1918–38: 3b, ss, manager, Hilldale, Homestead Grays, Darby Daisies, Pittsburgh Crawfords.
Personal: In 1923, Johnson married a schoolteacher, Anita T. Irons. They would have one daughter, Loretta, who later married Milwaukee Braves outfielder Billy Bruton. The nondrinker was nicknamed "Jingo" by premier slugger and teammate Josh Gibson. Johnson credits Hall of Fame infielder John Henry "Pop" Lloyd with his early development, saying: "He's the man I gave the credit to for polishing me, he taught me how to play third base and how to protect myself. John taught me more baseball than anyone else."

Respected by teammates as an excellent sportsman, Judy is a top-notch defensive third baseman. Possessing intelligence, cool and patience, Johnson is the consummate finesse player. He is also an excellent sign-stealer. Welding a 40-ounce bat, he is notorious for his clutch hits from an unorthodox batting stance.

Judy Johnson: Perhaps the game's best clutch hitter is also a top-notch, rock steady infielder. Although slight of build, Judy packs power (Courtesy of Todd Bolton).

A smart baserunner, Judy can stretch singles into doubles. An all-around performer, he is a paragon of baseball excellence.

1924 Season: This is his first great season in the big time. This year, he showed potential of being a cereal box cover boy. He had 10 games in which he gathered three or more hits and he led the club in doubles. He hit three of his four homers in July while batting .345 for the month. During this stretch, he banged three hits each in three successive games. This season, Johnson blitzed the Baltimore Black Sox for a .432 average and a .676 slugging percentage.

	G	AB	R	H	D	T	HR	AVG.	SLUG.
World Series	10	44	7	16	5	1	1	.364	.591

Scouting Reports: Connie Mack, owner of the Philadelphia A's, once told him, "If you were a white boy you could name your own price."

Rollo Wilson, sportswriter for the *Pittsburgh Courier*, wrote about his Most Valuable Player selection in 1929: "If you've ever seen him play and have marked his pep and ability you know why I chose him over all the rest. If colored athletes were as earnest generally as this boy, there would be a vast improvement in the game, the box offices would pick up, and everyone would prosper." Wilson added: "He was a great ball player and gentleman. Never argued about anything. Very seldom he argued a strike or a play on the bases. He was a gentleman all through those baseball years when baseball was just as rough as could be. He was the type of fellow that didn't try to hurt anyone. He just went along and played the game. You have respect for a man like that."

"Judy Johnson was the smartest third baseman I ever came across," Pittsburgh Crawfords outfielder Ted Page said. "A scientific ball player, did everything with grace and poise. You talk about playing third base—heck, he was better than anybody I ever saw. And I saw Brooks Robinson, Mike Schmidt and even Pie Traynor. He had a powerful accurate arm. He could do anything, come in for a ball, cut it off at the line, or range way over toward the shortstop hole. He was really something. Played a heady game of baseball, none of this just slugging the ball, a man on first base, and he just dies there because you didn't hit the ball up against the wall. Judy would steal your signals. He should have been in the major leagues 15 or 20 years as a coach. They talk about Negro managers. I always thought that Judy should have made perfect major league manager."

"That Judy, was like a rock [consistent]," noted former Crawfords teammate Jimmy Crutchfield, "a steadying influence on the club. Had a great brain, could anticipate a play, knew what his opponents were going to do. And nobody stole more signs."

James "Cool Papa" Bell said: "Johnson wasn't the best hitter among the four top third basemen in the Negro Leagues, but no one would drive in as many clutch runs as he would. He was a solid ballplayer, real smart, but he was the kind of fellow who could 'just get it done.' He was dependable, quiet, not flashy at all, but could handle anything that came up. No matter how much the pressure, no matter how important the play or the throw or the hit, Judy could do it when it counted." Bell added: "As a person, you could trust him in every way possible. I would trust him with my life and my money. He would never let you down. He was always up and optimistic. He brought sunshine into your life. When things got rough for us, Judy would always say, 'Somewhere the sun is always shining.' Judy and Jimmie Crutchfield are the two finest people I met in baseball."

"Judy Johnson was definitely one of the best," said Dick Powell, former owner and business manager of the Baltimore Elite Giants. "Good hitter too! Consistent hitter."

Lloyd Thompson, a former Hilldale scorekeeper, said: "Judy could do all that is required to make up a sterling third baseman and do it better than the rest of the field. A right-hand hitter, Judy developed a peculiar stance at the plate and hit the ball hard to all corners of the lot. Slight of build, this Hilldale luminary was a fielding gem, whose breath-taking plays on bunts and hard smashes are treasured among many fans' memories."

Newt Joseph: The intense competitor is prone to strike out. However, he normally hits for a high average but is a little slow afoot. Likes to play in tight at third base, a bona fide goosebump player (NoirTech Research).

Kansas City's "Red Hot Pepper"

NEWT JOSEPH
(Walter Lee Joseph)

Height 5'9", weight 165, bats right, throws right

Nicknames: Newt, Blood & Guts, Pep, Nimrod.
Born: October 27, 1899, Montgomery, Alabama.
Died: January 18, 1953, Kansas City, Missouri.
World Series Age: 24.
Career: 1922–39: 3b, manager, Kansas City Monarchs, Paige's All-Stars.
Personal: Married to Beatrice, Joseph is known as an intense competitor. An animated player and nonstop talker (he suffered a tonsillitis attack during the 1923 season), Joseph is the team's holler guy. He is called the team's best dresser.

Joseph hits for a high average but is prone to strike out. Although he has a strong and accurate arm, he has a reputation for playing the bunt very close. Because he likes to play in tight, Joseph is called the "Pepper Sauce of the Infield" by his teammates. He is a great sign stealer, providing the key to several Monarch victories. Not a gifted runner, he runs the basepaths like a turtle in quicksand. He may be slower than a holiday parade, but Joseph is a thrill to watch in the field, a bona fide goosebump player.

Joseph is also owner of the Paseo Taxi Cab company, which was later named the Monarch Cab company. He is a great hunter and fisherman and is known for shooting jackrabbits from the team bus for a quick happy meal.

1924 Season: Joseph is the Monarchs' surprise performer. In May, Newt was hotter than a potbelly stove, compiling a 12-game hitting streak with a .680 average (28 for 41), with eight doubles and two triples. Joseph hit 21 doubles, and had 12 games with three or more hits. Against the Indianapolis ABCs, he had two doubles and two triples, going 4-for-4. He added another 4-for-4 game against the Chicago American Giants. His second-longest hitting streak of the year was 11 games, banging out a .422 average. Overall, he scrambled the ABCs with a .588 average and an astounding 1.118 slugging percentage. Joseph hit three of his four homers against his hometown Birmingham Black Barons, while compiling a .467 average.

	G	AB	R	H	D	T	HR	AVG.	SLUG.
World Series	10	38	6	5	1	0	1	.132	.237

Scouting Reports: Teammate Newt Allen called him a student of the game: "Great sign stealer. He'd watch everybody on the other ball club, and in three innings, if there was any kind of sign, he'd have one or two of them."

Once asked by a radio announcer in Okmulgee, Oklahoma, "If you could go to the major leagues today, who would you take with you?" Joseph replied, "The entire Monarchs team."

"Joseph could go to his left or right equally well," said World Series fan Leo Ernstein.

"Newt was never known as a great hitter but won many a game for the club with drives that were natural home runs for most players—but Newt was lucky to get to third base," said Quincy Gilmore, business manager of the Monarchs. "Newt never could run, but Newt was the greatest defensive third sacker Negro baseball has ever known. No player, black or white, could handle bunts like Newt."

Hilldale's
"Purple Heart Beau"

Scrip Lee
(Holsey Scranton Lee, Sr.)

Height 6'3", weight 190, bats right, throws right

Nicknames: Scrip, Sparky, Scriptus.
Born: January 29, 1899, Washington, D.C.
Died: February 13, 1974, Washington, D.C.
World Series Age: 25.

Career: 1920–43: p, of, Norfolk Stars, Philadelphia Stars, Philadelphia Royal Giants, Hilldale, Norfolk Giants, Richmond Giants, Baltimore Black Sax, Bacharach Giants, Cleveland Red Sox, Philadelphia Giants; umpire, NNL.

Personal: Lee is a submarine pitcher with an ocean-in-the-motion delivery. From this angle he delivers a three-gears curve ball, a sinking fastball, and a butterfly knuckler. Lee has nothing but junk. He is an excellent fielding pitcher, along with being a good bunter. His rep is his ability to handle Josh Gibson's power. Lee is a very competitive competitor.

Lee is superstitious and prefers to wear white socks over the customary grays. He attended grade school with Duke Ellington. He also played club football with the famous Georgetown Athletes as a kicker/punter. Lee served in the all-black 372nd Infantry, stationed in Paris, France, where he won two medals, the coveted Meuse Argonne and Purple Heart.

1924 Season: Lee was used mostly as a relief pitcher. He did pitch complete games against the Brooklyn Royal Giants, giving up one run on five hits, and the Bacharach Giants, yielding four earned runs on 12 hits in a 10 inning loss. Lee once filled in admirably at third base for Mackey when Biz missed transportation connections.

Scrip Lee: The submarine pitcher likes to throw a lot of junk — a butterfly knuckler and a variety of curve balls (NoirTech Research).

	G	IP	H	R	BB	K	W	L	ERA
World Series	3	23⅓	19	9	4	10	0	2	3.09 **

Scouting Reports: Lee claimed his greatest thrill in baseball was "relieving Red Ryan in the 5th inning of the first Colored World Series [game 3], trailing 5 to 3 with the game ending 6 all after 13 innings."

"Scrip Lee was just a good ball player," said Dick Powell, former owner and business manager of the Baltimore Elite Giants. "Scrip could pitch and play outfield. A good hitter, too! He was a finesse type of pitcher."

Hilldale's
"Jolly Green Giant"

JOE LEWIS
(Joseph Herman Lewis)
Height 5'11", weight 195, bats right, throws right

Nicknames: Sleepy, Joe.
Born: January 17, 1895, Drakes Branch, Virginia.
Died: October 1986, Portsmouth, Virginia.
World Series Age: 29.
Career: 1919–36, 1939, 1942, 1946–48: c, 3b, manager, Baltimore Black Sox, Baltimore Grays, Washington Potomacs, Homestead Grays, Hilldale, Lincoln Giants, Quaker Giants, Darby Daisies, Bacharach Giants, Norfolk-Newport News Royals, Brooklyn Royal Giants, Belleville (Georgia) Grays.
Personal: He was born on the same day of the month as the boastful Muhammad Ali, but Lewis is a quiet man. He makes less noise than a Buckingham Palace guard.

Lewis is a journeyman catcher and utility player. Always the dependable performer, he is steady under pressure. He is known as a great handler of pitchers and is tough to steal on. Lewis can explode from the crouch position and throw out potential base stealers with missile-like accuracy. Base stealers should beware of his bionic arm. He is also a great handler of the knuckleball and has ability to go down in the dirt for errant pitches. Known as a pitcher's delight, Lewis is an original "rocking-chair-catcher." He calls a "good" game. Lewis runs like a catcher, which means slow.

He works as a riveter in the off-season. He loves his vittles and is known to weigh up to 260 pounds in the off-season. He likes sweet treats and cars—owns a vintage Hudson Roadster.
1924 Season: This is Lewis' first season with Hilldale. He came to the Hilldale club from the Homestead Grays, by way of the Washington Potomacs, where he suffered a broken leg. He saw limited action, playing behind catching legends Biz Mackey and Lou Santop and future Hall of Fame third baseman Judy Johnson.

	G	AB	R	H	D	T	HR	AVG.	SLUG.
World Series	7	17	1	3	1	0	0	.176	.235

"Pretty good catcher!" recalled Dick Powell, former owner and business manager of the Baltimore Elite Giants. "When we played our doubleheaders here in Baltimore, Doc Sykes and Lewis were the battery in the first game. [Nick] Logan and [Charley] Thomas would be the battery for the second game for the old Baltimore Black Sox. Joe Lewis was not an exceptional catcher. Joe was a good number two catcher. Joe batted right-handed, a pretty good hitter and could hit the ball out of the park on an occasion. Particularly in the Black Sox Park, there were no butterfly home runs. You had to hit the ball pretty good to get it out of the park, unlike the bandboxes today."

Biz Mackey: He is the standard for catchers in the league, but must play shortstop in the league to allow for Santop's spot in the lineup. A rarity among hitters, Biz is a power puncher who seldom strikes out (NoirTech Research).

Hilldale's
"Black Mack Attack"

BIZ MACKEY
(James Raleigh Mackey)
Height 6'0", weight 240, bats switch, throws right

Nicknames: Biz or Bizz (for Busy-Body).
Born: July 27, 1897, Eagle Pass, Texas.
Died: September 22, 1965, Los Angeles, California.
World Series Age: 27.
Career: 1918–48: c, ss, 3b, of, 2b, 1b, p, manager, San Antonio Giants, Indianapolis ABCs, Hilldale, Darby Daisies, Philadelphia Stars, Washington Elite Giants, Baltimore Elite Giants, Newark Eagles, Newark Dodgers, Nashville Elite Giants, Homestead Grays, San Francisco Sea Lions.
Personal: Mackey is one of the greatest catchers in baseball history. Some players claim he is better than his contemporaries, Josh Gibson, Louis Santop or Bruce Petway. Biz is a master defensive technician and superb handler of pitchers. He is an artist at framing pitches to influence the umpire's call. Mackey is a tough catcher to steal any base on, possessing a powerful bazooka-like throwing arm. He broke shortstop Jake Stephen's finger on a steal attempt by Bacharach's Luther Farrell in September 1926. Mackey has suffered many broken fingers during his career.

Mackey is probably the most feared

hitter on the team. A great clutch and contact hitter, he is difficult to strike out. Mackey dines daily on mistake pitches.

Mackey pitched briefly in 1921, showing his versatility. His only weakness as a player is his speed. He is a tortoise on the base paths — a slow slab of humanity.

As a player he is a hard-line competitor and takes no prisoners. He is also a jolly, good-natured player who constantly jabbers at batters in the box, making them lose concentration. Mackey really enjoys entertaining the fans. His trademark boyish grin is always with him.

1924 Season: Mackey started slowly because of a reinjured knee during spring training at the local Philadelphia YMCA. Last year, he hit .418 to help lead Hilldale to its first league title. This year, he had nine games with three or more hits. Throughout the season, he has been rumored to be jumping to the Homestead Grays. Mackey often used Louis Santop's superheavy bat to break out of a slump. He was elected to the league All-Star team by the *Pittsburgh Courier.*

Normally a catcher, Mackey played 33 games at shortstop to allow Santop's bat a spot in the line-up. At 210 pounds, he is the heaviest shortstop in the league. He also filled in at first base (24 games) when outfielder Briggs hurt his knee in August, when first baseman George Carr took his spot in right field. Biz also saw limited action at third base (nine games), and at catcher (five games).

Had a perfect 5 for 5 day against the Bacharach Giants. After going 8 for 8 in two games with two doubles, he named Harrisburg Giant's pitcher Charlie Henry, as president of his Mackey Fan Club. Mackey, consistent all year long, had a slugging percentage at home of .457, and .474 on the road.

	G	AB	R	H	D	T	HR	AVG.	SLUG.
World Series	10	41	7	10	0	1	0	.244	.293

Scouting Reports: "For combined hitting, thinking, throwing and physical endowment, there never has been another Biz Mackey," recalled Cumberland Posey, who managed the great Josh Gibson but rated Mackey as the No. 1 catcher of all time. "He was a tremendous hitter, a fierce competitor, although slow afoot he is the standout among catchers who have shown their wares in this nation."

Hilton Smith, the brilliant pitcher for the Kansas City Monarchs, got a chance to play catch with Mackey in the California Winter Leagues and had this to say about Biz: "Oooh, my goodness, I didn't know he was such a catcher! I think I struck out 15 guys. That guy was a marvelous catcher! I just — ooh, I just was on edge, and it looked like all my stuff was just working. He had the hitters looking like they didn't know what to do."

According to Hall of Famer Monte Irvin, "Mackey was the dean of teachers, he taught Campanella how to think like a catcher, how to set a hitter up — he'd throw a hitter his favorite pitch at a time when the hitter is not expecting it."

Dick Powell, former owner and business manager of the Baltimore Elite Giants, said: "Mackey was a large fellow. He did more playing infield and outfield than at catching, and that was because of Santop. Both of them couldn't catch. Because of the blue laws in Philadelphia, Hilldale couldn't play on Sunday when most of the doubleheaders were played. Usually when Hilldale came to Baltimore on Sunday, then Mackey and Santop got to catch a game each."

Roy Campanella was an aspiring 15-year-old catcher when he joined the Baltimore Elite Giants in 1937 and spoke highly of his mentor: "Biz was a great, great catcher in his day. He used to tell me how to handle pitchers, what to do in a certain situation. I gathered quite a bit from Mackey, watching how he shifted his feet for an outside pitch, how he threw with a short, quick, accurate throw without drawing back. I didn't think Mickey Cochrane [Philadelphia A's] was the master of defense that Mackey was."

Campanella added: "He caught as many as 10 games a week. Sometimes he would catch an afternoon game in Columbus and then rush to another city in Ohio, where he would catch another game that same night. He was tough. He'd catch a game on Monday, another on Tuesday, doubleheader on Wednesday, one on Friday, two on Saturday and another doubleheader on Sunday and then do the same thing all over again."

Ric Roberts, writer for the *Pittsburgh Courier*, spoke highly of Mackey. "He was sharp of eye, pugnacious of spirit and enormous in the clutch, no better handler of pitchers ever lived. Take a gander at his gnarled right hand — broken a dozen times, not one finger is free of smashed bones."

Frank (Doc) Sykes, pitcher for the Baltimore Black Sox and later a dentist, said: "Mackey was one of the best bunters we ever had. Had whole lot of baseball sense."

When infielder Judy Johnson was asked about Mackey's rifle arm, "You didn't have to move your glove six inches off the ground — his balls would just float in to third base."

Slugging first baseman for the Newark Eagles Lenny Pearson, who played with Biz towards the end of his career, offered: "He'd couldn't run a lick. He'd get a single and sort of wobble to first base. But he was an inspiration to us guys, because he was old enough to be our father and he made all of us get up and hustle a little bit more."

"Mackey was the greatest, smartest catcher," shortstop Jake Stephens said. "In 1925, I think, Snooks Dowd of Newark was the best baserunner in the International League — set a record, I think it still stands. We played the Newark club three games, and seven times Mackey threw him out — seven times! He'd shoot you out. Listen, please believe me, nobody — nobody — could catch as much baseball as Mackey. Mickey Cochrane couldn't carry his glove."

Lloyd Thompson, Hilldale scorekeeper, boasted: "If any receiver is entitled to the nonpareil of the wire mask, give the token to Mackey. The smoothest receiver in four decades with an unerring throwing arm, switch-hitting Bizz hit the ball hard from both sides of the plate. Also capable of playing any position in the infield and surprisingly agile for a big fellow, weighing over 200 pounds."

Kansas City's
"Brown Bomber"

HURLEY MCNAIR
(Allen Hurley McNair)

Height 5'4", weight 160, bats switch, throws right

Nicknames: Mac, Bugger, We We, Eric.
Born: October 28, 1888, Marshall, Texas.
Died: December 2, 1948, Kansas City, Missouri.
World Series Age: 35.
Career: 1911–46: of, Chicago Giants, Gilkerson's Union Giants, Chicago American Giants, Detroit Stars, Chicago Union Giants, Kansas City Monarchs, Cincinnati Tigers, All Nations, Kansas City (Kansas) Giants; umpire, NAL.

Personal: The original toy cannon, Air McNair is known for his aerial bombs. Hurley is a winning player with the ability to hit when down in the count. Despite his diminutive stature, McNair is a natural power hitter. Mac loves curves and low-ball pitches. He can hit to all fields. Because of his power and small strike zone, little Mac walks a lot.

He is the Monarchs' right field rifleman. McNair has powerfully strong wrists and Popeye-like arm strength. McNair plays a deep outfield and entertains the crowds with his shoestring catches. He is considered a great sun fielder, never using sunglasses. A speed merchant, McNair can go coast

Hurley McNair: The most dangerous two-strike hitter in the league. The toy cannon is an explosive low-ball lover and blessed with a rocket arm, desired by any right fielder (NoirTech Research).

to coast. He leads the league in excitement. His body is rumored to be "corked."

He married the former Emma Jackson in 1916 and is a member of the Prince Hall Masonic Lodge.

1924 Season: Mac was cleanup hitter for the Monarchs most of the season. He won a pair of the famous Dunlop shoes from a local haberdasher when he led the Monarchs in home runs with eight. He was injured in a game against the Chicago American Giants with a pulled leg muscle but hit 4 for 4. He had two four-hit games, and he had 14- and 15-game hitting streaks, batting .423 and .453 respectively. He was forced to pitch two innings against the American Giants when Allen, Hawkins, William Bell and Drake suffered ptomaine poisoning from home-made strawberry ice cream. He gave up one hit, striking out two batters during his brief assignment. Recognized for his abilities, he was voted to Cum Posey's All-Star team as a right fielder.

	G	AB	R	H	D	T	HR	AVG.	SLUG.
World Series	10	35	3	5	0	0	0	.143	.143

Scouting Reports: "That McNair was the oldest guy on the team, could place-hit the ball, a low-ball hitter, he murdered a low ball," said super fan Leo Ernstein. "He never swung hard, just made good contact. When they played the [Kansas City] Blues, he hit a home run off Jimmy Zinn — he seemed like he just golfed it. He hit a low curveball and it just took off."

Called the best two-strike hitter in baseball. According to teammate George Giles, "Mac could have taken two strikes on Jesus Christ and base-hit the next pitch."

Former teammate Chet Brewer says: "Hurley had strong wrists and big shoulders. He had sharp eyesight, once accidentally picked up a fungo bat and hit a home run."

Kansas City's "Cuban Blacksmith"

JOSE MENDEZ
(Jose De La Caridad Mendez)

Height 5'8", weight 170, bats right, throws right

Nicknames: Joe, Black Diamond, Black Matty, Mendy, El Diamante Negro, El Mono Amarillo.
Born: March 19, 1887, Cardenas, Cuba.
Died: October 31, 1928, Havana, Cuba.
World Series Age: 37.
Career: 1908–26: p, ss, 3b, 2b, manager, Cuban Stars (West), Stars of Cuba, All

Nations, Los Angeles White Sox, Chicago American Giants, Detroit Stars, Kansas City Monarchs, New York Cuban Stars.

Personal: Mendez is full of spirit and often temperamental. He speaks Spanglish, a combination of English and Spanish, yet everyone understands what he says.

The spirited one played cornet and guitar for the original touring Monarchs, the All-Nations Baseball Club. When the musician took his lounge act beyond the dugout he became a maestro on the mound. With his extremely long fingers, Mendez was able to generate great rotation on his slider and singing curveball that kept batters below the Mendoza line.

The Hispanic mechanic had all the tools to fix a win. He had a charcoal-activated fastball and could easily change velocity using the same pitching motion. Batters could hear the ball coming to the plate, but they couldn't see it. His arsenal also included a wicked screwball that made batters blush with shame.

Jose Mendez: One of the greatest Cuban pitchers in the game. After seeing Mendez beat aces Christy Mathewson and Nap Rucker in 1908, New York Giant manager John McGraw claimed, "I have just seen the greatest pitcher of all time." The Hispanic mechanic had all the tools to fix a win (Courtesy of Kimshi Productions).

With his creative musical ability exposed on the mound, he could beat the beats, making percussion his instrument. His pitching motion was smoother than elevator music, while his pitches lullabied batters to sleep.

Mendez started out as a catcher. He was one of the best shortstops that ever spiked a diamond. A great pitcher and hitter, he could play any position well, infield or outfield. Mendez pitched against John McGraw's New York Giants, who were the first team to go to Havana. He pitched the first day and was beaten 1–0. He turned around the next day and lost 3–2, two days in succession without being relieved.

Some players often call him the "10th Wonder of the World." Mendez can play every position on the field and is generally regarded, along with Martin Dihigo and Cristobal Torrienti, as the greatest Cuban players ever to play in the United States, before league integration. He treasures a red sports sweater given to him by McGraw.

1924 Season: A tough manager, he fired future Hall-of-Famer Oscar Charleston from the championship Santa Clara team in February 1924, after Charleston made two errors in one game. During the season, he was hospitalized at Phyllis Wheatley Provident for a minor, unknown operation. Team captain Lem Hawkins filled in as interim manager. Mendez was only able to start two games. A tough competitor, he won four games as a part-time starter and reliever. Although he hits like most pitchers, he did take one out of the park against the Indianapolis ABCs.

	G	IP	H	R	BB	K	W	L	ERA
World Series	4	19	11	4	5	6	2	0	1.42

Scouting Reports: Hall of Fame shortstop John Henry "Pop" Lloyd said, "I never saw a superior pitcher to Mendez."

Arthur Hardy, pitcher for the Topeka Giants and the Kansas City (Kansas) Giants, said: "The first time I met Mendez was in Chicago [1909] and boy, could he throw a ball! He had developed tremendous shoulders and biceps from chopping sugar cane. That ball was hopping! It looked like a pea coming up to the plate."

New York Giants manager John McGraw called him "sort of Walter Johnson and Grover Alexander rolled into one."

After a Cuban series against Almendares, second baseman Larry Doyle of the New York Giants said: "Mendez has wonderful speed, a tantalizing slow ball and perfect control. I've never seen a pitcher with better control." After Mendez beat aces Christy Mathewson and Nap Rucker in Cuba, McGraw wired back home, "I have just seen the greatest pitcher of all time. Were his skin other than black, I would sign him to a $10,000 a year contract."

"John McGraw was a great admirer of Mendez, he gave him a red sweater the first time his Giants went to Cuba when Jose pitched," said Monarch co-owner Tom Baird. "He played a fine brand of ball against the mighty Giants, and Mendez thought a lot of that old sweater — he kept it in his room and liked to show it. He must have shown it to me a dozen times. There have been a lot of stories about McGraw saying he would pay $10,000 for so and so if he were white. Mendez was the ball player that he really made the statement about."

Former Negro League umpire Billy Donaldson said: "Mendez was the old master of the Monarch pitching staff. Believe me, this old boy certainly knew how to handle a ballclub and was a master at breaking the visiting club's offense and defense."

"We can't help thinking what a sensation Mendez would be if it was not for his color," wrote W.A. Phelon of Cincinnati, Ohio. "But, alas, that is a handicap he can't outgrow."

Ira Lewis, sportswriter for the *Pittsburgh Courier*, recalled the greatest play he ever saw in his 1919 column: "The play to my mind which perhaps called for the extreme amount of quick thinking and rapid action occurred at Forbes Field, last summer in a game between the American Giants and C.I. Taylor's [Indianapolis] ABCs team. Jose Mendez, playing short for the Fosterites, was on the business end of this play.

"In the third inning of the second game of the series, with the Hoosiers leading by one run, Charleston, the speed merchant, on second and one out, when Powell, the Indianapolis catcher, swung on one of Whitworth's speeders and smashed a lightning grounder towards third. The pellet bounded off Francis' glove and rolled towards short. Mendez had moved over towards third at the crack of the bat and was at a decided disadvantage, as the ball caromed off the third baseman's glove in the direction of the former position. Right here was the spot where his speed and brains got busy.

"Realizing, evidently, what was in the mind of the winged heel of Charleston, Mendez made two or three greyhound leaps and captured the pill off balance and 'going away.' Without even hesitating a fractional part of a second as to what the situation presented, he uncorked the most remarkable throw to the plate it has ever been my good fortune to see. I had heard that the arm of Mendez had gone bad on him, but that throw which nipped the flying Charleston, as the latter hooked a fadeaway slide at the plate, was the fastest and most perfectly thrown I have ever seen. No one, other than a Charleston or a Cobb would have attempted to score on such a slim chance. This is one play which you would have to see, to fully appreciate."

**Kansas City's
"Sweet Georgia Brown"**

Dobie Moore
(Walter Moore)

Height 5'11", weight 230, bats right, throws right

Nicknames: Dobie, Freckle, Scoops, Black Cat.
Born: February 8, 1896, Atlanta, Georgia.
Died: Unknown.
World Series Age: 28.
Years Played: 1920–26: ss, Kansas City Monarchs.
Personal: Moore is a leather quality player, durable, consistent and rugged. He is an above average infielder. He had more range than Wyoming, an arm stronger than the law and knew the hitters better than their mothers. Adding a switchblade quick release and the ability to do deep in the hole, he was the best of the bunch at short. Faces would flush, toes would curl, and noses would sweat as fans watched Dobie do his duties. His only fault was a tendency to have memory lapses on the routine grounders. No doubt, the best shortstop in the league during the early Twenties.

Dobie Moore: The league's best shortstop was a bad-ball hitter and loved hitting the curveball. Some pitchers consider this quintessential money player the toughest out on the Monarchs (Courtesy of Kimshi Productions).

Moore started as a catcher for the hometown Atlanta Stars before joining the service in 1914. Moore played third base for the 25th Infantry team until 1918, when he was transferred to short after the regular shortstop's enlistment had expired.

Built like a locomotive with massive chest and arms, plus a grand caboose, Moore was a very aggressive runner. Like any freight train, the apple-cheeked Dobie ran on a straight line, ignoring any roadblocks. An all-around athlete, he also ran track for the Army team, specializing in the 440-yard relay and the long jump, plus finding time to play wide receiver on the service football team.

After an honorable discharge, Moore joined the Monarchs on the Fourth of July, 1920, under manager Jose Mendez. The manager immediately noticed

Moore's defensive deficiencies of overthrowing to first base and his inability to go to right with the same grace and ease that he displayed on hot grounders to his left. Mendez developed a regimen following the initial season while the club toured California that October. Moore practiced fielding grounds balls and throwing to first base for two hours each day, starting at 10 a.m. and continuing until noon. Every time Moore threw wide to first, the Cuban manager would add 15 minutes on to the practice session.

When Moore rejoined the team the following spring, he was able to go both ways equally well and throw to first with less speed but more accuracy.

The scouting report on Dobie was that he was a great curveball and bad-ball hitter. At times, Moore could get hotter than Gates' barbecue sauce. He was famously known for his line-drive homers. The quintessential money player, Moore was considered the toughest out on the Monarchs by many pitchers from the league's early years. Even tougher than the more celebrated Bullet Rogan.

In September 1923, the illiterate Moore married the former Francis Davis. Less than three years later, Moore decided to creep one night. On May 18, 1926, Moore was scheduled to be at a party for Monarch players and wives to celebrate an early season winning streak. Moore never appeared and was later found, shot in his left leg by girlfriend Elsie Brown. Brown claimed she mistook him for a prowler. Moore suffered compound fractures of the tibia and fibula. Hours later, team physician Dr. Bruce was unable to remove the bullet. The incident prevented him from playing baseball in the Negro Leagues again. It could be said that Moore's rugged lifestyle resembles a blues song.

Moore's only whistle stop in the Negro National League was with the Kansas City Monarchs. The league's best all-around shortstop's shelf life was only six seasons.

1924 Season: Moore is fully recovered from a serious hand injury (split finger) he suffered last season. He started with a bang, a 16-game hitting streak, hitting .429, and followed with streaks of 16 (the longest of any Monarch this year) for .382, 14 games at .422 and 15 games at .421. He is the most consistent hitter on the club. Moore only failed to get a hit in 10 games. He had 11 games where he had three or more hits this year. He was selected to Cum Posey's All-Star team as the league's premier shortstop. Posey said, "Moore is the peer of all shortstops, colored or white."

	G	AB	R	H	D	T	HR	AVG.	SLUG.
World Series	10	40	7	12	0	0	0	.300	.300

Scouting Reports: Former Yankee manager Casey Stengel said, "That Moore was one of the best shortstops that will ever live!"

Former teammate pitcher Chet Brewer recalls Dobie Moore as the greatest shortstop ever. "He could come up and hit the ball out of the park. That to my mind made him the best shortstop in league history. Willie Wells was a great fielder, but he didn't have the strong arm or the power Moore had. Sometimes the third baseman, Newt Joseph, would dive for a ball he just couldn't get to. Moore was on the edge of the grass, would scoop that ball up and throw a blue blazing strike from deep shortstop. Moore was the best I saw all around."

Teammate George Sweatt claimed: "Dobie may not have been as agile as some of them, but he had a rifle arm and made good plays. As far as fielding his position, and throwing and hitting, you couldn't beat him." Monarchs business manager Quincy Gilmore agreed: "Dobie Moore was in a class by himself at short."

Defensive catcher Frank Duncan of the Monarchs spoke of Moore's bad-ball hitting tendency: "I've seen them pitchers throw a curve ball to him, break in the ground, bounce up, and he'd hit it all up side the fence."

"Moore was mean and he was strong," says little Hilldale shortstop Jake Stephens. "He'd grab the belt of a runner rounding second. That half-stride the runner lost was often the difference between safe and out at third base or home."

Willie Grace, sensational outfielder for the Cleveland Buckeyes, remembered: "Dobie Moore had a great arm, played a deep short. Dobie hit like an outfielder, not an infielder."

Despite playing for many championship Monarch teams, the Santa Clara club of 1923 was given Moore's highest rating. "That club had everything," claimed Moore in a 1943 interview with writer Russ Cowan. "The infield was composed of Eddie Douglass at first, Frank Warfield at second, I played short, and Oliver Marcell was the third baseman. In the outfield were Oscar Charleston, [Estaban] Montalvo, [Alejandro] Oms and [Bernardo] Baro. The pitchers were Bill Holland, Rube Currie, Jose Mendez and Pedro Dibut. Frank Duncan and [Julio] Rojo were the catchers.

"The club won 26 and lost four in the first half, and won 14 and lost two before the second half closed. Santa Clara Leopardos were unbeatable." Their 11½ game margin of victory is the largest in Cuban League history.

"Marcell won the batting championship with an average of .392 just a point above my .391, the highest batting record I ever made. Marcell was given $500 and I won $100 for hitting the longest ball."

"Bill Holland won the pitching honors. I don't recall the number of games he won that season, but I do remember that he did not lose a game. He also won $500."

In a 1940 survey conducted by Monarch secretary Quincy Gilmore for the All-Time Monarch team, writer Cordell White claimed, "At shortstop, [Dobie] Moore was in a class by himself. [Hall of Famer Willie] Wells may have been more flashy, but I'll take Moore."

Milton Miller from Plattsburg, Missouri, concurred. "I picked Moore because he was naturally the best. The others don't compare to him."

Kansas City's "Golden State Hurler"

YELLOWHORSE MORRIS
(Harold Morris)

Height 5'11", weight 170,
bats right, throws right

Nicknames: Yellowhorse, Hal.
Born: February 16, 1896, Oakland, California.
Died: October 10, 1970, South San Francisco, California.
World Series Age: 28.
Career: 1924–36, 1946: p, Kansas City Monarchs, Detroit Stars, Chicago American Giants, Monroe (Los Angeles) Monarchs, San Francisco Sea Lions (co-owner).
Personal: Morris is married with two children. He is sometimes called the California Wonder because of his chiseled good looks and often called Yellowhorse by his teammates because of his light complexion and Native American heritage. Morris comes from the semipro Pierce Giants out of Oakland, California. He is rated as one of the best prospects in the league. Has a great sweeping curveball with radar control. His slow curve can be timed with a sundial.

Yellowhorse Morris: In his rookie season with the Monarchs and showing promise of a permanent spot in the starting rotation. His best pitch is a sweeping curveball (NoirTech Research).

1924 Season: Morris is enjoying his rookie year with the Monarchs. He had a 6–2 record at home with three complete games. Two of the complete games were against the powerful Birmingham Black Barons. He needs to establish a good record with the big boys of the Negro Baseball League to be able to stick in this league. He was unable to beat the rough Chicago American Giants, losing three times. But in relief of Jack Marshall against Chicago, Morris struck out the tough Bobby Williams, Bingo DeMoss and Leroy Grant in the final inning to regain his confidence. He later pitched a brilliant four-hitter against the Giants, only to lose 1–0 in the ninth inning. He also pitched a 5-hit shutout against the Birmingham Black Barons, beating the durable submariner Dizzy Dismukes. Morris pitched 26 scoreless innings against the Black Barons.

	G	IP	H	R	BB	K	W	L	ERA
World Series	1	1	2	0	0	0	0	0	0.00

Scouting Reports: "That Morris was a son-of-a-gun pitcher," said Chicago American Giants teammate Saul Davis.

"Oh, God, he had a great curve ball."

"Yellowhorse Morris pitched for the Monarchs some 20 or 25 years ago," wrote former co-owner of the Monarchs Tom Baird, "and was above in intelligent [*sic*] for a Negro."

Kansas City's
"Black Knight"

DEKE MOTHELL
(Carroll Ray Mothell)

Height 5'10", weight 175, bats switch, throws right

Nicknames: Deke, Dink.

Born: August 16, 1897, Topeka, Kansas.

Died: April 24, 1980, Topeka, Kansas.

World Series Age: 27.

Career: 1918–34: of, 2b, 1b, ss, c, p, All Nations, Kansas City Monarchs, Cleveland Stars, Chicago American Giants, Topeka Giants.

Personal: Mothell is a black knight in white satin. A dedicated disciple of the game, he is known for his line drive hits. Mothell is also an excellent fielder and can play every position. A cerebral player, Mothell is the master of versatility. He is a streak hitter, with an unbelievable knack for getting the clutch hit. His playing style sometimes represents "crumbling elegance"—he finds ugly ways to beat you.

Mothell is married with no children. He is a quiet, soft-spoken person, and leads by example.

1924 Season: Mothell pitched once, a complete game, a 15–3 victory over the lowly Cleveland Browns. He had five games with three or more hits and went 4-for-5 against the Birmingham Black Barons and 4-for-4 against the Detroit Stars. He was a great utility player who was a very valuable substitute when players were injured. He played 35 games in center field, 13 at first base, 11 at catcher, seven in right field, five in left field and third base and one game each as pitcher and second baseman. He played every position except shortstop.

	G	AB	R	H	D	T	HR	AVG.	SLUG.
World Series	7	13	0	2	1	0	0	.154	.231

Scouting Reports: Hall of Famer "Cool Papa" Bell said: "Mothell was the great-

Deke Mothell: The master of versatility is the best utility player in the game. He can play all nine positions and hit for a decent average. Mothell is on the right shaking hands with Monarch Eddie Dwight (NoirTech Research).

est utility man in the game. He could step in at any position except pitcher and you would never notice the regular player was missing."

The *Chicago Defender,* in 1932, wrote of the new double play combination of Willie Wells and Deke Mothell: "Could make more double plays than a crooked wife."

In the 1934 *Denver Post* Tournament, manager Sam Crawford spoke highly of his utility player when he put in John Donaldson as a pinch runner for Newt Joseph. After Donaldson advanced to second on a sacrifice fly, Crawford inserted Mothell for Donaldson. Crawford's explanation was "Donaldson was the fastest runner, but Mothell was the smarter man." Mothell scored.

Kansas City's
"Quicksilver"

BULLET ROGAN
(Charles Wilber[N] Rogan)

Height 5'7", weight 170, bats right, throws right

Nickname: Bullet.
Born: July 28, 1893, Oklahoma City, Oklahoma.
Died: March 4, 1967, Kansas City, Missouri.
World Series Age: 31.

Bullet Rogan: He is faster than a speeding bullet and hits like a Mack truck. The ace of the pitching staff who bats in the power spots of the lineup, Rogan can beat you in so many ways (NoirTech Research).

Career: 1917–46: p, of, 1b, 2b, 3b, ss, manager, Kansas City Colored Giants, All Nations, Los Angeles White Sox, Kansas City Monarchs; umpire, NAL.

Personal: Rogan is faster than a speeding bullet. He is the trigger that fires-up the Monarch team. As a pitcher, Rogan sometimes used a no windup delivery. His delivery is normally overhanded, with an occasional sidearm delivery. Rogan possesses a devastating fastball with a full array of curves. His fastball looks like a bar of hotel soap. Some players say Rogan has mastered three curves—a slider, a regular curve and a jug-handle curve that makes the ball look like it is dropping off the table. Rogan has a forkball, a palm ball and a spitter. Generally regarded by many baseball experts as the finest fielding pitcher in the league.

As a batter, he is a great low-ball and curveball hitter, like Ernie Banks. He uses a heavy bat. Rogan stands deep in the batter's box and attacks the pitch with his powerful wrist-type swing. He is considered a brainy player by his teammates.

Rogan married Kathryn in 1921 and they had a boy and a girl. Acknowledged as the best pool player on the team, he owns a recreation billiard parlor with the Monarchs' secretary, Quincy J. Gilmore, to generate a little off-season income. Rogan is rated as one the game's greatest all-around players.

1924 Season: Rogan enjoyed a 10–2 winning record at home, winning six games in a row. The former Giant killer of the Chicago American Giants was bombed for 44 runs in 69 innings. Called the "Iron Man" for his ability to pitch complete games, Rogan led club with 18 complete games in 22 starts. His only shutout came against the Memphis Red Sox, in August, on six hits and eight strikeouts.

Rogan had eight games with three hits. He had a four-hit game against the Cleveland Browns in July. He hit .529 against the Browns in four games. Rogan hit three of his five homers against the Detroit Stars. He riddled the Detroit team with an .870 slugging percentage. Hotter than a firecracker in July, Rogan batted a sizzling .488 with four homers, en route to a .976 slugging percentage. During the season he hit over .300 against every team and in every month. Rogan compiled a .423 average at home, and *only* .403 on the road.

As a pitcher	G	IP	H	R	BB	K	W	L	ERA
World Series	4	28	27	9	8	9	2	1	2.57

As a batter	G	AB	R	H	D	T	HR	AVG.	SLUG.
World Series	10	40	4	13	1	0	0	.325	.350

Scouting Reports: When asked how Rogan got his nickname, teammate Duncan replied, "He just threw that ball so hard that the name 'Bullet' stuck right to him and he never lost it."

In 1921, the *Chicago Whip* said: "There are few pitchers in the game today, regardless of color, who look as good on the mound as Rogan. He is a great twirler, we venture to say another Matty [Christy Mathewson] or [Rube] Foster."

Hall of Famer Judy Johnson said, "Satchel Paige was fast, but Rogan was smarter."

Bert Gholston, former umpire, said: "Bullet Rogan is the king of kings, I remember him pitching several shutout games one season [1923] in which he allowed from two to four hits. His one big feat was when he pitched a no-hit game against the Milwaukee Bears in Kansas City before 9,000 wild fans. He was robbed of another no-hit game against the [Indy] ABCs when [Oscar] Charleston hit a safety in the ninth after two were down."

Chet Brewer, former Kansas City Monarch pitching great who played with Paige and Rogan, insisted: "Rogan should have been put in the Hall of Fame before Satchel. Paige only had his fastball, but Rogan had a fastball and a curve also. Rogan could throw a curveball faster than most pitchers could throw a fastball. He was the best pitcher I ever saw in my life."

Brewer added: "He was raw-boned and tough as nails. Rogan had that running fastball. And he was the master of the palm ball. The same big delivery, and the ball just walked up to the plate. That pitch, right behind that fastball, was something!"

Jimmy Zinn, former Kansas City Blues star, recalled when Rogan was released from the army and joined the Monarchs. Joe was wearing the sharpshooter stripe he had earned in the service. "I asked him from how far away he could hit a person." Jimmy relates. "He said to me, 'Just give me his address and see.'"

Casey Stengel, former New York Yankees manager, was quoted as saying, "Rogan was one of the best — if not the best — pitcher that ever pitched."

Satchel Paige once said: "He was the onliest pitcher I ever saw, I ever heard of in my life, was pitching and hitting in the cleanup place. He was a chunky guy, but he could throw hard. He could throw as hard as Smokey Joe Williams — yeah. Oh yes, he was a number-one pitcher, wasn't any maybe so."

Hall of Fame umpire Jocko Conlon, who once saw Rogan beat the great Red Faber of the Chicago White Sox, said, "Rogan had an easy delivery, and fast — much faster than Paige."

Former 1940 and 1946 batting champion Buck O'Neil once said of Rogan: "You saw Ernie Banks hit in his prime, then you saw Rogan. He could hit that ball. He taught me quite a bit. He was the type of guy that stood a long way from the plate. Not too close, because they'd jam you. It really worked for me; my arms were kind of long anyway. And he taught me footwork, hit off the balls of your feet. He wouldn't only tell you, he did a pretty good job of demonstrating. He was very smooth — swung that bat good."

"Joe Rogan possessed as much natural ability as Smokey Joe or Satch, but his control was not up to theirs," wrote A.S. "Doc" Young, sportswriter. "Physically rugged, he was toughest when the chips were down."

"Rogan was the greatest pitcher that ever threw a ball," said teammate George Carr. "He had not only an arm to pitch with but a head to think with. Rogan was a smart pitcher with a wonderful memory. Once Rogan pitched to a batter, he never forgot that batter's weaknesses and strong points. And don't think Rogan was nicknamed 'Bullet' for nothing. That guy had a ball that was almost too fast to catch. He would really burn 'em in there."

"Yeah, that Rogan was the smartest pitcher you'd want to see. He'd throw you three straight changes of pace, and throw you strikes, then turn around and throw you three drop balls, you couldn't see them, and fastballs were right here at the knees all day long," boasted former World Series pitcher Jesse Hubbard.

Brooklyn Dodger outfielder Babe Herman played against Rogan in the Winter Leagues and Canada and stated: "He was the best colored pitcher I hit against. He had one of the best curveballs I ever saw and a good live fastball. I always said he was much better than Satchel Paige. Satchel was real fast, but he had a lousy curve and his fastball was pretty straight. Rogan's fastball was just alive!"

Country boy and show boater Dizzy Dean said: "Old Rogan was a showboat boy, a Pepper Martin type ball player. He was one of those cute guys, never wanted to give you a good ball to hit. Should be in the Hall of Fame."

Frank Duncan, a Monarch catcher who caught both Rogan and Paige, said: "Rogan was faster than Paige and a better athlete, but then, Satch could do a lot of things on that mound. I'll tell you how fast Rogan was. I used to buy two steaks before the game when he was going to pitch. You could buy a steak in those days for ten cents. I'd start the game catching Joe in the first inning with that steak next to my gloved hand. After five innings the steak would be beaten to shreds. So I'd replace it with a second steak."

"Satchel was easier to catch," added Duncan. "He could throw it in a quart cup. But Rogan was all over the plate — high, low, inside, outside. He'd walk five-six men, but he didn't give up many runs. Bullet had a little more steam on the ball than Paige — and he had a better-breaking curve. The batters thought it was a fastball heading for them and they would jump back from the plate and all of a sudden, it would break sharply for a strike. I would rank him with today's best. I have never seen a pitcher like him, and I have caught some of the best pitchers in the business."

"Shucks, Rogan was the toughest pitcher I ever faced, one of the smartest pitchers in the game," said George Giles, former All-Star first baseman.

Joe Rue, former Negro League umpire who saw them all, recalled: "The Monarchs had a wonderful ball club. They had a pitcher, Bullet Rogan. Oh, he could throw that ball. Outside of Bob Feller and Walter Johnson, who I worked behind in an exhibition game, Rogan was the fastest pitcher I've ever seen."

Willie Grace, former Cleveland Buckeye great, said: "Rogan had good control, good fastball, good change-up, good screwball. One of the best ever! No doubt about it."

Hilldale's
"Blue Print Pitcher"

RED RYAN
(Merven John Ryan)
Height 5'11", weight 160, bats right, throws right

Nickname: Red.
Born: July 11, 1897, Brooklyn, New York.
Died: August 1969, New York, New York.
World Series Age: 27.

Career: 1915–34: p, Pittsburgh Stars of Buffalo, Brooklyn Royal Giants, Hilldale, Harrisburg Giants, Bacharach Giants, Bal-timore Black Sox, Lincoln Stars, Newark Browns, Lincoln Giants, New York Black Yankees, Penn Red Caps of New York, Homestead Grays.

Personal: Ryan is a great control pitcher despite using a knuckleball as his major pitch. He uses a herky-jerky motion with a groundhog forkball. Ryan has a very bouncy fastball for a pitcher of his small stature. He is like a pound cake, simple in appearance, but his pitches pack a punch. Ryan is an excellent fielding pitcher and can play the outfield in a pinch. He is a good hitter for a pitcher. Ryan is the staff's No. 2 ace, behind Nip Winters.

On May 16, 1920, Ryan pitched the first shutout against the startup league when his Bacharach Giants defeated the Detroit Stars. Ryan gave up four hits in the win. Walks and strikeouts were not reported by the press.

Red Ryan: The knuckleball pitcher with the herky-jerky motion is number two in the pitching rotation. He hurled two of the team's four shutouts. With excellent control and groundhog forkball, he is tough to score against (From the Wm. Cash & Lloyd Thompson Collection, provided through the courtesy of the African American Museum in Philadelphia).

1924 Season: Ryan was used as a starter and middle reliever this season. He had 16 complete games, second on the team, behind Nip Winters' 21. He hurled two of the team's four shutouts. His excellent control is evident by his walking only 29 batters, about one per game.

	G	IP	H	R	BB	K	W	L	ERA
World Series	2	6⅓	8	7	2	3	0	0	8.53

Scouting Reports: "Red Ryan was quick afoot, with a quick pickup move," recalled Dick Powell, former owner and business manager of the Baltimore Elite Giants. "Good pitcher. Last time I saw him he was working as a skycap at Penn Station in New York."

Hilldale's
"Ole Grey Mare"

LOU SANTOP
(D. Louis Santop Loftin)

Height 6'4", weight 240,
bats left, throws right

Nicknames: Santop, Black Star Ranger, Big Bertha of the Bats, or Top; a.k.a. Louis Napoleon.
Born: January 17, 1889, Tyler, Texas.
Died: January 22, 1942, Philadelphia, Pennsylvania.
World Series Age: 35.
Career: 1909–31: c, manager, Fort Worth Wonders, Oklahoma Monarchs, Oklahoma City Giants, Philadelphia Giants, Lincoln Giants, Chicago American Giants, Lincoln Stars, Brooklyn Royal Giants, Hilldale, Santop's Broncos.
Personal: The former Navy man is married to Eunice. Santop is a registered Republican. He was nicknamed Big Bertha after the World War I German siege gun. A Sherman tank of a man, Santop has a howitzer for a bat. It has been reported that he hit tape-measure home runs during baseball's dead-ball era. Santop can hit the ball into the next zip code. He is a great curveball hitter. He is tem-

Louis Santop: The big burly Navy veteran could hit the ball into the next county. Columnist Red Smith wrote, "'Top caught a doubleheader with a broken thumb, and got four hits that day" (From the Wm. Cash & Lloyd Thompson Collection, provided through the courtesy of the African American Museum in Philadelphia).

peramental and a fierce competitor, making him a winner. Santop has extreme upper body strength, having a cannon for a throwing arm. A showman, Santop sometimes called out his home run. A big eater, he once consumed eight hard-boiled eggs on a bus trip from Newark to Paterson, New Jersey. He works in the stockyards in the off-season to build his awesome physique.
1924 Season: Santop began the season in superb condition. He started with a blast, with a homer in the first game, despite a few troublesome molars. He missed a few games in June because of tendonitis in his left shoulder. He later went 4 for 4 against both the Bacharach Giants and the Baltimore Black Sox. He

punished the Brooklyn Royal Giants with a .417 batting average. He hit .418 on the road, but only .298 at home.

	G	AB	R	H	D	T	HR	AVG.	SLUG.
World Series	9	24	2	8	0	0	0	.333	.333

Scouting Reports: "Now this Santop," said Frank Forbes of the New York Lincoln Giants. "You haven't got a man in baseball today like him. Tex hit a ball 999 miles! We were playing, I never will forget, he hit a ball off Doc Scanlan down in Elizabethport, New Jersey, in 1912, and it went over the fence, and it was 500-some feet away. They put a sign on the fence where he hit it. The balls they hit today are a joke; you get these boys 150–160 pounds, hit the ball out, forget it. That's a golf ball!"

Teammate Judy Johnson remembers Santop as a tough guy to get to know. "Louis Santop was a little tougher to get along with. He was a big star and one of the best hitters I ever saw. He could hit a ball a country mile."

"Santop was all the talk at the time as a catcher," said Dick Powell, former owner and business manager of the Baltimore Elite Giants. "He is a big strapping fellow. He could hit the long ball. Had a good throwing arm. I didn't think too many fellows would have challenged him coming to the plate."

Former pitching great Arthur Hardy of the Topeka Giants recalls: "Santop was great, he could really slam the ball. He is a very consistent hitter. As a catcher, very few players stole on him."

Teammate Scrip Lee boasted: "Santop had a better arm than anybody I've ever seen. You could stand at home plate and throw the ball into the center field bleachers."

Owner Ed Bolden claimed, "Top was the greatest star and the best drawing card we ever had."

"Santop was a big, chunky guy," recalls pitcher Webster McDonald. "Didn't like a low-pitched ball. But a curve ball breaking away out there — it was gone!"

"One of the greatest hitters, black or white, of all time," wrote columnist Red Smith. "That 'Top was a tough kid, caught a doubleheader with a broken thumb, and got four hits that day. A triple in the first game and a homer in the second game."

Jesse "Mountain Man" Hubbard, former pitcher, recalled, "Santop hit the ball farther than anybody, I said anybody — [John] Beckwith, Mule Suttles, Josh [Gibson], anybody."

"The big Top, because of his size and build, lacked both speed on the bases and agility behind the plate, but his great hitting power and mighty throwing arm awed many opponents," said Lloyd Thompson, former Hilldale scorekeeper. "A real money player when the chips were down, his driving influence often times inspired teammates to feats seemingly beyond their capabilities."

William E. Clark of the *New York Age* wrote: "Santop, the 'Big Bertha' of baseball, wasn't the greatest receiver in the world, but he was a wonderful drawing card and the hardest hitting catcher I ever saw. He was a forerunner of Babe Ruth and was feared by all pitchers, especially when men were on base."

Hilldale's
"Golden Retreiver"

JAKE STEVENS
(Paul Eugene Stephens)

Height 5'6", weight 145, bats right, throws right

Nicknames: Country Jake, Steve, Stevie, Speed.
Born: February 10, 1900, Pleasureville, Pennsylvania.
Died: February 5, 1981, York, Pennsylvania.
World Series Age: 24.

Jake Stephens: A great shortstop with a sticky glove is a superb bunter but a weak hitter. Country Jake was sometimes called the Wizard of York (NoirTech Research).

Career: 1921–37: ss, Hilldale, Philadelphia Giants, Homestead Grays, Pittsburgh Crawfords, Philadelphia Stars, New York Black Yankees.

Personal: The Wizard of York is what they call Country Jake. A small, flashy, aggressive and acrobatic infielder, Stephens was in the mode of the Cardinals' Ozzie Smith. He was known for his "poster plays." Stephens had gluey hands and sticky glove. He was Hilldale's main man up the middle, and a real smooth operator. Stevie has bicycle speed on the basepaths.

Stephens is a weak hitter and lacks power. He just can't hit the curveball. But he is a great bunter. He can pick the ball out of the catcher's glove and send a slow roller anywhere on the infield. Country Jake sent Hilldale owner Ed Bolden a letter stating, "I am the best short fielder that ever matriculated among the White Roses of York, Pa." He got the job! Jake just may be the greatest player in the world, according to barbershop lore.

1924 Season: Since joining Hilldale in 1921, Stephens has been riding the pine. He is still learning the game. He was farmed out earlier in the year to Danny McClellan's Philadelphia Giants for a little seasoning. Stephens rejoined the team in July and finished batting a poor .183.

	G	AB	R	H	D	T	HR	AVG.	SLUG.
World Series	1	2	0	0	0	0	0	.000	.000

Scouting Reports: Third sacker and teammate Judy Johnson marveled at the fielding of Stephens: "A lot of times that ball was hit past third, it would go right past me. He'd say 'Duck, Jing!' and throw the runner out."

Scrip Lee, submarine pitcher, called little Jake "the smallest man on the club and best glove I know of. If the ball hopped badly, he'd hop with it. Yes sir, he'd rounded those balls up and be in position to throw, where another man would be out of position."

Dick Powell, former owner and business manager of the Baltimore Elite Giants, said: "Jake Stephens was a darn good infielder. They use to try to compare him with Dick Lundy, but his height was against him. Balls that Dick Lundy would catch at his chest would perhaps go over Jake's head, unless he was able to get a hand up and snare it. But Jake was a damn good shortstop. In fact, he was good enough to move Judy [Johnson] out at short."

Kansas City's "Bronze Star"

GEORGE SWEATT
(George Alexander Sweatt)
Height 6'2", weight 195, bats right, throws right

Nicknames: Never, The Teacher, Big Sweat, Sharkey.

Born: December 7, 1893, Humboldt, Kansas.

Died: July 19, 1983, Los Angeles, California.

World Series Age: 30.

Years Played: 1921–28, 1931: 3b, 2b, of, Chicago Giants, Kansas City Monarchs, Chicago American Giants.

Personal: George sweats 'til he gets wet. A superb physical specimen and considered one of the finest athletes in the country, Sweatt is probably the finest athlete on the Monarch team. After suffering from infantile rheumatism as a child and told he would never walk, he became a superb athlete. He played halfback on his undefeated high school football team and played point guard on the school basketball team. He also helped his high school win the district track championship.

Sweat is a varsity letterman in football, basketball and track at Kansas State Normal College in Emporia. He is considered the fastest man on the team and plays both infield and outfield positions.

George Sweatt: The brains on the team could play all three outfield positions and fill in sometimes in the infield. The fastest player on the Monarchs, he can be the x-factor in the game (NoirTech Research).

Sweatt is a streak hitter, icy hot. He is an extremely popular player with both teammates and fans. He served in the 92nd Division, 816th Pioneer Infantry, in Romain, France. After signing with the Monarchs in 1921, he married the former Evelyn L. Groomer. He also testified on behalf of attorney Elisha Scott of Topeka, Kansas, in Scott's attempt to desegregate schools in Coffeyville, Kansas. Scott won the case, and Sweatt lost his teaching job.

After baseball, Sweatt moved to Chicago and retired as a mail carrier and served as a Scoutmaster for Troop 30. He later coached Little League baseball in Los Angeles and became a certified bowling instructor. He was elected president of the Old Tyme Ball Players Club of Los Angeles. The club included former Negro Leaguers Quincy Trouppe, Vic Harris, Chet Brewer, Jesse Hubbard, Buster Haywood, Andy Porter, Lou Dials and Lonnie Summers as board members.

1924 Season: Sweatt is on leave from the all-black high school in Coffeyville, Kansas, where he is principal. He could not join the club until June because of educational commitments. Sweatt was benched after an initial 2 for 21 slump. He came back in July, going 6 for 14, with two home runs against the Detroit Stars. His longest hitting streak was seven games in July, batting .382. He is using his baseball earnings to pay for medical school.

	G	AB	R	H	D	T	HR	AVG.	SLUG.
World Series	5	18	0	5	1	2	0	.278	.556

Scouting Reports: In an interview with historian John Coates, Sweatt said, "The greatest players I ever saw were Oscar Charleston, shortstop Willie Wells, catcher Bruce Petway and pitcher Smokey Joe Williams. My biggest thrill in baseball was being fortunate to have been one of the only two players to have played in the first four Colored World Series." (Rube Currie was the other.)

Clint Thomas: Called by some the black Joe DiMaggio because of his fielding ability and clutch hitting. A five-tool player who is an underrated talent (From the Wm. Cash & Lloyd Thompson Collection, provided through the courtesy of the African American Museum in Philadelphia).

Hilldale's "Gold Standard"

CLINT THOMAS
(Clinton Cyrus Thomas)

Height 5'8", weight 185, bats right, throws right

Nicknames: Clint, Hawk, Buckeye.
Born: November 25, 1896, Greenup, Kentucky.
Died: December 2, 1990, Charleston, West Virginia.
World Series Age: 27.
Career: 1920–38: of, 2b, Brooklyn Royal Giants, Columbus Buckeyes, Detroit Stars, Hilldale, Bacharach Giants, Lincoln Giants, Darby Daisies, New York Black Yankees, Newark Eagles, Philadelphia Stars, New York Cubans, Chicago American Giants.
Personal: Thomas married Ellen O'Dell Bland Smith in 1963. He

spends his winters in Detroit working for the Ford Motor Company and some-times drives a truck for the Ballantine Scotch Company in the off-season. He later operated a small real estate office.

An all-around ball player, Thomas has more dimensions than the twilight zone. His combination of power, speed, quick bat and go-get-'em defense makes him a superstar. Always a tough out, he has booming power to all fields.

Hawk was his name, the baseball was his prey, soaring effortlessly. Superb defensively, he has outstanding range in the outfield, goes back on the ball well and cuts off the gaps. Blessed with a great arm, Thomas can throw you out from the parking lot. An excellent base stealer, he has an invisible first step. Thomas will steal in key situations and take the extra base on daydreamers. He is a very underrated talent.

1924 Season: Thomas had 21 games with two or more hits. He enjoyed a 12-game hitting streak, batting .375. Thomas slammed the Royal Giants with a .394 bat-ting average and a .788 slugging percentage. He hit .324 on the road and .275 at home and was selected to the *Pittsburgh Courier's* All-Star first team as a leftfielder.

	G	AB	R	H	D	T	HR	AVG.	SLUG.
World Series	10	38	6	9	1	0	0	.237	.263

Scouting Reports: Former Pittsburgh Crawford outfielder Ted Page raved: "Offensively, Clint was very aggressive. He attacked the ball the way a dog attacks raw meat. Defensively, Clint went all out, he would chase the ball into another world. He was a colorful player."

Leo Ernstein, a lifelong Monarch fan, said: "He could go backwards for a ball hit over his head, with the best, including Oscar Charleston. That Thomas was a great center fielder."

"Clint was a Pete Rose–type player," Monte Irvin explained. "He always went all out. He was the black Joe DiMaggio."

Dick Powell, former owner and business manager of the Baltimore Elite Giants, said: "Thomas is an exceptionally good center fielder and great all-around ball player. Good on the base paths, good throwing arm, Clint was just a top-flight ball player."

Hall of Famer Buck Leonard said: "He was a heck of a player, shucks, when he got on base, we knew what was in his mind. He had stealing on his mind."

Judy Johnson recalls: "I called him 'Racehorse' because he ran to first base so fast that he almost had to turn around backwards to stop."

Roy Campanella: "Man! How he could play."

When speaking of his many all-star accomplishments, Thomas said: "The Hilldale Giants' victory over Kansas City Monarchs in 1925 was the highlight of my baseball career."

Thomas added, "In 1930, we were playing an all-star team that had Dizzy

Dean pitching for them. In the top of the ninth, there was no score and I was the first batter. I hit a ball that rolled all the way to the wall and I slid into third with a triple. I danced off the bag on the first two pitches and then I mentioned to their third baseman that I was going to steal home on the next pitch. He went and told Dizzy and he just looked over and waved at me. The next pitch, I went. Made it pretty easy. Dizzy was mad as he could be."

"The only time I ever got mad at a ballplayer was one Sunday I got mad at Satchel. Judy Johnson was playing on the other team and I heard him yell at Satchel when I came up, 'Throw one at him, Satch.' Well, Satch did and my spikes had got caught in the mud, it would have killed me. I got up and looked at Judy and he was snickering behind his glove. I hit the next pitch so hard it like to tore the scoreboard down. That was the hardest line drive I ever hit."

In an interview with sportswriter Billy Reed, Thomas recalled his greatest catch: "The best catch I ever made? Well, I guess it was one off Josh Gibson, one day in Pittsburgh. He hit one 500 feet to left-center, I had to run a mile. When I got near the wall, the left fielder was running alongside me and he kept sayin', 'Got it, Hawk? Got it?' I didn't say a word, but I finally put my glove up to the top of the wall and there it was. I could play ball, if I do say so myself."

Hilldale's
"Red Ball of Fire"

FRANK WARFIELD
(Francis Xavier Warfield)
Height 5'7", weight 150, bats right, throws right

Nicknames: Weasel, Frank.
Born: April 24, 1898, Christian County, Kentucky.
Died: July 24, 1932, Pittsburgh, Pennsylvania.
World Series Age: 26.
Career: 1914–32: 2b, manager, St. Louis Giants, Indianapolis ABCs, Kansas City Monarchs, Detroit Stars, Hilldale, Baltimore Black Sox, Washington Pilots, Bowser's ABCs, Dayton Marcos.
Personal: Warfield is a Catholic. He is known for his leadership ability and is the starch of the Hilldale Club. Warfield, with his cold eyes, has a combative personality. His ferocious, fiery disposition makes for a lot of chin-to-chin confrontations, and he is reported to have bitten off the nose tip of another quick and fiery tempered teammate, Oliver (Ghost) Marcell, in a fight over a card game, in Santa Clara, Cuba. Marcell demanded his money back, resulting in a battle. Marcell ended up in the hospital and Warfield in jail.

Warfield is a smart baserunner and an above-average hitter. He possesses a slick stick and is an excellent hit-and-run hitter who can protect runners on steal attempts. Warfield is the prototype two-strike hitter as well as a perennial all-star.

He is an excellent fielding and hustling second baseman. Warfield likes to throw underhand with a unique snap release to the bag. He makes the double-play pivot like a ballerina. Warfield is also the master of the hidden-ball trick. Don't let him clean off second base — he might tag you out!

1924 Season: He is Hilldale's team captain. Warfield played in every game. During the season, he went six for eight in a doubleheader against the Lincoln Giants. Warfield had two or more hits in 27 games. He also led the team in stolen bases with 35 (only 22 were recorded). He liked the confines of home, hitting .310, and living out of luggage roll with a .316 average. This year, he was selected to the *Pittsburgh Courier's* all-star team, at second base, edging out his former tutor, the legendary Elwood "Bingo" DeMoss.

Frank Warfield: The team captain and spark plug on the field is an above-average hitter for most second basemen. He also has good speed, durability, and is an excellent number two batter (courtesy of Kimshi Productions).

	G	AB	R	H	D	T	HR	AVG.	SLUG.
World Series	10	38	5	9	2	0	0	.237	.289

Scouting Reports: "He wasn't a big man," claimed catcher Frank Duncan, "but he came into home plate like a Mack truck."

"Warfield was always ready for a fight," said Baltimore pitcher Laymon Yokely. "He would rush in when his players were arguing with the umpires. He'd rush in and take the argument over himself."

"I would give Warfield the call over [Bingo] DeMoss by a very slight margin," said former Homestead Grays owner Cumberland Posey.

"Frank [Warfield] was a little fellow," said Dick Powell, former owner and business manager of the Baltimore Elite Giants. "I don't think he weighed over 150 pounds. He stood about five-six or something like that. He was a brainy ball player and excellent second baseman. And was successful as a manager, with both Hilldale and the [Baltimore] Black Sox."

Nip Winters: The toughest southpaw in the Eastern Colored League. His drop ball is unhittable and his fastball is invisible. Pitches every three days and sometimes pinch-hits to show off (NoirTech Research).

Hilldale's "Agent Orange"

NIP WINTERS
(James Henry Winters)

Height 6'5", weight 220, bats left, throws left

Nicknames: Nip, Big Jim, Jess, Jesse.
Born: April 29, 1899, Washington, D.C.
Died: December 12, 1971, Hockessin, Delaware.
World Series Age: 25.
Career: 1919–33: p, Washington Braves, Norfolk Stars, Bacharach Giants, Norfolk Giants, Hilldale, Philadelphia Stars, Harrisburg Giants, Lincoln Giants, Darby Daisies, Newark Browns, Washington Pilots, Baltimore Black Sox, Philadelphia Royal Giants, Mohawk Giants.
Personal: Winters' pitching is deadly to enemy batters. Considered by some baseball experts the finest southpaw in baseball today, he is rated as one of the most consistent pitchers in the league. Winter has superior mound intelligence and is a superb pitching machine. He brings a tough mental approach to the game. With his mastery of the drop ball, he can throw a belt-high heater, when suddenly the bottom will fall out. He also possesses a lively fastball with a bit of a tail on it, plus a slinky curve. Superstitious, Winters never wears a toe plate, standard equipment for pitchers.

He fields his position well because of quickness and agility. Winters also has a silky smooth pick-off move. As a batter, he is always a dangerous hitter in the clutch. He is often summoned to pinch-hit in late innings. Winters also has good speed and is a threat to steal at any time.

1924 Season: Winters is the only southpaw on the staff. He comes to Hilldale from the Cuban Almendares team, winners of the second half in the Cuban winter season. A marquee quality performer, Winters pitches most of his games at home. He led the team in innings pitched, strikeouts, wins and complete games. Winters pitched 21 complete games in 24 starts with two shutouts. He was the Eastern Colored League leader with a 20–5 record in league play, which included two wins in relief. Winters' fine season included a no-hit, no-run performance in September against the Harrisburg Giants. An error by normally flawless shortstop Stephens off a "Fats" Jenkins grounder prevented a perfect game. Winters was unbeaten by the Baltimore Black Sox, Cuban Stars and the Harrisburg Giants. He won seven straight games, from June 15 to July 24. He then lost two games and came back and won the last six games in league play. Winters has not lost a game since August 3 going into the Series. He finished the season with two shutout victories. He is a reliable hitting pitcher with four home runs to his credit. The *Pittsburgh Courier* selected Winters to the league's All-Star team.

	G	IP	H	R	BB	K	W	L	ERA
World Series	4	38⅔	27	9	8	21	3	1	1.16

Scouting Reports: "Nip Winters had a helluva curve like [Bullet] Rogan. He could hit for a pitcher, too," recalled Monarch fan Leo Ernstein. "His pitches would break down and in on you, especially on a right-handed batter. And when you got a left-hander up there, he'd pitch outside, you couldn't do nothing with him."

When asked to pick the greatest left-handed pitcher ever, Cum Posey, owner of the Homestead Grays, said, "Willie Foster, I think, was the top lefty we have produced. Dave Brown was right next to him and close behind them are Slim Jones and Nip Winters."

Dick Powell, former owner and business manager of the Baltimore Elite Giants, said: "Nip was the ace of the staff. Nip was an exceptionally good pitcher. The fastball was his best pitch — he could fire it. I would put in the category with left-handers like Slim Jones of the Philadelphia Stars or Jonas Gaines of the Baltimore Elite Giants.

Lloyd Thompson, Hilldale scorekeeper, had this scouting report on Winters: "Nip was a towering left-hander and the ace of port-siders, throwing a modified cross-fired fastball with tremendous speed, combined with one the sharpest breaking curves in baseball. A good first baseman and possessing amazing power at bat for a pitcher."

4

The Ten Games

GAME 1

Rogan vs. Cockrell

Friday, October 3, 1924
Philadelphia, PA

Game Conditions
Temperature: 76 degrees
Humidity: 67 percent
Winds: Northeast, 6 miles per hour
Forecast: Light fog, but clear

Park
Baker Bowl
Baker Street (N), Gold Street (W),
Calhoun Street (S), Pennsylvania Avenue (E)
Built: 1895
Capacity : 18,000
Dimensions: Left field, 335 feet; Center field, 408 feet;
Right center, 300 feet; Right field, 272 feet

Around high noon, the Monarchs took to the diamond for infield practice. The visitors looked flashy in their gray and red uniforms with black trimmings. They were greeted by a large contingent of hometown fans, who had traveled, by car and train, over 1,200 miles to Philadelphia from Kansas City. The roar from the crowd made it pleasurable for the road warrior Monarchs. While the Monarchs' home record was a sensational 34–7 (.829), they struggled modestly on the road to a 21–15 (.583) record.

Earlier, rainy weather threatened the start of the historic game. By 11:00 the

The first game of the first Colored World Series was played in Philadelphia at Baker Bowl. It was the best of nine, and to be played in four cities, instead of the two customary home fields. Shown is an advertising poster from the historic event (From the Wm. Cash & Lloyd Thompson Collection, provided through the courtesy of the African American Museum in Philadelphia).

sky had stopped crying and the sun was chasing the tears away. Despite having the home field advantage in their back yard at the Baker Bowl, the Hilldale Club, dressed in off-white uniforms with ruby red pinstripes, would be hard pressed to match the tremendous reception by the Monarchs fans. The men from Darby had an impressive home record of 34–11 (.756) and a road record of 13–12 (.520).

The Monarchs assigned the opening game to their staff leader, Bullet Joe Rogan (16–5), while most Philly fans were assured their twenty game winner, Nip Winters, would start. Over in front of the Hilldale dugout, the drama unfolded with Red Ryan, Phil Cockrell and Winters warming up. Which of these men would get the starting assignment? Right-hander Ryan, who compiled a 13–8 record, was a tough competitor known for his fastball, knuckler and a sinking forkball. Cockrell, another right-hander, had a flashing fastball and a nasty spitter to go with his excellent control. Proven veteran Winters, a lefty, was the league's win leader and expected to start.

At 2:00, game time, Bolden announced that Hilldale would start spitball pitcher and ten-game winner Phil Cockrell. His decision was as puzzling as a Walter Mosley mystery. Winters has not lost a game since August 3. He had also pitched six complete games in his last seven starts, giving up fewer than 2 runs per game. Meanwhile, Cockrell's last defeat came on June 15 to the Lincoln Giants. He had won his last eight games in nine appearances, completing seven of them. Cockrell, at 10–1, had the best won-lost percentage on the team. But Cockrell had not pitched in a league game since September 4, while Winters' last league appearance came on September 13 — ten days after his no-hitter. Perhaps Bolden feared his team going head-to-head against such a rugged competitor like Bullet Rogan or figured the Monarchs would have a more difficult time against a spitballer like Cockrell.

During the season the Monarchs had lost three of their 22 games to George Harney, a spitball pitcher for the Chicago American Giants. If Hilldale could win this first game with Cockrell pitching and come back with the dependable Winters in Game Two, the Monarchs may never overcome a two-game setback. This bold move by Chief Bolden could change the complexion of the entire series, creating second-guessing by fans around the town.

Hilldale also announced that their crack shortstop, Jake Stephens, would not be available for the entire series because of a stress fracture of his ankle. (He would later play.) The injury forces Bolden to shift adolescent Judy Johnson to shortstop from third and move catcher (and the less agile) Biz Mackey to third base. He would also start weak-hitting, but defensively strong Tom Allen at first base, in place of George Carr, a good stick.

On the white side of the baseball world, the World Series was getting under way between the Washington Senators and the New York Giants. The white series, like the black series, was not without conflict. Today, Ban Johnson, president of the American League, sent Clark Griffith, president of the Washington Senators, a telegram saying he would not attend the World Series. He said he had no desire to see the National League Giants as representative because of the "Intolerable condition that has permeated the club" and asserted the Brooklyn (Dodgers) club should have been selected to represent the National League.

"I have no desire to take anything away from Washington, which won its championship honestly, but I have no desire to see the Giants engage the Senators," Mr. Johnson added. "It is my opinion, the Philadelphia players, in addition to John 'Heinie' Sand, were approached to have games thrown." Sand, a shortstop for the Philadelphia club, told his manager Arthur Fletcher that Giant outfielder Jimmy O'Connell had offered him $500 not to play his best against the

Giants in a series at the Polo Grounds. O'Connell readily admitted his guilt when charged by commissioner Judge Landis, accusing Coach Cozy Dolan, Frank Frisch, George Kelly and Ross Youngs of having induced him to make the offer.

The white major leagues were still recovering from the Black Sox Scandal of 1919, when eight members of the Chicago White Sox took bribes to throw the series against the Cincinnati ballclub. Buck Weaver, one of the infamous Chicago Eight, had sworn he didn't have anything to do with throwing the 1919 World Series games. Although cleared in federal court, he was given a lifetime suspension by Commissioner Landis for admitting he knew about the incident but didn't come forth with the news. Sand, knowing of Weaver's expulsion and not wanting to suffer a similar fate, revealed what he knew.

O'Connell made no attempt to deny the charges by Sand. He claimed Dolan had told him to make the offer. Just before the white major leagues opened their series, O'Connell was banished from baseball forever — technically placed on the ineligible list. The "O'Connell-Dolan Affair," as the press called it, had shaken the public's faith in the American pastime once again.

So far, the colored baseball leagues had been able to avoid controversy of this magnitude. The series' first discord came in the first inning, setting the tone for relaxation of the rules. The Monarchs' first batter, Lem Hawkins, was down in the count, two strikes and one ball, when Cockrell loaded up and released his alluring spitter. Plate arbitrator McBride, a white umpire from the International League, raised both arms and immediately stopped play.

The spitter had been outlawed since 1919, when major leaguers like Happy Jack Chesbro and Burleigh Grimes had enjoyed tremendous success with the wet one. Umpire McBride disallowed the pitch, calling it a ball. Bolden, realizing the importance of Cockrell's most effective pitch, jumped from his box seat to appeal to the Western League Commissioner Rube Foster for sympathy. Despite previous personal disagreements between the two men, Foster waived the spitball rule with a couple puffs from his pipe and ordered umpire McBride to continue the game.

Spitball, emery ball, and cut balls were all legal in the Negro Leagues. Shaken by the unprecedented call, Cockrell delivers his next pitch down the middle of the plate and Hawkins smacks a stinging double to left field for the first hit of the Colored World Series. Still attempting to overcome series jitters, Cockrell is greeted by Newt Allen's ripping line drive to left-center. But speedy outfielder Dibo Johnson snares the liner with a diving catch as Hawkins hustles back to second base, barely avoiding the double play. Cockrell gets out of the inning, getting Joseph on strikes and the dangerous McNair to ground out. Rogan has an easy time as he puts the Hilldale Club down 1–2–3 in their half of the first inning.

In the Hilldale half of the second, Santop starts the inning by singling up the middle off of Rogan. Rogan strikes out Thomas before Judy Johnson singles to right field. With runners now on first and second an unusual play happens.

Working from the stretch, Rogan steps off the rubber and whirls toward second base, faking a throw, and then fires to first, attempting to catch Judy Johnson by surprise. Rogan's throw smacks Johnson in the head, sending him to the turf. Hilldale pitcher Bill Campbell is sent in to run for the ailing Johnson, as he is helped off the diamond.

Despite the rules of substitution, after the inning is over, future Hall of Famer Johnson is allowed to re-enter the game. A World Series without the great Judy would not be a World Series. The Monarchs were extending all the courtesies to their rival Eastern team. Rube Foster's benevolent acceptance of his red carpet treatment was a jolt to Eastern fans, who had heard about his reprehensible and unyielding character.

Starting pitchers Phil Cockrell and Bullet Rogan sail along easily in the third, fourth and fifth innings. For five innings, Cockrell has pitched flawless baseball. So far he has given up only two hits, a first inning double by Hawkins and a second inning single by Rogan. He has struck out two batters and walked one. But in the sixth inning Hawkins bounces a wicked line-drive off Cockrell's glove hand for a hit, visible shaking up Sir Philip. Capturing the moment, Newt Allen lays down a perfect bunt along the first baseline and Cockrell in his haste throws the ball over first baseman Tom Allen's head. After Joseph forces Hawkins at third, both runners advance when Cockrell's pickoff attempt hits Joseph on the leg. With the cleanup hitter "Air" McNair coming to bat, Bolden and Cockrell agree to walk McNair, filling the sacks. The next batter, Dobie Moore, hits a routine grounder to Frank Warfield at second that is fumbled, allowing Allen and Joseph to score the first runs of the series. Cockrell commits his third error on a pickoff attempt of McNair at second, as McNair goes to third on the wild throw. Bullet Rogan singles, scoring McNair, with Moore going to third. Rogan immediately steals second base uncontested, putting two men in scoring position. The traumatized Cockrell crosses up Santop, allowing Moore to score on a passed ball. After Heavy Johnson goes down on strikes, George Sweatt singles to right field, scoring Rogan. Frank Duncan ends the inning with a pop up to Allen at first base. A disastrous inning for Cockrell as he commits three errors and is bombed for five runs.

Hilldale attempts a comeback in the sixth with singles by Mackey and Santop with only one out. But Clint Thomas kills the rally by hitting in the series' first double play, Allen to Moore to Hawkins.

In the ninth inning the Monarchs add a run when Hawkins reaches first on shortstop Mackey's throwing error. Then Hawkins steals second as Newt Allen strikes out on a hit-and-run play. And Hawkins comes home with run number six, when Cockrell commits his fourth error of the game, on an easy hopper back to the mound and misfires to Allen at first.

Bullet Rogan enters the bottom of the ninth having allowed only six hits and no runs. After Santop grounds out, Thomas works Rogan for a walk. A now healthy and vengeful Judy Johnson doubles to left, with Thomas taking no chances, pulling up at third. After George Johnson pops up to Newt Allen, pitcher Nip Winters comes to the plate to pinch-hit for Tom Allen. Winters hits a sizzling single between shortstop Dobie Moore and second baseman Newt Allen, scoring Thomas and Judy Johnson, breaking up the Rogan shutout. Rogan gets pinch-hitter Joe Lewis on a ground ball to Newt Allen to capture the first world series victory.

The Eastern Colored League champions do not play like league winners before their hometown fans. They commit six errors, four by their pitcher Phil Cockrell. Nip Winters, pinch-hitting in the ninth inning, saves Hilldale from being shut out when he singles in two runs. Meanwhile, the Monarchs' Bullet Rogan scatters eight hits, drives in a run, and steals a base. He is voted "Player of the Game" by the local press.

Bullet Rogan: He pitches an eight-hitter, striking out five, and goes 2 for 4 at the plate (NoirTech Research).

1

Friday, October 3, 1924
Baker Bowl, Philadelphia, PA

Monarch Batting	AB	R	H	2b	3b	HR	RBI	SB	SO	BB	AVG
Hawkins, 1b	5	1	2	1	0	0	0	1	0	0	.400
Newt Allen, 2b	4	1	1	1	0	0	0	0	1	0	.250
Joseph, 3b	4	1	0	0	0	0	0	0	1	1	.000
McNair, cf	3	1	0	0	0	0	0	0	1	1	.000
Moore, ss	4	1	0	0	0	0	1	0	0	0	.000
Rogan, p	4	1	2	0	0	0	1	1	0	0	.500
Oscar Johnson, rf	3	0	0	0	0	0	0	0	1	1	000
Sweatt, lf	4	0	1	0	0	0	1	0	0	0	.250
Duncan, c	4	0	0	0	0	0	0	0	1	0	.000
Totals	**35**	**6**	**6**	**2**	**0**	**0**	**3**	**2**	**5**	**3**	**.171**
Hilldale Batting	**AB**	**R**	**H**	**2b**	**3b**	**HR**	**RBI**	**SB**	**SO**	**BB**	**AVG**
Briggs, rf	3	0	1	1	0	0	0	1	0	1	.333
Warfield, 2b	4	0	0	0	0	0	0	0	1	0	.000
Mackey, 3b	4	0	2	0	0	0	0	0	0	0	.500
Santop, c	3	0	2	0	0	0	0	0	0	0	.667
Thomas, lf	3	1	0	0	0	0	0	0	2	1	.237
Judy Johnson, ss	3	1	2	1	0	0	0	0	0	1	.667

Hilldale Batting	AB	R	H	2b	3b	HR	RBI	SB	SO	BB	AVG
George Johnson, cf	4	0	0	0	0	0	0	0	1	0	.000
Tom Allen, 1b	3	0	0	0	0	0	0	0	1	0	.000
Winters, ph*	1	0	1	0	0	0	2	0	0	0	1.000
Cockrell, p	3	0	0	0	0	0	0	0	0	0	.000
Lewis, ph†	1	0	0	0	0	0	0	0	0	0	.000
Totals	32	2	8	2	0	0	2	1	5	3	.250

*Winters singles for T. Allen in 9th.
†Lewis grounds out for Cockrell in 9th.

Kansas City	000	005	001	6	
Hilldale	000	000	002	2	

Monarch Pitching	IP	H	R	ER	BB	K	HB	WP	SAV	F/G	BF
Rogan (W, 1–0)	9	8	2	2	3	5	0	0	0	9–8	37

Hilldale Pitching	IP	H	R	ER	BB	K	HB	WP	SAV	F/G	BF
Cockrell (L, 0–1)	9	6	6	2	3	5	0	1	0	6–9	40

Game-Winning RBI: Dobie Moore
Errors: Warfield, Mackey, Cockrell (4)
Left on Base: Hilldale — 7, Kansas City — 7
Double Plays: Allen to Moore to Hawkins (6th)
Sacrifices: KC — McNair, N. Allen Hilldale — Santop
Hit By Pitcher: N. Allen by Cockrell
Umpires: McBride, Freeman, Doolan, McDevitt
Attendance: 5,366
Time: 2:00

Summary

Main man: Bullet Rogan pitches an eight-hitter, striking out five, and goes 2 for 4 at the plate.

Turning point: An error by Frank Warfield in the sixth inning with the bases loaded allows two runs to score, opening the door for a five-run inning.

Silent stats: Four errors by pitcher Phil Cockrell contribute to Hilldale's demise, when the Monarchs score four unearned runs, the margin of victory.

Game 1, Out by Out

First Inning

Kansas City
Hawkins doubles to left (first hit of the series).
1 — Newt Allen hits liner to left-center; G. Johnson makes a great one-handed catch.
2 — Joseph strikes out swinging.
3 — McNair grounds out, Warfield to Tom Allen.
H-1, R-0, LOB-1, E-0

Hilldale
1 — Briggs flies out to McNair in left center.
2 — Warfield rolls out to Hawkins unassisted.
3 — Mackey pops up to Newt Allen.
H-0, R-0, LOB-0, E-0

Second Inning

Kansas City

1— Moore grounds out Judy Johnson to Tom Allen.
     Rogan singles.
2 — Oscar Johnson fouls out to Santop.
3 — Sweatt lines out to Briggs.
                 H-1, R-0, LOB-1, E-0

Hilldale

     Santop singles to center.
1— Thomas strikes out.
     Judy Johnson singles to right field.
2 — George Johnson strikes out swinging.
3 — Tom Allen lines out to right field.
                 H-2, R-0, LOB-2, E-0

Third Inning

Kansas City

1— Duncan strikes out on a count full.
2 — Hawkins rolls out to Judy Johnson.
3 — Newt Allen bunts out, Santop to Tom Allen.
                 H-0, R-0, LOB-0, E-0

Hilldale

1— Cockrell bounces out to Moore at shortstop.
     Briggs works Rogan for a walk and steals second.
2 — Rogan picks off Briggs, tag by Moore.
3 — Warfield out, Newt Allen to Hawkins.
                 H-0, R-0, LOB-0, E-0

Fourth Inning

Kansas City

     Joseph walks on full count.
1— McNair sacrifices, Cockrell to Tom Allen.
2 — Moore rolls out to Tom Allen unassisted.
3 — Rogan drives George Johnson to the warning track.
                 H-0, R-0, LOB-1, E-0

Hilldale

     Mackey singles to right.
1— Santop lays down a nice sacrifice bunt, Joseph to Hawkins.
2 — Thomas strikes out.
     Judy Johnson walks on four straight pitches.
3 — George Johnson flies out to McNair in center.
                 H-1, R-0, LOB-2, E-0

Fifth Inning

Kansas City

1— Oscar Johnson out, Judy Johnson to Tom Allen.

2 — Sweatt lines out to Tom Allen, who robs him of a sure extra-base hit.
3 — Duncan out, Mackey to Tom Allen.

H-0, R-0, LOB-0, E-0

Hilldale

1 — Tom Allen grounds out to Newt Allen.
2 — Cockrell flies out to Oscar Johnson.
3 — Briggs out, Moore to Hawkins.

H-0, R-0, LOB-0, E-0

Sixth Inning

Kansas City

Hawkins bounces a hit off Cockrell's glove hand.

Newt Allen lays down a sacrifice bunt, safe at first, on Cockrell's throwing error.

1 — Joseph forces Hawkins at third, Santop to Mackey.

Both runners advance when Cockrell's pickoff attempt hits Joseph on the leg. Cockrell's second error.

McNair is intentionally walked, loading the bases.

Warfield makes an error on Moore's grounder, Newt Allen and Joseph score.

Cockrell commits third error on pickoff attempt of McNair at second, McNair goes to third.

Rogan singles to center, McNair scores, Moore to third.

Rogan steals second. Moore scores on passed ball.

2 — Heavy Johnson fans.

Sweatt singles to right, scoring Rogan.

3 — Duncan pops to Tom Allen.

H-3, R-5, LOB-1, E-4

Hilldale

1 — Moore throws out Warfield.

Mackey singles to left.

Santop singles to center.

2,3 — Thomas hits into the first double play of the series. Allen to Moore to Hawkins.

H-2, R-0, LOB-1, E-0

Score after six innings, Monarchs 5, Hilldale 0.

Seventh Inning

Kansas City

1 — Hawkins pops to Warfield.

Newt Allen doubles to left center.

2 — Joseph grounds outs, Mackey to Tom Allen.
3 — McNair flies out to George Johnson in center.

H-1, R-0, LOB-1, E-0

Hilldale

1 — Judy Johnson flies out to Oscar Johnson.
2 — George Johnson lines out to Moore at short.
3 — Tom Allen strikes out on three pitches.

H-0, R-0, LOB-0, E-0

Eighth Inning

Kansas City

1— Moore grounds out Warfield to Tom Allen.

2 — Rogan grounds out, Cockrell to Tom Allen.

    Oscar Johnson walks on four straight pitches.

3 — Sweatt drives a high long fly into Briggs' hands.

                H-0, R-0, LOB-1, E-0

Hilldale

    Morris warming up for Kansas City.

1— Cockrell bunts out, Duncan unassisted.

    Briggs doubles to right field.

2 — Warfield fans.

3 — Mackey fouls out to Joseph.

                H-1, R-0, LOB-1, E-0

Ninth Inning

Kansas City

1— Duncan rolls out, Judy Johnson to Tom Allen.

    Hawkins safe on Mackey's throwing error.

2 — Newt Allen strikes out, on hit and run, Hawkins stealing second.

    Joseph safe on Cockrell's throwing error (fourth of the game), Hawkins scoring.

3 — McNair strikes out.

                H-0, R-1, LOB-1, E-2

Hilldale

1— Santop grounds out.

    Thomas works Rogan for a walk.

    Judy Johnson doubles to left, Thomas pulls up at third.

2 — George Johnson pops to Newt Allen.

    Winters bats for Tom Allen and singles in right center, scoring Thomas and
        Johnson (wrecking shutout).

3 — Lewis to bat for Cockrell. Lewis grounds sharply to Newt Allen.

                H-2, R-2, LOB-1, E-0

          Final score: Kansas City 6, Hilldale 2

GAME 2
McCall vs. Winters

Saturday, October 4, 1924
Philadelphia, PA

Game Conditions
Temperature: 72 degrees
Humidity: 36 percent
Winds: Northeast 5 miles per hour
Forecast: Light fog, low clouds

Park
Baker Bowl

The second game of the series is played again in the roomy Baker Bowl. Down one game in the series, Bolden must now go to his twenty-game winner Nip Winters. No questions asked! The Monarchs will start left-hander Bill McCall. McCall had come to the Monarchs in September from the Birmingham Black Barons. He has defeated every team in the league this season. McCall was recruited by the Monarchs as a possible Giant killer in the event the Monarchs had to face the American Giants in the playoffs. As a Black Baron, McCall had limited the powerful Giants to just six hits in three games. During his short stay with the Monarchs, McCall won two games, beating the American Giants and the St. Louis Stars. A journeyman pitcher, McCall was known around for his blazing fastball but at times experienced control problems. As the only left-hander on the Monarch staff, he figures to play a prominent role during the series.

Nip Winters, the "Eastern Assassin," led the league with a 20–5 record and has not lost a game since August 3. Winters, who finishes what he starts, pitched 21 complete games plus two shutouts and a no-hitter. His regular catcher, the power-hitter Louis "Big Bertha" Santop whose season average was .343 and who got two hits yesterday, is surprisingly not in the lineup today. We can only guess; Bolden figures Winters prefers Joe Lewis as his backstop.

The action starts in the bottom of the first inning, when Hilldale's Otto Briggs walks on four straight pitches. McCall falls behind Frank Warfield, 3 and 0, and then clips him on the shoulder. With men on first and second, Biz Mackey singles to right field, scoring Briggs with Warfield going to third. Manager Mendez quickly pulls McCall and calls in Plunk Drake for damage control. The first batter for Drake is Clint Thomas, who taps the ball to the shortstop Dobie Moore, with Warfield running from third. Moore's throw to the plate is late, as Duncan and Warfield collide. Hilldale 2, Kansas City 0. Thomas takes second on the fielder's choice. After Judy Johnson bounces an easy roller back to the mound, George Johnson doubles to center field, scoring Mackey and Thomas, for runs 3 and 4. Drake then gets Lewis to pop up, but Tom Allen singles to center, scoring George Johnson. Nip Winters closes out the outburst by bouncing out to Lem Hawkins at first base for the third out. After one inning, Hilldale leads comfortably, 5–0.

In the second inning, Hilldale comes right back with two more runs. Drake, known for hitting batters, plunks the baggy-pants Briggs in the butt, sending him to first base. Later in the inning, Briggs is caught in a rundown between third and home when Biz Mackey hits a liner to Moore at shortstop. With Mackey on first, Thomas singles to right. Judy Johnson also singles, scoring Mackey from third. Mendez says enough is enough: Drake is sent to the showers and Mendez takes his place on the mound. George Johnson greets Mendez's first pitch with a single to center field. Thomas scores Hilldale's seventh run. Mendez gets Lewis to fly out to deep center to close out another explosive inning by Hilldale. After only two innings, the Darby dandies are 7-up on the scoreboard.

Yet the Hilldales were not finished. In the third inning Tom Allen doubles to left field and Winters beats out a bunt to aging warrior Mendez. Otto Briggs doubles to left center, scoring Tom Allen. Winters, attempting to score from first on the double, is thrown out at the plate by McNair to Moore to Duncan. Briggs goes to third on the play. Hilldale plays "tricky" baseball when Warfield and Briggs execute a suicide squeeze successfully, with Warfield bunting to Mendez, scoring Briggs from third base. Mackey closes out the inning with a fly to McNair. The Giants from Hilldale now have a commanding lead of 9–0.

Mendez and Winters escape the fourth and fifth innings with no problems. However, in the sixth inning, Hilldale strikes again. After one out, Mackey triples off the center field wall. Thomas brings him home with a long sacrifice fly to McNair in center. Judy Johnson doubles to center and takes third base on McNair's boot and scores when third baseman Joseph fumbles McNair's relay throw. Hilldale adds two more runs in this frame, increasing the blowout to 11-zip.

The sixth inning proves to be an exhausting affair for outfielder Hurley McNair. Warfield leads off with a humpback liner of which McNair makes a great shoestring catch. Mackey then hits one off the center field wall, and McNair chases it down to hold Biz to a triple. Hurley then runs down a long Clint Thomas sacrifice drive for the second out. Judy Johnson then doubles to center and a somewhat tired McNair slightly bobbles the ball as Judy heads for third base, Hurley makes a strong throw to Newt Joseph, but Newt fails to field the throw, as Judy skips home. Finally, Joe Lewis skies another one to center that McNair pockets. A very tired athlete tosses his glove to the side and wobbles into the dugout. A gallant effort from a ball player whose team was down by nine runs when the inning started.

The Monarchs go down in order in the seventh inning, failing to get the ball past the Hilldale infield. In the eighth and ninth innings the Monarchs get only one hit, going down to a devastating defeat to the great Nip Winters. Nip's sinking fastball was the star of today's game. He held the Monarchs to four stingy hits, two by Lem Hawkins, while getting 17 batters to ground out. The teams will travel to Baltimore for the third game of the series.

2

Saturday, October 4, 1924
Baker Bowl, Philadelphia, PA

Monarch Batting	AB	R	H	2b	3b	HR	RBI	SB	SO	BB	AVG.
Hawkins, 1b	4	0	2	0	0	0	0	0	1	0	.444
Newt Allen, 2b	4	0	0	0	0	0	0	0	0	0	.125
Rogan, lf	3	0	0	0	0	0	0	0	0	1	.286
McNair, cf	4	0	0	0	0	0	0	0	0	0	.000
Moore, ss	4	0	1	0	0	0	0	0	0	0	.125
Joseph, 3b	4	0	1	0	0	0	0	0	1	0	.125

Monarch Batting	AB	R	H	2b	3b	HR	RBI	SB	SO	BB	AVG.
Oscar Johnson, rf	3	0	0	0	0	0	0	0	0	0	.000
Duncan, c	2	0	0	0	0	0	0	0	0	1	.000
McCall, p	0	0	0	0	0	0	0	0	0	0	.000
Drake, p	0	0	0	0	0	0	0	0	0	0	.000
Mendez, p	3	0	0	0	0	0	0	0	1	0	.000
Morris, p	0	0	0	0	0	0	0	0	0	0	.000
Totals	31	0	4	0	0	0	0	0	3	2	.129
Hilldale Batting	AB	R	H	2b	3b	HR	RBI	SB	SO	BB	AVG.
Briggs, rf	3	2	1	1	0	0	1	1	0	1	.333
Warfield, 2b	2	1	0	0	0	0	1	0	0	0	.000
Mackey, 3b	5	3	2	0	1	0	1	0	0	0	.444
Thomas, lf	4	2	2	0	0	0	2	0	0	0	.286
Judy Johnson, ss	5	1	3	1	0	0	1	0	0	0	.625
George Johnson, cf	4	1	3	1	0	0	3	0	0	1	.375
Lewis, c	4	0	0	0	0	0	0	0	0	0	.400
Tom Allen, 1b	4	1	2	1	0	0	1	0	0	0	.286
Winters, p	4	0	2	0	0	0	0	0	1	0	.600
Totals	35	11	15	4	1	0	10	1	1	2	.429

Kansas City	000	000	000	0		
Hilldale	522	002	00x	11		

Monarch Pitching	IP	H	R	ER	BB	K	HB	WP	SAV	F/G	BF
McCall (L, 0–1)	0	1	3	3	1	0	1	0	0	0–0	3
Drake	1⅓	4	4	4	0	0	1	0	0	1–4	11
Mendez	5⅓	8	4	3	1	1	0	0	0	9–5	24
Morris	1	2	0	0	0	0	0	0	0	3–0	5
Totals	8	15	11	10	2	1	2	0	0	13–9	43
Hilldale Pitching	IP	H	R	ER	BB	K	HB	WP	SAV	F/G	BF
Winters (W, 1–0)	9	4	0	0	2	3	0	0	0	5–17	33

Game-Winning RBI: Biz Mackey

Errors: KC — McNair, Joseph; Hilldale — Warfield, J. Johnson

Left on Base: Hilldale — 8, Kansas City — 6

Double Plays: Mackey to Warfield to T. Allen; Judy Johnson to Warfield to T. Allen

Sacrifices: Warfield — 2; Thomas — 1

Hit by Pitcher: Warfield by McCall; Briggs by Drake

Umpires: McDevitt, McBride, Freeman, Doolan

Attendance: 8,661

Time: not available.

SUMMARY

Main man: George Johnson drives in three of the 11 runs, with three hits, including a double.

Turning point: Hilldale scores five runs in the first inning on only three hits, a walk, one hit batter and no Monarch errors.

Silent stats: Nip Winters pitches a four-hitter, not allowing a Monarch to reach third base.

Game 2, Out by Out

First Inning

Kansas City

1— Hawkins out on strikes.

    N. Allen safe on Warfield's error.

    Rogan walks.

2 — McNair bounces to Winters, N. Allen is forced at third.

3 — Moore flies out to George Johnson in center field.

H-0, R-0, LOB-2, E-1

Hilldale

    Briggs walks on four pitches.

    Warfield is issued three balls and then is struck by the pitch.

    Mackey singles to right field, scoring Briggs, Warfield to third.

    Drake goes to the mound and McCall to the showers.

    Thomas taps one to short, Warfield is safe in a collision at the plate. The throw to the plate was too late. Fielder's choice for Thomas.

1— Judy Johnson out, Drake to Hawkins.

    George Johnson doubles to center, Mackey and Thomas scoring.

2 — Lewis pops up to Moore.

    Tom Allen singles to center, scoring George Johnson.

3 — Winters out to Hawkins unassisted.

H-3, R-5, LOB-1, E-0
Score after one inning: Monarchs 0, Hilldale 5

Second Inning

Kansas City

    Joseph singles to right field.

1— Oscar Johnson forces Joseph at second.

2,3 — Duncan hits into a fast double play, Mackey to Warfield to T. Allen.

H-1, R-0, LOB-0, E-0

Hilldale

    Briggs is hit by pitched ball.

1— Warfield is out on a sacrifice bunt, Drake to Hawkins. Briggs advances to second on throw.

    Briggs steals third.

2 — Mackey hits to Moore, Briggs out in rundown between third and home plate.

    Thomas singles to right.

    Judy Johnson singles to right scoring Mackey.

    Drake to the showers, Mendez now pitching with two outs.

    George Johnson hits the first pitch for a single to center, Thomas scoring.

      Both runners advancing.

3 — Lewis flies out to McNair in center field.

H-3, R-2, LOB-2, E-0
Score after two innings: Monarchs 0, Hilldale 7

Third Inning

Kansas City

1— Mendez out, Winters to Tom Allen.

       Hawkins singles to center.

2 — Newt Allen out, Winters to Tom Allen.

3 — Rogan rolls out to Judy Johnson.

H-1, R-0, LOB-1, E-0

Hilldale

       Tom Allen doubles to left.

       Winters beats out bunt to Mendez, who tries to hold Allen.

       Briggs doubles to left-center, scoring Tom Allen.

1— Winters is out at the plate, McNair to Moore to Duncan, Briggs to third.

2 — Warfield bunts to Mendez on squeeze play, Briggs scores.

3 — Mackey flies out to McNair.

H-3, R-2, LOB-1, E-0

Score after Three Innings: Monarchs 0, Hilldale 9

Fourth Inning

Kansas City

1— McNair out, Winters to T. Allen.

       Moore singles to left.

2,3 — Joseph hits into a double play, J. Johnson to Warfield to Tom Allen.

H-1, R-0, LOB-0, E-0

Hilldale

1— Thomas fouls out to Hawkins.

2 — Judy Johnson flies out to McNair.

       George Johnson beats out a hit to Moore.

3 — Lewis skies to Rogan in left field.

H-1, R-0, LOB-1, E-0

Fifth Inning

Kansas City

1— Oscar Johnson rolls out to T. Allen.

       Duncan walks on full count.

2 — Mendez is called out on strikes.

3 — Hawkins flies out to Thomas in left field.

H-0, R-0, LOB-1, E-0

Hilldale

1— Tom Allen pops up to Moore.

2 — Winters strikes out swinging.

3 — Briggs bounces out, Moore to Hawkins.

H-0, R-0, LOB-0, E-0

Sixth Inning

Kansas City

       Newt Allen safe on J. Johnson's error.

1— Rogan forces out Allen at second. Rogan beats outs double play ball.

2 — McNair forces Rogan at second, Judy Johnson to Warfield.

3 — Moore forces McNair at second, Judy Johnson to Warfield.

H-0, R-0, LOB-1, E-1

Hilldale

1— Warfield out on a great catch by McNair in short center.

    Mackey triples to the center field wall.

2 — Thomas's sacrifice fly to McNair scores Mackey.

    Judy Johnson doubles to center, takes third on McNair's fumble

       and scores on Joseph's error of McNair's throw at third.

    George Johnson works Mendez for a walk.

3 — Lewis flies out to McNair.

H-2, R-2, LOB-1, E-2
Score after Six Innings: Monarchs 0, Hilldale 11

Seventh Inning

Kansas City

1— Joseph grounds out to Warfield.

2 — O. Johnson grounds out to Warfield.

3 — Duncan bounces out to Winter.

H-0, R-0, LOB-0, E-0

Hilldale

1— T. Allen rolls out to N. Allen.

    Winters singles to center,

2 — but is out at second trying to stretch it into a double.

    McNair to Moore.

3 — Briggs rolls out to Moore.

H-1, R-0, LOB-0, E-0

Eighth Inning

Kansas City

1— Mendez fouls out to Tom Allen near first base box seats.

    Hawkins singles to left.

2 — Newt Allen forces Hawkins at second.

3 — Rogan pops up to Judy Johnson.

H-1, R-0, LOB-1, E-0

Hilldale

Yellowhorse Morris now pitching for the Monarchs

1— Warfield pops up to Duncan near screen.

2 — Mackey fouls out to Hawkins near Monarchs dugout.

    Thomas singles to center.

    Judy Johnson singles to left.

3 — George Johnson flies out to McNair.

H-2, R-0, LOB-2, E-0

Ninth Inning

Kansas City
1— McNair hits deep drive to center for out.
2 — Moore out, Warfield to Tom Allen.
3 — Joseph strikes out.

H-0, R-0, LOB-0, E-0
Final Score: Kansas City 0, Hilldale 11

GAME 3
W. Bell vs. Ryan

Sunday, October 5, 1924
Baltimore, MD

Game Conditions
Temperature: 62 degrees
Humidity: 77 percent
Winds: North, 1 mile per hour
Forecast: Early dense fog, foggy

Park
Maryland Baseball Park (a.k.a. Black Sox Park)
On Westport Boulevard, between Russell and Bush
streets on edge of the suburb Cherry Hill
Built: 1921
Capacity: 3,500 to 5,000
Dimensions: Unknown

The teams travel 100 miles by car to play the third game of the series in Maryland Baseball Park. Philadelphia, the City of Brotherly Love, bans Sunday baseball, forcing fans go to the Monument City of Baltimore. The suburban park in nearby Westport, on Westport Boulevard between Russell and Bush streets, is no band box. It has an extremely large outfield, with approximately 3,800 covered seats and several thousand grandstand seats. Today, grounds are in fierce condition with a much smaller crowd anticipated.

Today's game is scheduled to start promptly at 1:00 P.M., with darkness due around 5:30 P.M. One man who attended the game was Richard "Dick" Powell.

Powell was responsible for bringing the Baltimore Elite Giants to the city in 1938. Powell served as their general and business manager for several years. As a lad he attended this game. Here is a condensed interview of Powell's recollection of what it was like that day at the ball park (from Monday, July 22, 1996 interview).

I never gave it any thought to getting to the ball park by subway. It was always by street car. The fare was only a nickel. My father would give me enough money for a round trip, two nickels, plus perhaps a quarter or so to buy a hotdog, which only cost a dime, and maybe a candy bar that cost a nickel. And from time to time, they would advertise what they called today, an extra-long hotdog. A hotdog back then that cost a dime, was actually longer than the extra-long hotdogs sold today. Shucks, the hotdog stuck out of both ends of the bun. Plus the fact, this was during a period of prohibition, and they sold what they called "near" beer. It wasn't real beer, but very similar to beer. It was very similar to the beer they authorized at various military posts. I got my first taste of beer at the ballpark. Sometimes, a friend of father, Mr. Ross, would take me to the ball park. I recalled one Sunday [in 1924], not during the series, I got thirsty and said to Mr. Ross, I wanted some water. They didn't have water fountains like they do today at the ballpark. So anyway he called the fellow over who was selling the beer. He had a regular ice bucket, with maybe eight or ten bottles of beer, no cans back then. I told Mr. Ross I didn't want any beer, "I want some water." But he told me to go ahead and drink it, claiming, "It wasn't a damn thing but water anyway." And that was my first experience with any semblance of alcohol....

But back to the World Series, I was aware of the fact that it was a championship game and it was on a Sunday. I went to the ball park on a routine basis, especially on Sundays. Now on Monday, it was a different story, I had to go to school and of course after school, I may have had chores around the house to do. And I may not have had the price of admission after spending all my money the day before.

The baseball park was located in south Baltimore. And I lived in northwest Baltimore. Oh I would say it was easily about three miles from where I lived to the ball park. It was the Maryland Baseball Park, home of the Baltimore Black Sox.

Maryland Ball Park was an open field where some wooden stands were constructed. A grandstand was behind home plate. You had considerable area for the outfield, in fact I've heard old-timers say, it was once an area for dumping. They were just looking for an open field to put up a ball park. It was enclosed. I don't think there were more than three gates. You got your tickets up front, even if you entered on the sides. Also during that period, there was prohibition on Sunday baseball as well. You could not charge a fee to enter the ball park on Sunday. How they circumvented the law was, they made up scorecards, that were maybe about five by eight inches. And you went to the window and you put in your fifty cents and you got a scorecard. Around that time, general admission was about fifty cents, with box seats about a buck and a quarter. When you came to the front gate with your scorecard in your hand, that admitted you. This was done during the world series game. I remember so well that Alex Pompez [owner of the Cuban Stars] watching to see that the two fellows on the gate wasn't allowing their buddies in. Otherwise, somebody would slip them a quarter and sneak in without a scorecard. I don't remember whether I stole in or carried somebody's bag. I just wanted to see that ball game....

In fact during the early forties when the Depression was about to end, when I was traveling with the ball team, I got seventy-five cents a day for meal money. The players got a dollar. We got two meals. We could go to a restaurant in New York city and get bacon and eggs and coffee for forty cents. Then we hold back fifteen cents to go to the Apollo. Then you had thirty or forty cents left to go to dinner.

I don't remember whether I walked home from the game or took the street car. If I didn't use the extra nickel to buy some candy, I'd take the street car home. Every now and time, there was an extra buddy along, we would just walk back. To tell you the truth, kids like us would get on the bus with no fare. We would just get in with the crowd and try to steal a free ride for a few blocks. We were just typical kids. After we got put off, we would just walk home.

Back then, placards to a large degree were used. They were placed in the barber-shop and hair dresser salons, and wooden telegraph poles. I would probably hear more about the game in the barbershop than anywhere else. I also lived in an area, near Smith Hotel, where the ball players came into that particular [barber]shop, and I might hear some exchange of rapport on various players. In fact, I saw Jack Johnson once in that barbershop. He was there having a shave. There was a lot of people milling around and looking through the window of Mr. Goobie's shop.

It was a prohibition era and bootleg whiskey was sold. And there were ladies of the evening. It was in an area of high black activity. Mr. Smith's hotel where these fellows stayed, was a noted politician at that time. This was where most of the sporting life took place. Thomas R. Smith was a black man. All the top black enter-tainers stayed there, especially stage performers, like Noble & Sissle, Florence Mills, Eubie Blake, Bert Williams, and film producer Oscar Michaeux. We saw shows like "Dixie to Broadway" and "Shuffle Along."

I distinctly recalled seeing Jose Mendez, the team manager, standing on top the visiting teams dugout in this tie game, trying to see the end of the game. Mendez was a very dark fellow and had several gold teeth. The fans had moved from their seats to standing on the field. A lot of people, by this time, had gotten on the field. I remember being on the third base side, in the pavilion, and I maneuvered myself around to the visiting team's dugout, stood on the dugout with him.

That was a lot of word-of-mouth about outstanding ball players at that time, and remembered a fellow named Bullet Rogan. This being a rail-road city [Baltimore]. And hav-ing the Chesapeake Bay, in which boats sailed to Virginia and surrounding areas, and therefore a lot of the waiters and porters who got around, talked about various sports, race horses and prize fighters and baseball. And therefore being a little boy around my dad who mingled in the sporting circle, that's where I heard about Bullet Rogan and Frank Wickware. That Rogan had quite a reputation back then.

Dick Powell: As a youngster growing up in Balti-more, he recalls his experience at the World Series game in Maryland Baseball Park (Courtesy of Bar-bara Golden).

Starting pitchers for today's game are Red Ryan for Hilldale and William Bell for Kansas City. During the season, Ryan had been used mostly as the third starter and sometimes middle reliever. Ryan is best known for his knuckleball and forkball of which he has excellent control. He's credited with two of four staff shutouts and has the lowest walks per innings ratio on the team. Although small in stature, Ryan has a bouncy fastball and is a fine batter, for a pitcher.

Texan William Bell is known as a control pitcher who can paint the corners. His repertoire includes a better than average fastball, a slow-breaking curve and a nice slider. Three of his 10 wins came against the tough Chicago American Giants. And Bell gave up less hits (117) than innings (118⅔) pitched during the season, a testament to his excellent control.

The Monarchs initially strike in the third inning with two outs, when Ryan becomes uncharacteristically wild, walking Hawkins and hitting Allen. When Santop can't hold a pitch to Rogan, the runners move up a base on the passed ball. Rogan then makes Ryan pay for his wildness and promptly singles to center, scoring both men. Ryan settles down to strike out clean-up hitter Hurley McNair to close out the inning. The Hilldale Club scores one run in their half of the inning when Tom Allen singles up the middle. After Allen goes to second on a sacrifice bunt by pitcher Ryan and to third on a ground out, Warfield brings him home with a single to center field. Monarchs 2, Hilldale 1.

In the fourth inning, Heavy Johnson lays into a pitch and belts it for a double off the right field wall. Ryan then hangs a curve ball to Newt Joseph, who enjoys a victory lap with a blast over the center field pavilion, giving the Monarchs a four-to-one lead.

Starting the fifth inning, Bolden replaces Ryan with submariner Scrip Lee and Joe Lewis takes over the catching duties for Louis "Big Bertha" Santop. Hilldale comes back in the bottom of the fifth inning with three runs. George Johnson leads off with a double to center field and goes to third on an error by third baseman Newt Joseph, on Allen's tapper. Johnson then scores on Duncan's passed ball. Bell, unusually wild in the inning, walks pitcher Scrip Lee on four straight pitches. Briggs then bunts the runners up, but Warfield hits to Joseph with the runners holding. With the tying runs on base, the notorious Biz Mackey comes to the plate. Taking no chances, Bell gives Mackey a courtesy pass to first base, loading the bases for Joe Lewis, who hit a very respectable .333 in limited action during the season, but lacks the power of Big Bertha. The Monarchs' strategy backfires when Lewis doubles home Tom Allen and Scrip Lee, tying the game.

After six innings, with the score tied, Mendez sends in the all-purpose Mothell to play right field in place of the slower Heavy Johnson. Hilldale quickly mounts a rally after Briggs singles and scores on Warfield's ground rule double into the right field seats. With runners on second and third and only one out, Bell must face Biz Mackey again. Refusing the challenge, Bell gives Mackey a second free pass to first base. With the bases loaded, Bell gets Lewis out on strikes, while Clint Thomas puts a scare into the Monarchs, hitting a sinking line drive that defensive specialist Mothell snares on the run.

Going to the top of the ninth inning, the score remains tied at 4–4. Hilldale ace Lee has held the Monarchs to only three hits since taking over in the fifth inning. The inning starts with Lee beaning Dink Mothell. Mothell is carried off the field and replaced by George Sweatt. Joseph is also hit by a pitch, putting the Monarchs in a position to win the game and take the lead in the series. Frank Duncan attempts a sacrifice bunt, but the quick Lee grabs the slow roller and fires to third, getting swift Sweatt for the first out of the inning. But Joseph scores when Judy Johnson throws away William Bell's slow roller on a check swing. Duncan notices that Judy's throw bounces to the outfield and attempts to pad the one-run lead by pilfering home. George Johnson scoops up the errant throw and fires to Frank Warfield, who relays the peg to Lewis at home for the second out of the inning, virtually killing the rally.

With the sun disappearing, the Monarchs have a chance to win this thriller but must now face the heart of the Hilldale lineup. Working carefully, Bell reluctantly gives up a leadoff walk to Warfield. The always dangerous Mackey hits a bullet down the line to Joseph at third, who back hands the drive and throws wildly to first base pulling Hawkins off the bag. Fueling the error, Hawkins fires back to Joseph in a futile attempt to catch the sneaky Warfield trying to get over to third. Hawkins' wayward throw allows Warfield to score the tying run. Though Bell gets the side out, the game is going into extra innings.

In the twelfth inning, with two outs, Newt Allen's double and Bullet Rogan's single give the Monarchs the lead again, only to have Hilldale tie it when Clint Thomas walks and Judy Johnson doubles, putting runners on second and third, with no outs. George Johnson grounds out to third with Joseph holding the runners. Nip Winters pinch-hits for Tom Allen, but Mendez orders Bell to give Winters first base. With the bases loaded, George Carr bats for Lee and works Bell for a walk, forcing in the tying

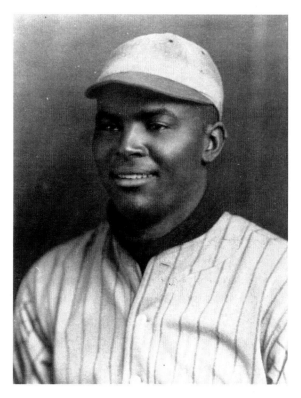

Biz Mackey: Three intentional walks to Mackey by Monarch pitchers kept Hilldale from busting loose for more runs and a possible victory (NoirTech Research).

run. Now, with one out and the bases still loaded, Otto Briggs sends a deep drive to left field. Hurley McNair catches the drive and whirls in time and throws a perfect strike to catcher Duncan, nipping Judy Johnson at the plate, ending the inning. A golden opportunity is lost for the Hilldale Club.

The thirteenth and final inning, Hilldale sends Rube Currie to the mound, while the Monarchs go with Rogan. Currie cruises through his inning. Rogan gets Judy Johnson for the final out, withstanding two uneventful errors by his team-mates, after two Hilldale outs. Neither pitcher gives up a hit as the game is called on account of darkness.

The Kansas City Monarchs were able to dodge the Hilldale bullets through-out the game. In the fifth, seventh and eleventh innings, they intentionally walked the great Biz Mackey, who hit .332 during the season with a .464 slugging per-centage, to keep Hilldale at bay. Despite their fielding lapses of six errors, the Monarchs were lucky to walk away from the game with a tie. And with William Bell struggling for twelve innings and the Monarchs having to use their top pitcher Rogan for the final inning, the Monarchs pitching corps may be in trouble if the series goes the distance.

The local press reports that Jack Hendricks, Cincinnati Reds manager on his way to Seattle, thought today's game was well played. Despite the poor fielding conditions, Hendricks expressed his delight in watching talented defensive plays by second basemen, Frank Warfield and Newt Allen, hot corner man Newt Joseph, and catcher Frank Duncan.

3

Sunday, October 5, 1924
Maryland Baseball Park, Baltimore

Monarch Batting	AB	R	H	2b	3b	HR	RBI	SB	SO	BB	AVG.
Hawkins, 1b	4	1	0	0	0	0	0	0	1	2	.308
Newt Allen, 2b	4	2	2	2	0	0	0	0	0	0	.250
Rogan, cf-p	5	0	3	0	0	0	3	0	0	1	.417
McNair, lf	5	0	0	0	0	0	0	0	2	1	.000
Moore, ss	6	0	0	0	0	0	0	0	0	0	.071
Oscar Johnson, rf	3	1	1	1	0	0	0	0	1	0	.111
Mothell, rf (a)	0	0	0	0	0	0	0	0	0	0	.000
Sweatt, rf-cf (b)	2	0	0	0	0	0	0	0	0	0	.167
Joseph, 3b	4	2	1	0	0	1	2	0	2	1	.167
Duncan, c	6	0	1	0	0	0	0	0	1	0	.083
W. Bell, p-rf (c)	3	0	0	0	0	0	0	0	1	0	.000
Totals	42	6	8	3	0	1	5	0	8	5	.190
Hilldale Batting	**AB**	**R**	**H**	**2b**	**3b**	**HR**	**RBI**	**SB**	**SO**	**BB**	**AVG.**
Briggs, rf	5	1	1	0	0	0	0	1	0	0	.273
Warfield, 2b	5	1	2	1	0	0	1	0	1	1	.182
Mackey, 3b	4	0	0	0	0	0	0	0	0	3	.308
Santop, c	2	0	0	0	0	0	0	0	0	0	.400
Lewis, c (f)	5	0	1	1	0	0	2	0	1	0	.100

Hilldale Batting	AB	R	H	2b	3b	HR	RBI	SB	SO	BB	AVG.
Thomas, lf	6	1	1	0	0	0	0	0	0	1	.231
Judy Johnson, ss	7	0	3	2	0	0	0	0	0	0	.533
George Johnson, cf	5	0	1	1	0	0	0	0	2	0	.308
Tom Allen, 1b	5	2	1	0	0	0	0	0	0	0	.250
Winters, ph (d)	0	0	0	0	0	0	0	0	0	1	.600
Ryan, p	0	0	0	0	0	0	0	0	0	0	.000
Lee, p	2	1	0	0	0	0	0	0	1	2	.000
Carr, ph-1b (e)	0	0	0	0	0	0	1	0	0	1	.000
Currie, p	0	0	0	0	0	0	0	0	0	0	.000
Totals	46	6	10	5	0	0	4	1	5	9	.217

(a) Mothell replaces O. Johnson in right field in 7th inning.
(b) Sweatt pinch-runs for Mothell in 9th inning, and goes to right.
(c) William Bell goes to right field, Sweatt to center field and Rogan to pitch in 13th inning.
(d) Winters walks for T. Allen in 12th inning.
(e) Carr walks for Lee in 12th inning.
(f) Lewis replaces Santop at catching in 5th inning.

Kansas City	002	200	001	001	0	6
Hilldale	001	030	001	001	0	6

13 innings—game called because of darkness

Monarch Pitching	IP	H	R	ER	BB	K	HB	WP	SAV	F/G	BF
W. Bell	12	10	6	4	9	4	1	0	0	7–22	56
Rogan	1	0	0	0	0	1	0	0	0	2–0	5
Totals	13	10	6	4	9	5	1	0	0	9–22	61

Hilldale Pitching	IP	H	R	ER	BB	K	HB	WP	SAV	F/G	BF
Ryan	4	3	4	3	2	2	1	0	0	4–6	18
Lee	8	5	2	1	2	6	2	0	0	3–12	32
Currie	1	0	0	0	1	0	0	0	0	0–2	3
Totals	13	8	6	4	5	8	3	0	0	7–20	53

Game-Winning RBI: none
Errors: KC — Hawkins, Moore, Joseph (3); Hilldale — J. Johnson
Left on Base: Hilldale — 15, Kansas City — 8
Double Plays: Moore to Hawkins; Allen to Moore to Hawkins; McNair to Duncan
Sacrifices: KC — N. Allen, W. Bell; Hilldale — Briggs Warfield, G. Johnson, Ryan.
Hit by Pitcher: Joseph and Mothell by Lee; N. Allen by Ryan; Briggs by W. Bell.
Passed Balls: Duncan, Santop, Lewis
Umpires: Freeman, Dolan, McDevitt, McBride
Attendance: 5,503
Time: not available

SUMMARY

Main man: Bullet Rogan provides clutch hitting driving in three runs with three hits to keep the Monarchs in the game.

Turning point: Entering the ninth inning, the Monarchs are up by one run. After a leadoff walk and an infield single, a throwing error by Lem Hawkins allows Frank Warfield to score the tying run, sending the game into extra innings.

Silent stats: Three intentional walks to Biz Mackey by Monarch pitchers

kept Hilldale from busting loose for more runs and a possible victory by Hilldale.

Game 3, Out by Out

First Inning

Kansas City

    Hawkins walks.

1 — Newt Allen sacrifices Hawkins to second.

2 — Rogan out, Warfield to Tom Allen.

3 — McNair bounces out to Warfield.

H-0, R-0, LOB-1, E-0

Hilldale

1 — Briggs flies to McNair in left.

2 — Warfield out to Hawkins, unassisted.

3 — Mackey pops to Newt Allen.

H-0, R-0, LOB-0, E-0

Second Inning

Kansas City

1 — Moore out to J. Johnson.

2 — Oscar Johnson pops up to Santop.

3 — Joseph flies out to Briggs in right.

H-0, R-0, LOB-0, E-0

Hilldale

1 — Santop out to Newt Allen.

2 — Thomas out to Newt Allen.

    Judy Johnson doubles to right.

3 — George Johnson strikes out.

H-1, R-0, LOB-1, E-0

Third Inning

Kansas City

1 — Duncan is called out on strikes.

2 — Wm. Bell grounds out to Warfield.

    Hawkins works Red Ryan for a walk.

    Newt Allen is hit by a pitched ball.

    Santop lets one of Ryan's pitches get away from him and it rolls to the screen.

      Hawkins going to third and Allen to second. Passed ball on Santop.

    Rogan singles to center, Hawkins and Allen score.

3 — McNair strikes out.

H-1, R-2, LOB-1, E-0

Hilldale

    Tom Allen singles to center.

1 — Ryan advances Allen with sacrifice bunt, great play by Bell.

2 — Briggs grounds out, Allen to Hawkins.

Warfield singles up the middle and Tom Allen scores.
3 — Mackey grounds out, William Bell to Hawkins.
H-2, R-1, LOB-1, E-0
Score after Three Innings: Monarchs 2, Hilldale 1 —

Fourth Inning

Kansas City
1 — Moore flies out to George Johnson.
Oscar Johnson doubles into the right field pavilion, for a ground rule double.
Joseph hits the ball over the center field fence for a home run, scoring Johnson.
2 — Duncan out, Judy Johnson to Tom Allen.
3 — William Bell grounds out, Warfield to Tom Allen.
H-2, R-2, LOB-0, E-0

Hilldale
1 — Santop grounds out on sensational play by Newt Allen.
Thomas singles to right.
2,3 — J. Johnson bounces into double play, Newt Allen to Moore to Hawkins.
H-1, R-0, LOB-0, E-0
Score after Four Innings: Monarchs 4, Hilldale 1

Fifth Inning

Kansas City
Lee, the submarine pitcher, now pitching for Hilldale, with Lewis catching.
1 — Hawkins strikes out.
Newt Allen doubles into the pavilion seats in right field.
Rogan bunts to Lee. Lee's throw to third for the attempted out on Allen
is not in time. (Rogan credited with a hit.)
2 — Lewis juggles ball but recovers in time to putout Rogan trying to steal second,
Warfield makes tag. Allen holding at third base.
3 — McNair out to Judy Johnson.
H-2, R-0, LOB-1, E-0

Hilldale
George Johnson doubles to center.
Tom Allen taps to Bell, G. Johnson is safe at third when Joseph drops the ball.
Duncan lets one of Bell's pitches get away and George Johnson scores.
Lee walks on four straight balls.
1 — Both runners advance on Briggs' sacrifice.
2 — Warfield bounces out to Joseph.
Mackey is intentionally walked, filling the bases.
Lewis' double scores Tom Allen and Lee.
3 — Thomas out, Moore to Hawkins.
H-2, R-3, LOB-2, E-1
Score after Five Innings: Monarchs 4, Hilldale 4

Sixth Inning

Kansas City
1 — Moore grounds out, Warfield to Tom Allen.

2 — Heavy Johnson strikes out.

3 — Joseph strikes out also.

H-0, R-0, LOB-0, E-0

Hilldale

1 — J. Johnson grounds out to Bell.

2 — G. Johnson goes down swinging.

3 — Tom Allen grounds out, Moore to Hawkins.

H-0, R-0, LOB-0, E-0

Seventh Inning

Kansas City

Duncan pushes a soft hit past Lee that J. Johnson could not handle.

1 — Bell is out on a near-perfect bunt, sacrifice.

2 — Hawkins lines into Mackey's hands.

3 — Newt Allen grounds out, Warfield to Tom Allen.

H-1, R-0, LOB-1, E-0

Hilldale

Mothell is now playing right field in place of Oscar Johnson.

1 — Lee is out on strikes.

Briggs singles to right.

Warfield doubles into the extra seats in right, scoring Briggs.

Umpire sends him back to third on the ground rule double.

Mackey is again intentionally walked, filling the bases.

2 — Lewis strikes out.

3 — Thomas is out when Mothell takes his drive on the run.

H-2, R-0, LOB-3, E-0

Eighth Inning

Kansas City

1 — Rogan rolls out, Warfield to Tom Allen.

2 — McNair out on strikes.

3 — Moore out, J. Johnson to T. Allen.

H-0, R-0, LOB-0, E-0

Hilldale

Judy Johnson beats out a hit to Moore.

1 — George Johnson sacrifices, Hawkins to N. Allen.

2 — T. Allen out, Bell tossing to Hawkins.

Lee walks on full count.

3 — Briggs grounds out, Bell to Hawkins.

H-1, R-0, LOB-2, E-0

Ninth Inning

Kansas City

Mothell is hit by pitch and carried from field; Mothell is replaced by George Sweatt.

Joseph is also hit by pitch.

1 — Duncan attempts a sacrifice, Lee forces Sweatt at third.

     William Bell safe on throwing error by J. Johnson, Joseph scoring.

2 — Duncan is out at the plate trying to score on the same play. George Johnson to Warfield to Lewis.

     Bell to second on play.

     Lewis accidentally kicks ball to screen. Bell to third.

     Passed ball on Lewis.

3 — Hawkins grounds out to Judy Johnson.

H-0, R-1, LOB-1, E-1

Hilldale

     Warfield walks.

     Mackey safe on Joseph's throwing error.

     Hawkins makes bad throw back to Joseph in attempt to get
        Warfield going to third.

     Warfield scores, when ball gets away from Joseph.

1 — Lewis flies out to Johnson.

2 — Thomas grounds out to N. Allen.

3 — J. Johnson out to Hawkins unassisted.

H-0, R-1, LOB-1, E-2

Score after Nine Innings: Monarchs 5, Hilldale 5

Tenth Inning

Kansas City

1 — N. Allen out, Warfield to Tom Allen.

     Rogan walks.

2 — McNair grounds out Warfield to Tom Allen.

3 — Moore lines to Briggs in right.

H-0, R-0, LOB-1, E-0

Hilldale

1 — George Johnson flies to Rogan, who makes a nice catch.

2 — Tom Allen pops out to Newt Allen.

3 — Lee bounces out to Newt Allen.

H-0, R-0, LOB-0, E-0

Eleventh Inning

Kansas City

1 — Sweatt grounds out, Lee to Tom Allen.

2 — Joseph strikes out.

3 — Duncan's foul fly is caught by Warfield.

H-0, R-0, LOB-0, E-0

Hilldale

     Briggs is hit by pitch.

1 — Warfield is out, Bell to Hawkins, on a sacrifice bunt.

     Mackey ordered intentionally walked for the third time.

2,3 — Lewis bounces into double play, N. Allen to Hawkins.

H-0, R-0, LOB-1, E-0

Twelfth Inning

Kansas City

1 — William Bell strikes out.

2 — Hawkins flies out to left field.

   Newt Allen lines a double into the seats in right field.

   Rogan singles to center and Allen scores.

   Rogan takes second on the throw to the plate.

   McNair intentionally walked by Lee.

3 — Moore grounds out weakly to T. Allen.

H-2, R-1, LOB-2, E-0

Hilldale

   Thomas walks.

   Judy Johnson doubles to center.

1 — G. Johnson grounds out to Joseph.

   Winters is sent to bat for Tom Allen and is intentionally walked.

   Carr bats for Lee and is walked, forcing in tying run.

2 — Briggs flies out to McNair in left field.

3 — Judy Johnson is out at the plate, McNair to Duncan.

H-1, R-1, LOB-2, E-0

Score after Twelve Innings: Monarchs 6, Hilldale 6

Thirteenth Inning

Kansas City

Rube Currie goes to the mound for Hilldale.

Carr is playing first base.

1 — Sweatt grounds out, Lewis to Carr.

   Joseph walks.

2 — Joseph is out stealing second, Lewis to Warfield.

3 — Duncan out to Warfield on close play.

H-0, R-0, LOB-0, E-0

Hilldale

Rogan goes to the mound for the Monarchs.

Sweatt is moved to center field and William Bell takes right field.

1 — Rogan fans Warfield.

2 — Mackey lines out to Bell.

   Lewis is safe on Joseph's error.

   Thomas safe on Moore's throwing error to N. Allen at second.

   First and second base are occupied.

3 — J. Johnson hits liner to Newt Allen for final out.

H-0, R-0, LOB-2, E-2

The game is called on account of darkness. It will be played off tomorrow.

Score after Thirteen: Kansas City 6, Hilldale 6

GAME 4

C. Bell vs. Ryan

Monday, October 6, 1924
Baltimore, MD

Game Conditions
Temperature: 66 degrees
Humidity: 89 percent
Winds: Southwest, 2 miles per hour
Forecast: Light fog, clear

Park
Maryland Baseball Park (a.k.a. Black Sox Park)

Once again the two teams would meet on neutral grounds in Baltimore's spacious Black Sox Park. After Sunday's somewhat cool weather, less than 600 fans show up for today's contest.

Bolden, realizing the missed opportunities in Game Three as Hilldale left 15 runners stranded on the bases, decides to shake up his lineup. The Monarchs were able to kill three potential rallies by walking the always dangerous Biz Mackey. They chose to face either Santop or Lewis in the lineup. Santop was past his prime and Lewis may never reach his prime. Bolden moves Judy Johnson, who had eight hits with four doubles in the first three games, to the cleanup spot. Behind Judy, Bolden puts Dibo Johnson, who had three hits in game two plus three ribbies. Putting Johnson and Johnson behind Mackey presented a formidable lineup that would keep the Monarch pitchers busy. Hilldale also put George Carr at first, benching Tom Allen, adding even more power to the lineup.

Today's game will see Red Ryan return to the mound for Hilldale, while the Monarchs will start Cliff Bell for the first time. Although not a hard thrower, Ryan had pitched four innings in yesterday's game, giving up three earned runs. Once again, Bolden's selection of starting pitchers is questioned by baseball aficionados. Now, Bell's best pitch is a screwball, and he was primarily used by the Monarchs as a spot starter, or middle reliever, during the season. He started the season by pitching three complete games in three starts, including a shutout against the Detroit Stars. Unfortunately, Bell developed a sore arm, and his last league appearance was on July 22 against the same Detroit team, pitching only two innings and giving up four runs. The Monarchs were taking a gamble with an unproven, although a well-rested, pitcher for this crucial game. The Monarchs anticipated that Hilldale would bring back Winters in Game Five and they could counter with Bullet Rogan in an attempt to neutralize their ace.

The Monarchs were the first team out of the chute, scoring two runs in the first inning with back-to-back doubles by N. Allen and Rogan, with Dobie Moore singling in Rogan. The Monarchs scored another run in the third inning, when N. Allen doubles again and Rogan drives in his second run of the game, for a 3–0 lead. At this point, Bolden brings in pitcher Rube Currie, who had pitched the 13th inning of yesterday's marathon.

Hilldale comes right back in their half of the third when Joe Lewis singles to left, but turns his ankle going to second. The speedy Campbell goes in for the injured Lewis, while Carr walks. Campbell and Carr surprise the Monarchs with a double steal putting runners on second and third. Currie grounds out to second baseman Newt Allen, scoring Campbell. Otto Briggs doubles, scoring Carr, and takes third base on Rogan's fumble in the outfield. After Thomas hits weakly back to the mound, Biz Mackey comes up representing the go-ahead run, with two outs and the tying run on third base. However, Briggs surprises everyone, including Mackey, and steals home, tying the game, 3–3. Cliff closes out the inning by retiring Mackey on a grounder.

As pitchers Bell and Currie settle into a groove, they hold each team scoreless until the ninth inning. In the top of the ninth, the Mon-

Otto Briggs: His steal of home plate in the third inning with Biz Mackey at bat shocks everyone. His theft ties the game, setting the stage for Hilldale to win the game in the ninth inning (NoirTech).

archs' Newt Joseph doubles to right field. With first base open, former Monarch pitcher Rube Currie pitches around the dangerous Heavy Johnson and gives him a free pass to first base. Currie prefers to pitch to Frank Duncan and gets him to ground into a fast 4–6–3 double play, with Joseph going to third. Now with two outs and the go-ahead run at third, Mendez decides not to send switch hitter Dink Mothell to the plate for pitcher Bell. Mothell, a fine .282 clutch hitter during the season, stays on the pine, while Cliff, who had only 11 at bats during the regular season, strolls to the plate. Seizing the moment, veteran Currie easily gets C. Bell to ground weakly to first base and escapes a potential loss.

Hilldale starts off their half of the ninth with two walks against C. Bell, which results in a mound conference between manager Mendez, Bell and the entire infield. The next batter, Warfield, hits one back to the mound and Bell throws to third for the force play, but he is too late. The bases are now loaded with no outs. With the infield drawn in, Santop hits a routine grounder to Newt Allen at second and Allen throws wildly to catcher Duncan, allowing Judy Johnson to score the ugly, but winning, run.

Except for Bell's inability to hold Briggs at third base in the third frame, he pitched a fine game. And Mendez's failure to pinch-hit for Bell in the ninth was a fatal decision. The unearned run in the ninth inning because of two Monarch throwing errors will be a bitter pill for Kansas City to swallow tomorrow morning.

4

Monday, October 6, 1924
Maryland Baseball Park, Baltimore

Monarch Batting	AB	R	H	2b	3b	HR	RBI	SB	SO	BB	AVG.
Hawkins, 1b	4	0	0	0	0	0	0	0	0	0	.235
Newt Allen, 2b	4	2	3	2	0	0	0	0	0	0	.375
Rogan, cf	4	1	2	1	0	0	2	0	0	0	.438
McNair, lf	4	0	0	0	0	0	0	0	0	0	.000
Moore, ss	4	0	1	0	0	0	1	0	0	0	.111
Joseph, 3b	4	0	1	1	0	0	0	0	2	0	.188
Oscar Johnson, rf	3	0	1	0	0	0	0	0	0	1	.167
Duncan, c	4	0	0	0	0	0	0	0	0	0	.063
Cliff Bell, p	4	0	0	0	0	0	0	0	1	0	.000
Totals	35	3	8	4	0	0	3	0	3	1	.229

Hilldale Batting	AB	R	H	2b	3b	HR	RBI	SB	SO	BB	AVG.
Briggs, rf	4	1	1	1	0	0	1	1	1	0	.267
Thomas, lf	4	0	0	0	0	0	0	0	0	0	.176
Mackey, 3b	4	0	0	0	0	0	0	0	0	0	.235
Judy Johnson, ss	3	1	0	0	0	0	0	0	1	1	.444
George Johnson, cf	3	0	2	0	0	0	0	0	0	1	.375
Warfield, 2b	3	0	0	0	0	0	0	0	0	0	.143
Lewis, c	1	0	1	0	0	0	0	0	0	0	.182
Campbell, pr (a)	0	1	0	0	0	0	0	1	0	0	.000
Santop, c (b)	3	0	0	0	0	0	2	0	0	0	.250
Carr, 1b	2	1	0	0	0	0	0	1	1	1	.000
Ryan, p	0	0	0	0	0	0	0	0	0	0	.000
Currie, p	3	0	0	0	0	0	0	0	1	0	.000
Totals	30	4	4	1	0	0	3	3	4	3	.133

(a) Campbell ran for Lewis in 3rd inning.
(b) Santop replaces the injured Lewis in 4th inning.

Kansas City	201	000	000	3
Hilldale	003	000	001	4

None out when the winning run scored.

Monarch Pitching	IP	H	R	ER	BB	K	HB	WP	SAV	F/G	BF
C. Bell (L, 0–1)	8	4	4	3	3	4	1	2	0	6–13	34

Hilldale Pitching	IP	H	R	ER	BB	K	HB	WP	SAV	F/G	BF
Ryan	2⅓	5	3	3	0	1	0	0	0	0–6	12
Currie (W, 1–0)	6⅔	3	0	0	1	2	0	0	0	10–7	24
Totals	9	8	3	3	1	3	0	0	0	10–13	36

Game-Winning RBI: Santop
Errors: KC — N. Allen, Rogan, McNair, C. Bell; Hilldale — J. Johnson
Left on Base: Hilldale — 3, Kansas City — 6
Double Plays: Warfield to J. Johnson to Carr
Sacrifices: Currie
Hit by Pitcher: Warfield by C. Bell
Umpires: Freeman, Dolan, McDevitt, McBride
Attendance: 584
Time: not available.

SUMMARY

Main man: Rube Currie, who came in relief for Ryan, shuts down the Monarchs over the last six and two-thirds innings.

Turning point: Otto Briggs' steal of home in the third inning with Biz Mackey at bat shocks everyone. His surprise theft ties the game, setting the stage for Hilldale to win the game in the ninth inning.

Silent stats: The Monarchs wasted a fine batting effort by Newt Allen, who gathers three hits, including two doubles. Unfortunately, Allen's ninth inning error turns him from Hero to Goat.

Game 4, Out by Out

First Inning

Kansas City
1 — Hawkins out, J. Johnson to Carr.
  Allen doubles to left.
  Rogan slams a double to right, Allen scoring.
2 — McNair out Warfield to Carr.
  Moore singles, scoring Rogan.
3 — Joseph forces Moore at second, Judy Johnson to Warfield.
  H-3, R-2, LOB-1, E-0

Hilldale
1 — Briggs out on strikes.
2 — Thomas grounds out to Moore.
3 — Mackey out to McNair in left field.
  H-0, R-0, LOB-0, E-0
  Score after One Inning: Monarchs 2, Hilldale 0

Second Inning

Kansas City
1 — O. Johnson grounds out to Warfield.
2 — Duncan out to J. Johnson.
3 — Cliff Bell fans.
  H-0, R-0, LOB-0, E-0

Hilldale
1 — J. Johnson grounds out to Moore.

2 — G. Johnson rolls out to Bell.

3 — Warfield out, Allen to Hawkins.

H-0, R-0, LOB-0, E-0

Third Inning

Kansas City

1 — Hawkins out, Warfield to Carr.

    Allen doubles to left.

    Rogan singles to center and Allen scores.

    Currie now pitching for Hilldale.

2 — McNair pops up to Warfield.

3 — Moore flies out to Briggs in right.

H-2, R-1, LOB-1, E-0

Hilldale

    Lewis singles to left but turns his ankle going to second.

    Campbell running for Lewis.

    Carr walks.

    Campbell and Carr complete double steal.

1 — Currie out, Allen to Hawkins, Campbell scores.

    Briggs doubles, Carr scores. Briggs advances to third on Rogan's error.

2 — Thomas breaks his bat and is out, Bell to Hawkins.

    Briggs steals home when Bell fails to hold him close at third base.

3 — Mackey grounds out to N. Allen.

H-2, R-3, LOB-0, E-1

Score after Three Innings: Monarchs 3, Hilldale 3

Fourth Inning

Kansas City

Santop now catching for Hilldale.

1 — Joseph fans.

    Oscar Johnson singles sharply to right.

2 — Duncan fouls out to Santop.

3 — Cliff Bell pops up to Judy Johnson.

H-1, R-0, LOB-1, E-0

Hilldale

1 — J. Johnson rolls out to Moore.

    George Johnson singles to left, goes to second on McNair's error.

2 — Warfield out to Hawkins unassisted.

3 — Santop flies to George Johnson.

H-1, R-0, LOB-1, E-0

Fifth Inning

Kansas City

1 — Hawkins out, Currie to Carr.

    Newt Allen gets third hit, a single to center.

2 — Rogan grounds out to Warfield.

3 — McNair grounds out to Warfield.

H-1, R-0, LOB-1, E-0

Hilldale

1 — Carr strikes out.

2 — Currie out, Allen to Hawkins.

3 — Briggs out on a splendid play by Joseph.

H-0, R-0, LOB-0, E-0

Sixth Inning

Kansas City

1 — Moore out, Warfield to Carr.

2 — Joseph strikes out swinging.

3 — Oscar Johnson flies out to Briggs.

H-0, R-0, LOB-0, E-0

Hilldale

1 — Thomas pops up to Duncan.

2 — Mackey grounds out, Joseph to Hawkins.

3 — Judy Johnson is out on strikes.

H-0, R-0, LOB-0, E-0

Seventh Inning

Kansas City

1 — Duncan skies to Thomas.

2 — Bells fouls out to Santop.

3 — Hawkins out, Warfield to Carr.

H-0, R-0, LOB-0, E-0

Hilldale

George Johnson singles a hard shot off Moore's glove.

Warfield hit by pitch.

1 — Santop pops up to Allen.

2 — Carr flies out to Rogan in center.

3 — Currie strikes out.

H-1, R-0, LOB-2, E-0

Eighth Inning

Kansas City

1 — Allen flies out to Thomas.

Rogan safe on Judy Johnson's error.

2 — McNair flies to Thomas.

3 — Moore lines out to Briggs.

H-0, R-0, LOB-1, E-0

Hilldale

1 — Briggs out, Allen to Hawkins.

2 — Thomas flies out to Oscar Johnson.

3 — Mackey fouls out to Duncan.

H-0, R-0, LOB-0, E-0

Ninth Inning

Kansas City

> Joseph doubles to right.
>
> Oscar Johnson walks.

1,2 — Duncan hits into double play, Warfield to J. Johnson to Carr.

> Joseph remains at third.

3 — Cliff Bell out to Carr unassisted.

H-1, R-0, LOB-1, E-0

Hilldale

> J. Johnson walks.
>
> G. Johnson walks.
>
> Bell, Mendez, Moore, Allen and Hawkins have mound conference.
>
> Warfield safe on Bell's late throw to third to get J. Johnson. Error on Bell.
> Bases loaded.
>
> Santop hits grounder to N. Allen. Allen makes wide throw to Duncan at the
> plate, J. Johnson scores the winning run. Error on N. Allen (no outs).

H-0, R-1, LOB-X, E-2

Final Score: Kansas City 3, Hilldale 4

GAME 5

Rogan vs. Winters

Saturday, October 11, 1924
Kansas City, Missouri

Game Conditions

Temperature: 82 degrees
Humidity: 50 percent
Winds: South, 8 miles per hour
Forecast: Clear

Park

Muehlebach Park
22nd Street (1st base) (S), 2128 Brooklyn Avenue (right field) (E),
21st Street (left field) (N), Euclid Avenue (3rd base) (W)
Built: 1923
Capacity: 17,476
Dimensions: Left field, 350 feet; Left center, 408 feet;
Center field, 450 feet; Right center, 382 feet; Right field, 350 feet

The Monarchs return home after four games as the visiting team in eastern
cities. Down two games to one and having stranded six men on base in the last
game and nine in the third game, the Monarchs decide to shake up their lineup.

They insert George Sweatt in center field and bat him second, taking Newt Allen's spot in the order. In limited series action Sweatt has been hitting some sizzling line drives, but, unfortunately, right at someone. The hot Allen moves to cleanup, having gone 5-for-8 with four doubles in the last two games. The Monarch's regular cleanup batter, switch-hitter Hurley McNair, is a pitiful 0 for 16, having deserted 15 men on the base paths. So far in the series "Air" McNair's bat has been grounded by the Hilldale Club.

In turn, Hilldale keeps basically the same lineup, but moves power hitter Louis Santop to cleanup behind the menacing Biz Mackey. With Mackey, Santop and Judy Johnson in the heart of the lineup the Monarch pitchers will have a hard time pitching around this threesome.

This will be Nip Winters' second start of the series, while Rogan makes his third series appearance, one start and one inning of relief. The much anticipated matchup between the two star marquee pitchers is now here: power versus power, flame thrower versus flame thrower.

Winters has not pitched since the second game, on October 4, seven days ago. After Rogan easily retires Hilldale in order, a rusty Winters walks Lem Hawkins on a full count. Sweatt sacrifices Hawkins to scoring position and Joseph promptly knocks Sweatt in for the first run of what was supposed to be a pitcher's duel. Manager Bolden rushes to the bullpen to have Scrip Lee warm up. Meanwhile, Joseph is out trying to steal second, but Newt Allen doubles again and Dobie Moore brings him home with a single to center field. Winters escapes further damage when Rogan grounds out to Warfield ending the inning. Monarchs 2, Giants zip.

Hilldale does not score until the fourth inning when Santop hits a mean liner off of Joseph's glove at the hot corner. Judy Johnson singles to center and Clint Thomas advances the runners to second and third with a sacrifice bunt. With one out, Rogan intentionally walks George Johnson to load the bases. Tom Allen then sends a high fly to McNair in right field. McNair rifles an impeccable peg to Duncan at the plate, yet the huge Santop somehow manages to slide around him for Hilldale's first score. Winters grounds out, ending the inning with Hilldale down by a run.

In the eighth inning, Rogan gets into trouble when Hilldale loads the bases again, this time with no outs, because of two errors and an infield hit. George Johnson hits a sharp grounder to Moore at short and Moore forces pinch-runner Cockrell at the plate. George Carr pinch-hits for Tom Allen and hits another infield bouncer to Hawkins, forcing Judy Johnson out at the plate. Unable to help his cause, Winters strikes out with the bases loaded. An excellent pitching job by Rogan yields no runs, escaping serious damage.

With the guts of the Monarchs' batting order coming up in the bottom of the eighth, hometown fans anticipate excitement. Just before Duncan hits an opposite-field double, Winters slips three strikes by heavy hitters McNair and

Johnson and gets Hawkins on a fly ball, killing the challenge. Before Duncan's double, Winters had retired 21 batters in a row, a series record.

With a one run lead going into the top of the ninth, Mendez makes a defensive move by yanking the slower Heavy Johnson and putting in versatile Dink Mothell in left field. The first batter, Briggs with his baggy pants, is nicked by a Rogan pitch, taking first base. After Warfield pops up for the first out, Mackey singles to left field. Briggs goes to third and Mackey to second, when usually dependable Mothell kicks the ball for an error. Mothell's error is contagious. Joe Lewis hits the next pitch to Moore at short, who juggles the ball long enough to miss the flying Briggs at the plate, tying the game, but tosses to Hawkins in plenty of time to get Lewis at first. Only Hawkins is daydreaming and not on the bag.

Rogan and Allen yell at him but when Hawkins finally reaches the sack, Lewis has beaten him. The damage continues by Hilldale. The Monarchs pull their infield and outfield in tight to cut off the go-ahead run. Judy Johnson upsets the strategy by hitting a liner over George Sweatt's head in center for an inside-the-park homer, putting Hilldale up by three runs. After Thomas adds another single, Rogan shuts down the four-run burst by getting George Johnson and George Carr out.

In the Monarchs' last hurrah they go down in order, 1–2–3, losing 5–2. It was a bitter defeat for the hometown Monarchs. Winters had only allowed four hits, three of them in the first inning. Against Winters' drop ball, the Monarchs were only able to hit four balls out of the infield. The Monarchs had disappointed their fans with another poor performance in the field with four costly errors, and were now down three games to one.

Nip Winters: He nails down his third World Series win. Winters gives up one earned run and seven singles and an extra base hit in capturing the victory (Kimshi Productions).

Judy Johnson: Hits a three-run homer in the ninth to put Hilldale in the lead for good. (Courtesy of Todd Bolton)

5

Saturday, October 11, 1924
Muehlebach Park, Kansas City, Missouri

Hilldale Batting	AB	R	H	2b	3b	HR	RBI	SB	SO	BB	AVG.
Briggs, rf	4	1	0	0	0	0	0	0	0	0	.211
Warfield, 2b	3	0	1	0	0	0	0	0	0	2	.176
Mackey, 3b	5	1	1	0	0	0	0	0	1	0	.227
Santop, c	4	1	1	0	0	0	0	0	0	0	.250
Cockrell, pr (a)	0	0	0	0	0	0	0	0	0	0	.000
Lewis, c (b)	1	1	1	0	0	0	1	0	0	0	.250
Judy Johnson, ss	5	1	3	0	0	1	3	0	0	0	.478
Thomas, lf	4	0	2	0	0	0	0	0	0	0	.238
George Johnson, cf	4	0	0	0	0	0	0	0	0	1	.300
Tom Allen, 1b	2	0	0	0	0	0	1	0	1	0	.214
Carr, 1b (c)	1	0	0	0	0	0	0	0	1	0	.000
Winters, p	4	0	1	0	0	0	0	0	2	0	.444
Totals	37	5	10	0	0	1	5	0	5	3	.270

Monarch Batting	AB	R	H	2b	3b	HR	RBI	SB	SO	BB	AVG.
Hawkins, 1b	3	1	0	0	0	0	0	0	0	1	.200
Sweatt, cf	3	0	0	0	0	0	0	0	1	0	.111
Joseph, 3b	4	0	1	0	0	0	1	0	1	0	.200
Newt Allen, 2b	4	1	1	1	0	0	0	0	1	0	.350
Moore, ss	3	0	1	0	0	0	1	1	1	0	.143
Rogan, p	3	0	0	0	0	0	0	0	0	0	.368
McNair, rf	3	0	0	0	0	0	0	0	1	0	.000
Oscar Johnson, lf	3	0	0	0	0	0	0	0	1	0	.133
Mothell, lf (d)	0	0	0	0	0	0	0	0	0	0	.000
Duncan, c	3	0	1	1	0	0	0	0	1	0	.105
Totals	29	2	4	2	0	0	2	1	7	1	.138

(a) Cockrell pinch runs for Santop in 8th inning.
(b) Lewis replaces Santop at catching in 8th inning.
(c) Carr replaces T. Allen at first base in 8th inning.
(d) Mothell replaces O. Johnson in left field in 9th inning.

Hilldale	000	100	004	5
Kansas City	200	000	000	2

Monarch Pitching	IP	H	R	ER	BB	K	HB	WP	SAV	F/G	BF
Rogan (L, 1–1)	9	10	5	4	3	5	1	0	0	3–18	46

Hilldale Pitching	IP	H	R	ER	BB	K	HB	WP	SAV	F/G	BF
Winters (W, 2–0)	9	4	2	2	1	7	0	0	0	5–13	31

Game-Winning RBI: Judy Johnson
Errors: Hilldale — Santop; KC — Moore (2), Rogan, Mothell
Left on Base: Hilldale — 12, Kansas City — 2
Double Plays: None
Sacrifices: KC — Sweatt; Hilldale — Thomas, T. Allen
Hit by Pitcher: Briggs by Rogan
Umpires: McGrew, Anderson, Costello, Goeckel
Attendance: 3,891
Time: 1:57

Summary

Main man: Judy Johnson hits a three-run homer in the ninth to put Hilldale in the lead for good.

Turning point: Defensive replacement Dink Mothell makes a fielding error in the top of the ninth inning, putting runners in the tying and winning positions, opening the door for a Hilldale victory.

Silent stats: Nip Winters retires 21 batters in a row and only allowed one hit after the first inning scare by the Monarchs. Winters strikes out every Monarch starter except Rogan and Hawkins.

Game 5, Out by Out

First Inning

Hilldale
1 — Briggs out, Moore to Hawkins.

2 — Warfield grounds out to Hawkins.

3 — Mackey out to deep short, Moore to Hawkins.

H-0, R-0, LOB-0, E-0

Kansas City

Hawkins walks on full count.

1 — Sweatt sacrifices Hawkins to second. Tom Allen makes the out.

Joseph singled to left, Hawkins scoring.

2 — Joseph was out stealing, Santop to Warfield.

Newt Allen doubles into right field corner.

Moore singles to center, scoring Newt Allen.

Moore steals second and goes to third when Santop's throw hits
    him and rolls into the outfield.

3 — Rogan out, Warfield to Tom Allen.

H-3, R-2, LOB-1, E-1

Score after One Inning: Hilldale 0, Monarchs 2

Second Inning

Hilldale

1 — Santop rolls out, Joseph to Hawkins.

J. Johnson hits a smash to Hawkins, credited with a hit.

2 — Thomas out, Rogan to Hawkins.

3 — George Johnson out on a high foul fly to Duncan.

H-1, R-0, LOB-1, E-0

Kansas City

1 — McNair fouls out to Thomas, who makes running catch.

2 — Heavy Johnson rolls out to T. Allen unassisted.

3 — Duncan called out on strikes.

H-0, R-0, LOB-0, E-0

Third Inning

Hilldale

1 — Tom Allen called out on strikes.

Winters singles to left center.

2 — Briggs forces Winters at second, Hawkins to Moore.

Warfield walks on four straight balls.

3 — Mackey strikes out.

H-1, R-0, LOB-2, E-0

Kansas City

1 — Hawkins out on a sensational leaping catch by Mackey, at third.

2 — Sweatt strikes out, on three pitches.

3 — Joseph out, Warfield to Allen.

H-0, R-0, LOB-0, E-0

Fourth Inning

Hilldale

Santop lines a single off Joseph's glove.

J. Johnson's second hit, a single to center field. Santop stopping at second base.

1 — Thomas sacrifice bunts, Rogan to Hawkins.

George Johnson intentionally passed, loading bases.

2 — Tom Allen sent a sacrifice fly to right field.

McNair's throw had Santop at the plate, but Duncan allows Santop to slide around him.

3 — Winters out, Moore to Hawkins.

H-2, R-1, LOB-2, E-0

Kansas City

1 — Newt Allen strikes out on full count.

2 — Moore strikes out swinging.

3 — Rogan bounces out to Winters.

H-0, R-0, LOB-0, E-0

Score after Four Innings: Hilldale 1, Monarchs 2

Fifth Inning

Hilldale

1 — Briggs out, Moore to Hawkins.

Warfield singles to center.

2 — Mackey forces Warfield at second.

Santop safe on Moore's error.

3 — Judy Johnson grounds out, Newt Allen to Hawkins.

H-1, R-0, LOB-2, E-1

Kansas City

1 — McNair bounces out to Tom Allen.

2 — Oscar Johnson taps weakly to the pitcher's mound.

3 — Duncan rolls out, Judy Johnson to Tom Allen.

H-0, R-0, LOB-0, E-0

Sixth Inning

Hilldale

1 — Thomas out, Newt Allen to Hawkins.

2 — George Johnson out, Newt Allen to Hawkins.

3 — Tom Allen pops up to Newt Allen.

H-0, R-0, LOB-0, E-0

Kansas City

1 — Hawkins flies out to George Johnson.

2 — Sweatt out at first by Judy Johnson.

3 — Joseph struck out.

H-0, R-0, LOB-0, E-0

Seventh Inning

Hilldale

1 — Winters strikes out.

2 — Briggs grounds out to Moore.

Warfield walks for second time.

3 — Mackey out on a great play by Joseph on a slow roller.

H-0, R-0, LOB-1, E-0

Kansas City

1 — Allen flies out to right field.

2 — Moore out, Mackey to T. Allen.

3 — Rogan bounces out to Winters.

H-0, R-0, LOB-0, E-0

Eighth Inning

Hilldale

Santop safe on Moore's second error of the game.

Judy Johnson bunts, Rogan throws wild to second, both runners safe.
   Error on Rogan.

Cockrell in to run for Santop.

Thomas hits ball to Hawkins, who attempts to put out the speedy Cockrell
   at third, but to no avail.

Thomas credited with hit.

Bases loaded, no outs.

1 — George Johnson hits to Moore and Cockrell is forced out at the plate.

2 — Carr batting for Tom Allen and hits to Hawkins, forcing Judy Johnson
   out at the plate.

3 — Winters strikes out, with bases loaded

H-1, R-0, LOB-3, E-2

Kansas City

Carr now playing first base for Hilldale in place of Tom Allen.

Lewis is now catching in place of Santop.

1 — McNair called out on strikes.

2 — O. Johnson called out on strikes (Retired 21 batters in a row).

Duncan doubles to right field.

3 — Hawkins flies out to right field.

H-1, R-0, LOB-1, E-0

Ninth Inning

Hilldale

Mothell playing left field in place of Oscar Johnson.

Briggs was hit by pitch. Duncan protests call.

1 — Warfield pops up to Newt Allen back of first.

Mackey singles to left field.

Briggs goes to third and Mackey to second, when defensive replacement
   Mothell fumbles ball.

Error on Mothell.

Lewis hits to Moore, Moore hesitates, Briggs scores.

Moore throws to first, Hawkins is not on the base and Lewis is safe.
   Lewis credited with single.

Judy Johnson hits inside-the-park home run over Sweatt's head in center.

Thomas singles past Allen.
2 — George Johnson was thrown out at first base by Rogan.
3 — Carr strikes out.

H-4, R-4, LOB-1, E-1

Kansas City
1 — Sweatt flies out to Thomas.
2 — Joseph bounces out to Winters.
3 — N. Allen bounces out to Winters.

H-0, R-0, LOB-0, E-0

Final Score: Hilldale 5, Kansas City 2

GAME 6

Cockrell vs. W. Bell

Sunday, October 12, 1924
Kansas City, Missouri

Game Conditions
Temperature: 80 degrees
Humidity: 37 percent
Winds: South, 9 miles per hour
Forecast: Clear, scattered cloudiness

Park
Muehlebach Park

Down by two games, the Monarchs turn to William Bell, hoping that he regains his excellent control. Bell, who went 12 innings in the 13-inning tie game, will face spitballer Phil Cockrell, who has not pitched since the opener.

With momentum from yesterday's game, Hilldale quickly scores two runs in the first inning when Judy Johnson triples in the gap, scoring Mackey and Santop, after two are out. Down two runs to none, the Monarchs put together a walk and two cheap back-to-back singles, by Rogan and Joseph, to squeeze across a run. With one out, Rogan is out attempting to steal third base. Moore keeps the rally alive with a single. Meanwhile, the aggressive Monarchs will not be denied, as Moore and Joseph pull off a double steal, putting runners on second and third. McNair drives in his first run of the series with a shallow hit to right, scoring Joseph. Later, Moore scores, while McNair takes second on a wild pitch by Cockrell. Scrip Lee gets up quickly in the bullpen with George Sweatt coming to bat. After Sweatt takes two strikes, manager Bolden has seen enough and replaces him with Lee. Sweatt singles off of Lee's first pitch, scoring McNair, and the Monarchs are up four runs to two before Duncan hits a weak dribbler to third for the final out.

After a scoreless second, Hilldale comes back in the top of the third inning with singles by Briggs and Warfield. After Mackey forces Briggs out at third, Mackey

Left: Rube Foster: The controlling league president Foster wanted the pivotal games of the series to be played in hometown Chicago. The Monarchs protested, claiming, "Whose World Series is this, anyway?" Games six, seven and eight were played in Kansas City. *Above:* Dobie Moore: He gets three hits and scores two key runs in the Monarch victory (Both photographs NoirTech Research).

and Warfield politely show the Monarchs their speed with a double steal of second and third bases. Big Bertha Lou Santop is walked, loading the bases. Never shy with the bat, Judy Johnson drives in another run with a single. And Hilldale adds another run when Rogan misjudges Thomas' fly, allowing Mackey to score. W. Bell really bears down and gets Dibo Johnson and Tom Allen to hit grounders back to him. Hilldale ties the game 4–4, and it looks like another wild game is at hand.

Nevertheless, Kansas City fights back. In the bottom of the fourth, Duncan walks and steals second and comes home on William Bell's double. The contest continues as Hilldale ties the score in the sixth inning when Scrip Lee singles home Thomas, who had doubled off the left field wall. The pitchers for both clubs are leading the offensive charge.

Going into the eighth inning, Lee had only given up six hits since he took over for Cockrell in the troublesome first inning. Normally used as a middle reliever during the season, Lee is beginning to show signs of wear. Joseph drives George Johnson to the warning track before Moore singles sharply to right field. After McNair pops up to Mackey, Sweatt triples in the gap, scoring Moore with the eventual winning run.

After Bell gives up a leadoff single to pinch hitter Carr in the top of the ninth, Mendez sends Plunk Drake in to kill any thoughts of a Hilldale rally, with three straight pop ups. The Monarchs with aggressive baserunning, steal a 6–5 victory and are down by a game in the series.

6

Sunday, October 12, 1924
Muehlebach Park, Kansas City, Missouri

Hilldale Batting	AB	R	H	2b	3b	HR	RBI	SB	SO	BB	AVG.
Briggs, rf	5	0	1	0	0	0	0	0	0	0	.208
Warfield, 2b	5	1	1	0	0	0	0	1	0	0	.182
Mackey, 3b	4	2	1	0	0	0	0	1	0	1	.231
Santop, c	2	1	2	0	0	0	0	0	0	1	.357
Lewis, c (a)	2	0	0	0	0	0	0	0	0	0	.214
Judy Johnson, ss	4	0	2	0	1	0	3	0	0	0	.481
Thomas, lf	3	1	1	1	0	0	0	0	0	1	.250
George Johnson, cf	4	0	0	0	0	0	0	0	0	0	.250
Tom Allen, 1b	4	0	0	0	0	0	0	0	1	0	.167
Cockrell, p	0	0	0	0	0	0	0	0	0	0	.000
Lee, p	3	0	2	0	0	0	1	0	1	0	.400
Carr, ph (b)	1	0	1	0	0	0	0	0	0	0	.250
Totals	37	5	11	1	1	0	4	2	2	3	.297

Monarch Batting	AB	R	H	2b	3b	HR	RBI	SB	SO	BB	AVG.
Hawkins, 1b	2	0	1	0	0	0	0	1	0	0	.227
Mothell, 1b (c)	2	0	0	0	0	0	0	0	0	0	.000
Newt Allen, 2b	3	1	0	0	0	0	0	0	0	1	.304
Rogan, cf-lf (d)	4	0	2	0	0	0	0	1	0	0	.391
Joseph, 3b	4	1	1	0	0	0	1	1	1	0	.208
Moore, ss	4	2	3	0	0	0	0	0	0	0	.240
McNair, rf	4	1	2	0	0	0	1	0	0	0	.087
Sweatt, lf-cf (e)	4	0	2	0	1	0	2	0	0	0	.231
Duncan, c	3	1	0	0	0	0	0	1	0	1	.091
William Bell, p	3	0	1	1	0	0	1	0	0	0	.167
Drake, p	0	0	0	0	0	0	0	0	0	0	.000
Totals	33	6	12	1	1	0	5	4	1	2	.364

(a) Lewis replaces Santop at catching in 6th inning.
(b) Carr singles for Lee in 9th inning.
(c) Mothell replaces Hawkins at first base in 3rd inning.
(d) Rogan goes to left field in 8th inning.
(e) Sweatt to center field in 8th inning, McNair stays in right.

Hilldale	202	001	000	5
Kansas City	400	100	01x	6

Hilldale Pitching	IP	H	R	ER	BB	K	HB	WP	SAV	F/G	BF
Cockrell	⅔	4	4	4	1	0	0	1	0	1–0	7
Lee (L, 0–1)	7⅓	8	2	2	1	1	0	0	0	13–6	29
Totals	8	12	6	6	2	1	0	1	0	14–6	36

Monarch Pitching	IP	H	R	ER	BB	K	HB	WP	SAV	F/G	BF
W. Bell (W, 1–0)	8	11	5	4	2	2	0	0	0	7–13	37
Drake (S)	1	0	0	0	1	0	0	0	1	3–0	4
Totals	9	11	5	4	3	2	0	0	1	10–13	41

Game-Winning RBI: Sweatt
Errors: KC — Rogan
Left on Base: Hilldale — 8, Kansas City — 5
Double Plays: Mothell unassisted; Moore to N. Allen to Mothell
Sacrifices: none
Umpires: Anderson, Costello, Goeckel, McGrew
Attendance: 8,885
Time: 2:05

SUMMARY

Main man: George Sweatt drives in two runs, one in the big first inning and the winning run in the eighth inning.

Turning point: The game turned when manager Warfield allowed pitcher Scrip Lee to pitch more innings than his usual diet. Lee's fatigue resulted in a less than stellar performance in the fatal eighth inning.

Silent stats: Walter "Dobie" Moore gets three hits and scores two key runs in the Monarch victory.

Game 6, Out by Out

First Inning

Hilldale
1 — Briggs flies to Rogan in center, who makes a shoestring catch,
       turning somersaults.
2 — Warfield rolls out, Bell to Hawkins.
         Mackey singles to left.
         Santop singles to center, on hit and run play, Mackey on third.
         Judy Johnson triples to right center field, scoring Mackey and Santop.
3 — Thomas out, Moore to Hawkins.
                    H-3, R-2, LOB-1, E-0

Kansas City
1 — Hawkins flies to George Johnson in center field.
         Newt Allen walks.
         Rogan singles to right, Allen going to third.
         Joseph singles to center, scoring Allen. Rogan on second.
2 — Rogan caught stealing third.
         Moore singles.
         Moore and Joseph complete double steal.
         McNair singles to shallow right, Joseph scores, Moore on third.
         Moore scored and McNair took second on a wild pitch, by Cockrell.
         Cockrell get two strikes on Sweatt. Lee in for relief.
         Sweatt singles off Lee, to center, scoring McNair.
3 — Duncan out, Mackey to Tom Allen.
                    H-5, R-4, LOB-1, E-0
            Score after One Inning: Hilldale 2, Monarchs 4

Second Inning

Hilldale

1 — George Johnson out to Hawkins unassisted.

2 — T. Allen flies out to center.

3 — Lee takes strike three looking.

H-0, R-0, LOB-0, E-0

Kansas City

1 — W. Bell out to J. Johnson.

    Hawkins singles to center.

2 — Newt Allen lines out to Thomas.

    Hawkins steals second.

3 — Rogan flies out to G. Johnson in center.

H-1, R-0, LOB-1, E-0

Third Inning

Hilldale

Mothell playing first for Hawkins, who hurt his ankle sliding into second.

    Briggs singles to center.

    Warfield hits a smash off Joseph's glove.

1 — Mackey forces Briggs out at third, Bell to Joseph.

    Warfield and Mackey engineered a double theft, getting safely to third and second.

    Santop was walked, loading bases.

    Judy Johnson's single scores Warfield.

    Thomas safe on Rogan's error on fly ball. Mackey scores.

2 — George Johnson hit to Bell and Santop out at the plate.

3 — Tom Allen out, Bell to Mothell.

H-3, R-2, LOB-3, E-1

Kansas City

1 — Joseph out, Warfield to Tom Allen.

2 — Moore flies in Thomas in left.

    McNair beat out a hit to Judy Johnson.

3 — McNair caught stealing, Santop to Warfield.

H-1, R-0, LOB-0, E-0

Score after Three Innings, Hilldale 4, Monarchs 4

Fourth Inning

Hilldale

    Lee beats out bunt to Bell down first base line.

1 — Briggs forces Lee out at second.

2 — Warfield lines out to Mothell.

3 — Briggs was doubled up when Mothell steps on first.

H-1, R-0, LOB-0, E-0

Kansas City

1 — Sweatt flies out to G. Johnson.

    Duncan walks, steals second.

William Bell doubles to right center, Duncan scoring.

2 — Mothell bounces out to Lee, Bell going to third.

3 — N. Allen out on fine play by Warfield.

H-1, R-1, LOB-1, E-0

Score after Four Innings: Hilldale 4, Monarchs 5

Fifth Inning

Hilldale

1 — Mackey ground out to Moore.

    Santop singles over second.

2,3 — Judy Johnson hits into double play, Moore to Allen to Mothell.

H-1, R-0, LOB-0, E-0

Kansas City

    Rogan singles to left.

1 — Joseph fanned.

    Rogan steals second.

    Moore hit a hard liner off Warfield's glove for a hit.

    Rogan to third.

2 — Moore out on attempted steal of second.

3 — McNair flies out to Thomas in left.

H-2, R-0, LOB-1, E-0

Sixth Inning

Hilldale

    Thomas hit a smash off the left field wall for a double.

1 — George Johnson pops up to Newt Allen back of first.

2 — Tom Allen fans, losing his temper.

    Lee singles to right, scoring Thomas.

3 — Briggs flies out to McNair.

H-2, R-1, LOB-1, E-0

Kansas City

Lewis catching for Hilldale.

1 — Sweatt flies to Warfield.

2 — Duncan flies to George Johnson in center.

3 — William Bell pops up to Mackey.

H-0, R-0, LOB-0, E-0

Score after Six Innings, Hilldale 5, Monarchs 5

Seventh Inning

Hilldale

1 — Warfield out to Mothell unassisted.

2 — Mackey flies out to McNair to right.

3 — Lewis out, Moore to Mothell.

H-0, R-0, LOB-0, E-0

Kansas City

1 — Mothell out on long fly to G. Johnson.

2 — N. Allen lines out to Judy Johnson.

3 — Rogan fouls out to Mackey near Hilldale dugout.

H-0, R-0, LOB-0, E-0

Eighth Inning

Hilldale

The Kansas City outfield is switched. McNair stays in right, Sweatt goes to center and Rogan to left field.

1 — Judy Johnson out on pop up to Newt Allen.

    Thomas walks.

2 — George Johnson forces Thomas out at second.

3 — T. Allen out, Bell to Mothell.

H-0, R-0, LOB-1, E-0

Kansas City

1 — Joseph robbed of hit by George Johnson, on the warning track.

    Moore singles to right.

2 — McNair fouls out to Mackey.

    Sweatt triples between right and center field, Moore scores.

3 — Duncan out, Judy Johnson to Tom Allen.

H-2, R-1, LOB-1, E-0

Score after Eight Innings, Hilldale 5, Monarchs 6

Ninth Inning

Hilldale

Carr batting for Lee.

    Carr singles to center.

    Drake comes in for William Bell with no outs.

1 — Briggs fouls out to Joseph.

2 — Warfield pops up to N. Allen.

    Mackey walks.

    Duncan and Drake have a conference on the mound.

3 — Lewis fouls out to Joseph.

H-1, R-0, LOB-2, E-0

Final Score: Kansas City 6, Hilldale 5

GAME 7

Winters vs. C. Bell

Tuesday, October 14, 1924
Kansas City, Missouri

Game Conditions
Temperature: 79 degrees
Humidity: 26 percent
Winds: Southeast, 7 miles per hour
Forecast: Clear and mild

Park
Muehlebach Park

Today's game had been originally scheduled to be played yesterday. However, a benefit game sponsored by the *Kansas City Journal-Post* for Children's Mercy Hospital, featuring Babe Ruth and his All-Stars, caused the game to be rescheduled. Babe Ruth, America's most celebrated diamond star, was of course the main attraction. Ticket prices were $1.00 for the choice seats, with all proceeds donated to Mercy Hospital.

Today's matchup will feature the Monarchs' Cliff Bell against the tough Nip Winters of Hilldale. Winters has been practically unbeatable so far in the series, while Bell lost his only appearance in game four of the series. Early in the season, Bell pitched one of the four shutouts by the Monarchs pitching staff, but has struggled of late. And with the Monarchs facing the great Nip Winters, they could be down by two games after today. Moreover, Winters is pitching with only two days' rest, raising questions about Warfield's pitching selection.

Seasonal stats show Winters pitching three complete games in eight days, winning two and losing one. Later in the season, under hotter conditions, he pitched four complete games in 11 days, winning all four. This mule of a man had pulled the Hilldale tractor all season and is now being asked to pull the carriage to the church.

Warfield makes more lineup changes, putting Mackey behind the plate, and moving Carr to first. Making his first world series appearance is the flashy yet injured Jake Stephens at shortstop. This is the third game of the series to be played in Kansas City's Muehlebach Park and so far the hometown fellows have not taken advantage of it. With Bullet Rogan and Plunk Drake already warming up in the bullpen, the most crucial game of the series is about to begin.

Winters weathers another slow start, walking Newt Allen on five pitches. Sweatt bunts Allen safely to second and Rogan puts down another bunt for a single. After fanning Joseph on three pitches, Moore works Winters for a walk, loading the bases. The Monarchs' leading home run hitter, Hurley McNair, comes to the plate. McNair, hitting .087 so far in the series, is due for a big hit. But Winters wastes no time and gets Mac out swinging, leaving the bases full.

Seizing the failed opportunity, Hilldale comes back in the second inning with one out, with George Johnson tripling over Rogan in center field, scoring Judy Johnson, who had singled. Once again, Plunk Drake, with tobacco juice running down his jersey, comes in from the bullpen, replacing C. Bell. Warfield greets Drake with a single, scoring George Johnson, but Drake gets Carr and Winters on easy outs to end the inning. Hilldale is now up 2 runs to 0, with their ace on the mound, in this important game.

Earlier, little Jake Stephens had attracted the crowd's attention. Limping around, he showed great gameness in trying to play. He took Duncan's roller in the second, limped across the bag, forcing a runner, and then threw to first for a double play. He had two times at bat and was safe on Newt Allen's error in the third. Unfortunately, the popular Country Jake could not finish the game, retiring to the bench in the third inning.

The Monarchs attempt a comeback in the third inning when Newt Allen singles to right and steals second. Sweatt, who had been tattooing the ball hard the entire series, hits a sure double up on the right field slope. However, Briggs climbs that hill, robbing Sweatt of an RBI, spins and fires to second base, doubling Allen off the bag for a double play. After the game, Biz Mackey describes one of the greatest plays he had ever seen in his career: "The Kansas City club put on a rally in the third inning of the game. Newt Allen singles sharply to right and steals second. Then George Sweatt hits a long one to the gap in right center, and Briggs runs many feet up an embankment to intercept the ball and throw it back to Warfield at second, catching Newt Allen off second, for a double play." The steep hill in right field has always been a challenge for visiting outfielders, but Briggs showed why he is considered one of the best outfielders in the business.

Down by two runs, the Monarchs finally make a dent in Winters' armor in the fourth inning. Joseph smashes a hit down the first base line that tattoos Carr's chest. Carr, stunned on the play, fails to recover in time to get Joseph at first, and is charged with an error. Next, Moore gets an infield hit deep off third base, as Mackey can't make the play. With two runners on, McNair again fails to deliver, flying out to George Johnson in center. After Mothell looks at a third strike and two are out, Joseph and Moore combine for a double steal. Hilldale catcher Joe Lewis, befuddled, does not attempt a throw on the double steal, holding the ball like some kind of souvenir. When he nonchalantly throws back to the mound, Joseph steals home blindly. Winters loses his composure, as Duncan labors him for a walk, and pitcher Drake singles up the middle, scoring Moore with the tying run. The fans go crazy as the Monarchs are now playing their brand of up-tempo baseball.

The Monarchs score the go-ahead run in the bottom of the eighth, when Rogan walks and goes to third on Joseph's bunt and Moore's fly to center. This time, Mendez pinch-hits Heavy Johnson for McNair, who is 0 for 11 against Winters. Heavy hits the first pitch for a single to left field, scoring the motoring Rogan. For the first time in the series, the Monarchs are leading in a game in which Winters is pitching.

Unfortunately, their lead is short-lived as Judy Johnson starts off the ninth with a single to left and goes to second on Thomas' sacrifice bunt. With a runner in scoring position, Santop is sent in to bat for George Johnson but is given a free pass. Scrip Lee runs for Santop. Down by one run and two runners on, Warfield singles to right, scoring Judy with the tying run. A heated Mendez takes over mound duties to avoid any more Hilldale havoc. Mendez gets Carr on strikes before worriedly watching Winters drive Rogan to the warning track in deep center for the final out of the inning.

After nine innings of play, the Giants and Monarchs are tied at 3 all, with Winters still on the mound for Hilldale and Mendez doing duty for the Monarchs. Both men breeze through the tenth and eleventh innings. Entering the twelfth inning, there is some speculation that Winters may be tiring, after giving up a double to Sweatt in the tenth and a long fly out by Heavy Johnson in the eleventh. With merely two days' rest, Winters quiets all of the second-guessers by getting Mendez to bounce an easy one back to the mound and striking out Newt Allen to start the twelfth. However, Winters still has not found the formula to get Sweatt out. Sweatt legs out a triple over Briggs' head in right field but hurts his leg on a bang-bang play at third. William Bell goes in to run for Sweatt. With Mackey and Tom Allen guarding the foul lines, Rogan hits a high bouncer in the gap between Mackey and shortstop Judy Johnson. Judy grabs the bouncer deep on the infield dirt and fires a long throw to first baseman Tom Allen for the final out. But his throw pulls Allen off the bag, failing to get the speedy Rogan. Bell scores on the play, giving the Monarchs their first victory over Winters in the series.

A tired Winters pitched another excellent game, only allowing two earned runs, while striking out eight Monarchs. After four steals in Sunday's game, the Monarchs add five stolen bases in this game, showing the eastern fellows their style of play.

With the series tied at 3 all and the Monarchs scheduled to pitch Rogan in the next game, Kansas City is primed to take the series lead.

7

Tuesday, October 14, 1924
Muehlebach Park, Kansas City, Missouri

Hilldale Batting	AB	R	H	2b	3b	HR	RBI	SB	SO	BB	AVG.
Briggs, rf	5	0	0	0	0	0	0	0	0	1	.172
Stephens, ss	2	0	0	0	0	0	0	0	0	0	.000
Lewis, c	3	0	0	0	0	0	0	0	0	0	.176
Mackey, c-3b	5	0	0	0	0	0	0	0	0	0	.194
J. Johnson, 3b-ss	5	2	2	0	0	0	0	0	0	0	.469
Thomas, lf-cf	3	0	1	0	0	0	0	0	0	0	.259
George Johnson, cf	2	1	2	0	1	0	1	0	0	0	.308
Santop, ph (a)	0	0	0	0	0	0	0	0	0	1	.357
Lee, pr (b)	0	0	0	0	0	0	0	0	0	0	.400
Cockrell, lf	1	0	0	0	0	0	0	0	0	0	.000
Warfield, 2b	4	0	2	0	0	0	2	0	0	0	.231
Carr, 1b	4	0	0	0	0	0	0	0	2	0	.125
Tom Allen, 1b	1	0	0	0	0	0	0	0	0	0	.158
Winters, p	4	0	0	0	0	0	0	0	1	1	.308
Totals	39	3	7	0	1	0	3	0	3	3	.179
Monarch Batting	**AB**	**R**	**H**	**2b**	**3b**	**HR**	**RBI**	**SB**	**SO**	**BB**	**AVG.**
Newt Allen, 2b	5	0	1	0	0	0	0	1	1	1	.286
Sweatt, lf-rf	5	0	2	1	1	0	0	0	1	0	.278
William Bell, pr (c)	0	1	0	0	0	0	0	0	0	0	.167

Monarch Batting	AB	R	H	2b	3b	HR	RBI	SB	SO	BB	AVG.
Rogan, cf	5	1	3	0	0	0	1	1	1	1	.429
Joseph, 3b	3	1	0	0	0	0	0	2	2	1	.185
Moore, ss	4	1	1	0	0	0	0	1	0	1	.241
McNair, rf	3	0	0	0	0	0	0	0	1	0	.077
Oscar Johnson lf (d)	2	0	1	0	0	0	1	0	0	0	.176
Mothell, 1b	3	0	1	0	0	0	0	0	1	0	.200
Hawkins, ph-1b (e)	2	0	0	0	0	0	0	0	0	0	.208
Duncan, c	4	0	1	0	0	0	0	0	0	1	.115
Cliff Bell, p	0	0	0	0	0	0	0	0	0	0	.000
Drake, p	3	0	1	0	0	0	1	0	0	0	.333
Mendez, p	2	0	0	0	0	0	0	0	1	0	.000
Totals	41	4	11	1	1	0	3	5	8	5	.268

(a) Santop walks for George Johnson in 9th.
(b) Lee pinch-runs for Santop in 9th inning.
(c) Bell pinch-runs for the injured Sweatt in 12th inning.
(d) O. Johnson singles for McNair in 8th inning.
(e) Hawkins pops out for Mothell in 8th inning.

Hilldale	020	000	001	000	3	
Kansas City	000	200	010	001	4	

Hilldale Pitching	IP	H	R	ER	BB	K	HB	WP	SAV	F/G	BF
Winters (L, 2–1)	11⅔	11	4	2	5	8	0	1	0	9–13	50

Monarch Pitching	IP	H	R	ER	BB	K	HB	WP	SAV	F/G	BF
C. Bell	1⅓	2	2	2	0	0	0	0	0	0–4	6
Drake	7	5	1	1	2	2	0	0	0	8–9	27
Mendez (W, 1–0)	3⅔	0	0	0	1	1	0	0	0	9–1	12
Totals	12	7	3	3	3	3	0	0	0	17–14	45

Game-Winning RBI: Rogan
Errors: Hilldale — Carr; KC — N. Allen
Left on Base: Hilldale — 7, Kansas City — 8
Double Plays: KC — Drake to Joseph to Moore; Hilldale — Stevens to Carr; Briggs to Warfield
 Warfield to Carr to Thomas
Sacrifices: KC — Sweatt, Joseph; Hilldale — Thomas 2, Warfield, G. Johnson
Umpires: Costello, Goeckel, McGrew, Anderson
Attendance: 2,539
Time: 2:53

Summary

Main man: Bullet Rogan gets on base four times off his nemesis Nip Winters. His mini-offensive attack includes a bunt, two infield hits and a walk.

Turning point: Down by two runs in the fourth inning, the tortoise Newt Joseph steals home on Sleepy Lewis' mental error of not keeping the runners close to their respective bases. The gift run causes Winters to lose his composure, resulting in the second run of the inning on a Frank Duncan single.

Silent stats: The notoriously slow Newt Joseph steals two bases to keep Monarch rallies alive. Hilldale must toss out the scouting report on the slothful Joseph.

Game 7, Out by Out

First Inning

Hilldale

1 — Briggs out at first.

2 — Stephens out, Moore to Mothell.

3 — Mackey out, Joseph to Mothell.

H-0, R-0, LOB-0, E-0

Kansas City

　　　Allen walks on five pitches.

1 — Sweatt hit sacrifice bunt to Carr, Allen advances.

　　　Rogan bunts safely for a single.

2 — Joseph fanned on three straight pitches.

　　　Moore walks on four straight balls.

3 — McNair fans, with bases loaded.

H-1, R-0, LOB-3, E-0

Second Inning

Hilldale

　　　Judy Johnson singles sharply off Joseph's glove.

1 — Thomas sacrifices, Bell to Mothell.

　　　George Johnson triples over Rogan, scoring Judy Johnson.

　　　Bell to the dugout, Plunk Drake to the mound, one out.

　　　Warfield singles to center scoring George Johnson.

2 — Carr grounds out, Newt Allen.

3 — Winter strikes out.

H-3, R-2, LOB-1, E-0

Kansas City

1 — Mothell out on a great play by Stephens.

　　　Duncan singles to left.

2,3 — Drake hits into double play, Stephens to Carr.

H-1, R-0, LOB-0, E-0

Score after Two Innings, Hilldale 2, MONARCHS 0

Third Inning

Hilldale

1 — Briggs fly out to Rogan.

　　　Stephens safe on Newt Allen's error.

2 — Mackey flies to Sweatt.

3 — Judy Johnson pops up behind first to Duncan.

H-0, R-0, LOB-1, E-1

Kansas City

　　　Allen singles to right and steals second.

1 — Sweatt robbed of a two-base hit by Briggs.

2 — Briggs doubles Allen off second on the catch.

3 — Rogan fans.

H-1, R-0, LOB-0, E-0

Fourth Inning

Hilldale

    Thomas singles to center.

1 — George Johnson flies out deep to Rogan, Thomas advances to second on the out.

2,3 — Warfield hits a bouncer to Drake, who throws to Joseph at third for one out.

    and relays to Moore who runs down Warfield trying to get back to first.

H-1, R-0, LOB-0, E-0

Kansas City

    Mackey goes to third, Judy Johnson to short. Lewis goes behind the plate and Stephens leaves the game, due to severe pain in his injured leg.

    Joseph safe on error by Carr.

    Moore safe on hit back of third base.

1 — McNair out on short fly to George Johnson, Joseph holding at second.

2 — Mothell looks at strike three.

    Joseph and Moore combine on double steal, no throw by Lewis.

    When Lewis throws back to the mound, Joseph steals home.

    Duncan got to Winters for a walk.

    Drake singles to center, scoring Moore with the tying run.

3 — Newt Allen hits to Mackey for force out of Drake at second.

H-2, R-2, LOB-2, E-1
Score after Four Innings, Hilldale 2, Monarchs 2

Fifth Inning

Hilldale

1 — Carr called out on strikes.

2 — Winters out to Mothell unassisted.

    Briggs walks.

3 — Lewis out, Moore to Mothell.

H-0, R-0, LOB-1, E-0

Kansas City

1 — Sweatt out, Winters to Carr.

    Rogan beat out a hit to Judy Johnson.

2 — Rogan out trying to steal second.

    Joseph walks.

3 — Moore flies to Briggs.

H-1, R-0, LOB-1, E-0

Sixth Inning

Hilldale

1 — Mackey flies out to McNair in right.

2 — Judy Johnson flies out to McNair.

3 — Thomas flies out to Sweatt in left.

H-0, R-0, LOB-0, E-0

Kansas City

1 — McNair out, Judy Johnson to Carr.

    Mothell singles to left.

2 — Duncan rolls out, Warfield to Carr.

3 — Mothell overruns base and Thomas comes in from left field and tags him out on throw by Carr.

H-1, R-0, LOB-0, E-0

Seventh Inning

Hilldale

George Johnson drops a single between Allen and McNair into right.

1 — Warfield out on sacrifice, Drake to Mothell.

2 — Carr grounds out to Mothell.

3 — Winters pops up to Duncan.

H-1, R-0, LOB-1, E-0

Kansas City

1 — Drake grounded out to Carr unassisted.

2 — Newt Allen pops up to Judy Johnson.

3 — Sweatt fans on full count, after fouling off three pitches.

H-0, R-0, LOB-0, E-0

Eighth Inning

Hilldale

1 — Briggs out, Drake to Mothell.

2 — Lewis flies to McNair in right.

3 — Mackey grounds out, Moore to Mothell.

H-0, R-0, LOB-0, E-0

Kansas City

Rogan walks.

1 — Joseph sacrifice bunts, Winters to Carr, Rogan to second.

2 — Moore hit long fly to George Johnson, Rogan advancing to third.

Oscar Johnson batting for the slumping McNair, singles to left, Rogan scoring.

3 — Hawkins batting for Mothell, pops up to Carr near box seats.

H-1, R-1, LOB-1, E-0
Score after Eight Innings, Hilldale 2, Monarchs 3

Ninth Inning

Hilldale

Hawkins on first for Kansas City, Johnson in left and Sweatt in right; Mothell and McNair are out of the game.

Judy Johnson singles to left.

1 — Thomas out on sacrifice, Drake to Hawkins.

Santop batted for George Johnson, intentionally passed.

Lee runs for Santop.

Warfield singles to right, scoring Judy Johnson.

Mendez took the mound with one out and men on first and third.

2 — Carr strikes out.

3 — Winters is robbed of a base hit by Rogan in center.

H-2, R-1, LOB-2, E-0

Kansas City

    Tom Allen went to first for Hilldale, Cockrell to left, Thomas to center field.

1 — Duncan grounds out, Judy Johnson to Tom Allen.

2 — Mendez strikes out looking.

3 — Newt Allen flies to George Johnson.

H-0, R-0, LOB-0, E-0

Score after Nine Innings, Hilldale 3, Monarchs 3

Tenth Inning

Hilldale

1 — Briggs flies out to Sweatt in right.

2 — Lewis is out on Oscar Johnson's amazing catch in left.

3 — Mackey out, Newt Allen to Mothell.

H-0, R-0, LOB-0, E-0

Kansas City

    Sweatt doubles to right.

1 — Rogan forces Sweatt on an attempted sacrifice.

2 — Joseph fans, while Rogan steals second, on failed hit-and-run attempt.

3 — Moore hits line drive, Cockrell makes sensational shoestring catch, turning
    somersaults. Cockrell had to be assisted to the Hilldale dugout.

H-1, R-0, LOB-1, E-0

Eleventh Inning

Hilldale

1 — Judy Johnson lined out to Moore.

2 — Thomas fouls out to Duncan.

3 — Cockrell out on great catch by Oscar Johnson.

H-0, R-0, LOB-0, E-0

Kansas City

1 — Oscar Johnson robbed of a hit by Briggs.

2 — Hawkins out, Judy Johnson to Tom Allen.

3 — Duncan flies out to Briggs.

H-0, R-0, LOB-0, E-0

Twelfth Inning

Hilldale

1 — Tom Allen flies out to Rogan.

2 — Warfield out on another great catch by Oscar Johnson.
    Winters walks.

3 — Briggs flies to Rogan.

H-0, R-0, LOB-1, E-0

Kansas City

1 — Mendez rolls out to Warfield.

2 — Newt Allen strikes out.

    Sweatt triples over Briggs' head in right field. Sweatt injured on the
    collision at third.

William Bell to run for Sweatt.
Rogan hits one between third and short.
Shortstop J. Johnson's throw pulls T. Allen off the bag.
Rogan credited with a hit, W. Bell scores winning run.
H-2, R-1, LOB-, E-0
Final Score: Kansas City 4, Hilldale 3

GAME 8

Currie vs. Rogan

Saturday, October 18, 1924
Chicago, Illinois

Game Conditions
Temperature: 79 degrees
Humidity: 67 percent
Winds: Southwest, 12 miles per hour
Forecast: Partly cloudy

Park
Schorling Park (South Side Park), Chicago
Wabash, Wentworth (right field) (E), Princeton (W) and
Michigan Avenues at 39th Street (1st base) (S) (now Pershing Road)
Built: 1900
Capacity : 9,000–18,000
Dimensions: Left field, 357 feet; Center field, 400 feet;
Right field, 353 feet

Robert S. Abbott, owner of the *Chicago Defender*, opens the Chicago portion of the series by throwing out the first ball. He strides to the mound wearing Bullet Rogan's cap and glove to look the part of the legend. After a glorified windmill windup, he throws a perfect strike to the plate, just like Bullet would have.

Starters for today's game are former Monarch ace hard-luck Rube Currie and the sensational Bullet Rogan. Hilldale puts Mackey, Santop and Judy Johnson at the 3-4-5 lineup spots, while Newt Joseph is still batting cleanup for the Monarchs, with McNair down at the sixth spot. Bolden probably would have brought back Winters to pitch again on three days' rest, had he not pitched 11⅔ innings on Tuesday.

Rogan breezes along to the sixth inning with a three-hitter, when Warfield leads off with a single to right. With Mackey, Santop and Judy coming to bat, Hilldale is poised for a big inning. The switch-hitting Mackey pushes a bunt to first base, moving Warfield over to second. Santop completes the execution by dropping a hit over the infield, scoring Warfield for a 1–0 Hilldale lead. Rogan escapes the inning by getting Judy on a grounder and Clint Thomas on fly to McNair in center.

Nevertheless, Hilldale is not done. In the next inning, George Johnson greets Rogan with a triple and scores when George Carr flies out to Mothell in right field. With Hilldale up by two runs, the normally unlucky Rube Currie appears poised to win the lottery game. Rube enters the ninth inning, with total command on the mound having only yielded four singles and a double so far.

The Monarchs have been shut out over the first eight frames, with the last 14 batters failing to reach base. The ninth inning innocently starts with a lazy fly out by Mothell to Thomas. Yet, the always competitive Bullet Rogan beats out a slow roller to Biz Mackey at third, providing the Monarchs with their first base runner since the fourth inning. Normally, third sacker Judy Johnson, one of the greatest at charging balls, is at shortstop, because of Country Jake's injury. Still any hopes for a Monarch rally are quickly dashed when Newt Joseph grounds weakly to Frank Warfield at second for out number two. With the celebration about to begin, Dobie Moore hits a routine bouncer to Judy at short, but the ball takes an errant bounce over his head, putting two runners on the basepaths.

Coincidentally, during the seventh game of the white World Series, the Washington Senators captured their version of the world championship title when Earl McNeely hit a bad hop single in the 12th inning to New York Giants' Fred Lindstrom. The ball struck a pebble and bounced over Lindstorm's head at third base, resulting in a 4–3 Senator win.

Robert Abbott: Owner of the *Chicago Defender* opens the Chicago leg of the series by throwing out the ceremonial first pitch (NoirTech Research).

With two outs and the tying run on first base, manager Mendez must make his toughest decision in the series. His next batter is McNair, who is 3 for 29, a .103 average! Do you "dance with the one who brung you," or do you pinch hit? Regardless of McNair's outstanding play in the field, his bat has been invisible. He was the last man to hit the ball hard against Currie with his fourth inning single. For the series, Hurley is 1 for 7 against Rube. With the game on the line, Hurley McNair smashes a single to center scoring Rogan. Currie joins in the slapsticks by hitting wide-body Heavy Johnson in the seat of his pants, loading the bases. Now Mendez, realizing the opportunity to win the game with two outs, considers pinch-hitting for the young Frank Duncan, who hit only .267, but with no dingers this season. Down to their last cry, Mendez decides to send Duncan up to the plate. Like McNair, Duncan is also 3 for 29, batting a woeful .103 in the series. An ideal pinch-hit situation for steady Sweatt, but Mendez decides to go with his young rising star. A nervous Duncan hits a game-ending high pop foul near the screen that somehow veteran catcher Santop muffs. The baseball gods put Duncan at-ease and he capitalizes on what will become the infamous "Santop Drop" and he raps a bloop single past converted-catcher Biz Mackey at third. Fairy tales Moore and McNair score the tying and winning runs.

The Hilldale fans are stunned. Joe Lewis had earlier replaced Santop in Games Six, Five and Three, for defensive purposes. With Hilldale leading by two runs in the ninth inning, it would seem a perfect nod for a defensive replacement for Santop. Although still possessing a potent kick with the bat, the old grey mare had seen his best days behind the plate.

(An error of this magnitude would not be repeated until the 1941 World Series. Disaster struck the Brooklyn Dodgers, when catcher Mickey Owen dropped a third strike, that enabled the New York Yankees to come back to win the game, and eventually the Series the next day.)

Frank Duncan: Young Dunk stuns Hilldale with the winning RBI single in the ninth inning, after two outs and a helpful reprieve from Santop's drop (Courtesy of Kimshi Productions).

With a win today, and not since Game One, the Monarchs grab the lead in the series, four games to three. This heated, uphill battle with Hilldale continues tomorrow in Schorling Park with temperatures expected in the eighties.

8

Saturday, October 18, 1924
Schorling Park, Chicago, Illinois

Hilldale Batting	AB	R	H	2b	3b	HR	RBI	SB	SO	BB	AVG.
Briggs, rf	5	0	2	0	0	0	0	0	0	0	.206
Warfield, 2b	4	1	1	0	0	0	0	0	0	1	.233

Hilldale Batting	AB	R	H	2b	3b	HR	RBI	SB	SO	BB	AVG.
Mackey, 3b	2	0	1	0	0	0	0	0	0	1	.212
Santop, c	3	0	1	0	0	0	1	0	0	1	.353
Judy Johnson, ss	4	0	0	0	0	0	0	0	0	0	.417
Thomas, lf	4	0	0	0	0	0	0	0	0	0	.226
George Johnson, cf	4	1	1	0	1	0	0	0	1	0	.300
Carr, 1b	3	0	2	0	0	0	1	2	0	0	.273
Currie, p	4	0	1	0	0	0	0	0	2	0	.143
Totals	33	2	9	0	1	0	2	2	3	3	.273

Monarch Batting	AB	R	H	2b	3b	HR	RBI	SB	SO	BB	AVG.
Newt Allen, 2b	4	0	1	0	0	0	0	0	0	0	.281
Mothell, rf	3	0	0	0	0	0	0	0	0	0	.125
Rogan, p	4	1	1	0	0	0	0	0	0	0	.406
Joseph, 3b	4	0	0	0	0	0	0	0	1	0	.161
Moore, ss	4	1	3	0	0	0	0	0	0	0	.303
McNair, cf	4	1	2	0	0	0	1	0	0	0	.133
Oscar Johnson, lf	3	0	1	1	0	0	0	0	0	0	.200
Duncan, c	4	0	1	0	0	0	2	0	0	0	.133
Hawkins, 1b	3	0	0	0	0	0	0	0	0	0	.185
Totals	33	3	9	1	0	0	3	0	1	0	.273

Hilldale	000	001	100	2	
Kansas City	000	000	003	3	

2 outs when the winning run scored.

Hilldale Pitching	IP	H	R	ER	BB	K	HB	WP	SAV	F/G	BF
Currie (L, 1–1)	8⅔	9	3	1	0	1	1	0	0	10–14	35

Monarch Pitching	IP	H	R	ER	BB	K	HB	WP	SAV	F/G	BF
Rogan (W, 2–1)	9	9	2	2	3	3	0	0	0	13–9	37

Game-Winning RBI: Frank Duncan
Errors: Hilldale — Santop
Left on Base: Hilldale — 8, Kansas City — 4
Double Plays: none
Sacrifices: Hilldale — Carr, Mackey KC — Mothell
Hit by Pitcher: O. Johnson by Currie
Umpires: Goeckel, Moore, McGrew, Costello
Attendance: 2,608
Time: not available.

SUMMARY

Main man: Young Frank Duncan stuns Hilldale with the winning RBI single in the ninth inning, after two outs and a helpful reprieve from Santop's muff.

Turning point: With two outs in the ninth, Judy Johnson is unable to field Dobie Moore's bad hopper, putting the tying runs on base.

Silent stats: Rube Currie pitched a brilliant game, scattering nine hits over 8⅔ innings. Unfortunately, three fielding errors and a timely bad bounce proved to be lethal for Currie, as his hard luck continues.

Game 8, Out by Out

First Inning

Hilldale
1 — Briggs out to O. Johnson in left.
2 — Warfield accidentally taps one to Rogan.
    Mackey singles to left center.
3 — Santop forces Mackey at second.
                    H-1, R-0, LOB-1, E-0

Kansas City
    Allen singles to left center.
1 — Mothell sacrifices, Currie to Carr.
2 — Rogan flies out to Thomas.
3 — Joseph grounds out, J. Johnson to Carr.
                    H-1, R-0, LOB-1, E-0

Second Inning

Hilldale
1 — J. Johnson out, Allen to Hawkins.
2 — Thomas out, Moore to Hawkins on great play.
3 — G. Johnson flies out to McNair in center.
                    H-0, R-0, LOB-0, E-0

Kansas City
    Moore singles past Currie, up the middle.
1 — McNair flies to G. Johnson in center.
    Heavy Johnson doubles to right center.
2 — Moore out in rundown.
    G. Johnson to Warfield to Santop to Mackey.
3 — Duncan lines out to Mackey.
                    H-2, R-0, LOB-1, E-0

Third Inning

Hilldale
1 — Carr flies out to McNair in center.
    Currie singles past second.
2 — Briggs flies out to O. Johnson.
3 — Warfield out, N. Allen to Hawkins.
                    H-1, R-0, LOB-1, E-0

Kansas City
1 — Hawkins out, Mackey to Carr.
2 — N. Allen flies out to Briggs.
3 — Mothell lines out to Mackey.
                    H-0, R-0, LOB-0, E-0

Fourth Inning

Hilldale

> Mackey walks.
> Santop walks.

1 — Mackey out on steal attempt, Duncan to Moore to Joseph.

2 — J. Johnson flies out to O. Johnson.

3 — Thomas pops out to Rogan.

> H-0, R-0, LOB-1, E-0

Kansas City

1 — Rogan out, Currie to Carr.

2 — Joseph out, J. Johnson to Carr.

> Moore singles to center.
> McNair singles to right.

3 — Heavy Johnson out, Currie to Carr.

> H-2, R-0, LOB-2, E-0

Fifth Inning

Hilldale

1 — G. Johnson robbed of triple by Heavy Johnson.

> Carr singles to right. Steals second.

2 — Currie fans.

3 — Briggs flies to Mothell.

> H-1, R-0, LOB-1, E-0

Kansas City

1 — Duncan fouls out Thomas.

2 — Hawkins out to Currie.

3 — N. Allen grounds to J. Johnson.

> H-0, R-0, LOB-0, E-0

Sixth Inning

Hilldale

> Warfield singles to right.

1 — Mackey sacrifices.

> Santop singles, scoring Warfield.

2 — J. Johnson grounds out to Moore.

3 — Thomas flies out to McNair.

> H-2, R-1, LOB-1, E-0

Kansas City

1 — Mothell out, Warfield to Carr.

2 — Rogan pops up to J. Johnson.

3 — Joseph strikes out.

> H-0, R-0, LOB-0, E-0
> Score after Six Innings: Hilldale 1, Monarchs 0

Seventh Inning

Hilldale

> George Johnson triples.

1 — Carr hit sacrifice fly to Mothell, Johnson scores.
2 — Currie strikes out.
    Briggs beats out infield hit to Moore.
    Warfield walks.
3 — Mackey flies out to McNair.

H-2, R-1, LOB-2, E-0

Kansas City
1 — Moore grounds out to J. Johnson.
2 — McNair flies out to G. Johnson.
3 — Heavy Johnson lines out to Warfield.

H-0, R-0, LOB-0, E-0

Score after Seven Innings: Hilldale 2, Monarchs 0

Eighth Inning

Hilldale
1 — Santop grounds out to Hawkins unassisted.
2 — J. Johnson out on a shoestring catch by Heavy Johnson.
3 — Thomas out to N. Allen.

H-0, R-0, LOB-0, E-0

Kansas City
1 — Duncan grounds out, J. Johnson to Carr.
2 — Hawkins grounds out, J. Johnson to Carr.
3 — N. Allen grounds out to Carr unassisted.

H-0, R-0, LOB-0, E-0

Ninth Inning

Hilldale
1 — G. Johnson called out on strikes.
    Carr singles to left, steals second.
2 — Currie flies out to Mothell.
    Briggs singles to left.
3 — Carr out at the plate trying to score, Heavy Johnson to Duncan.

H-2, R-0, LOB-1, E-0

Kansas City
1 — Mothell flies out to Thomas.
    Rogan beats out roller to Mackey.
2 — Joseph out, Warfield to Carr.
    Moore safe on bad bouncer past J. Johnson.
    McNair singles to center, Rogan scoring.
    Heavy Johnson hit by pitch, bases loaded.
    Santop drops Duncan's foul.
    Duncan singles pass Mackey at third, scoring Moore and McNair.

H-4, R-3, LOB-X, E-1

Final Score: Kansas City 3, Hilldale 2

GAME 9

Winters vs. W. Bell

Sunday, October 19, 1924
Chicago, Illinois

Game Conditions
Temperature: 81 degrees
Humidity: 78 percent
Winds: West 7 miles per hour
Forecast: Partly cloudy

Park
Schorling Park (South Side Park)

Fans of Chicago continue to show support for their home team, forming a long line well before the gates are to open. With Rogan out of the way, Hilldale is favored by many to take the series, as Nip Winters is scheduled to pitch today for the Easterners. Winters has been practically unbeatable. He has yielded four earned runs in 29⅔ innings for a 1.21 ERA. His 18 strikeouts in three complete games against a power-packed Monarch lineup puts him in the pitching elite status of baseball.

Not having the luxury of a groundskeeper, the field, especially the infield, is in terrible condition from yesterday's game. Moreover, the players are accustomed to poor conditions and will struggle to fashion another professional performance for their fans.

Until now the lords of the diamonds have been smiling on the Monarchs. The Kansas City club has won the last three games, each by one sole run. All of this, after seeing Hilldale victorious in three previous games. The big question for today's game will be if Hilldale can reverse the emotional tide and win a game on western soil. The Giants would face William Bell again today. So far in the series, Bell has surrendered 21 hits and 8 earned runs in 20 innings of pitching. Normally possessing excellent control, Bell has given up eleven walks in his two previous appearances. Definitely not vintage Bell, but the Texas native has met the challenge several times before.

After winning three straight games, Mendez plays musical chairs with the lineup once again and moves his hitting machine Bullet Rogan to the lead-off position. Thus far in the series, Rogan is leading all Monarchs with a .406 average and Mendez figures he wants Rogan to get as many plate appearances as possible. In contrast, Newt Joseph, who is batting only .161, stays in the cleanup slot, followed by Dobie Moore with a steadier .303 average.

When Hilldale fails to score with two hits and two walks in the first two innings, the Monarchs strike first in the second inning. They score two runs, aided by George Carr's errors on grounders by Moore and Hawkins. Bell helps his cause by knocking in Hawkins with a single to center field. The Hilldale Club remains scoreless until the fifth inning, when Warfield leads off with a double to center and scores on Mackey's single to right field. Then cleanup hitter Santop singles to Rogan in right field. Rogan mishandles the liner and Mackey scores on the error. With no outs, here comes Plunk Drake again from the bullpen. After being bombed in the second game of the series, Drake has been unhittable over the last eight innings of relief.

With two runs in for the 2–2 tie and one runner on base, Drake gets the dangerous Judy Johnson to ground out, Thomas to strike out, and George Johnson to weakly tap one back to the mound, retiring the side.

Neither club threatens until the eighth inning when Hilldale attacks first. After George Johnson and Carr go down on strikes, Winters works Drake for a walk. He scores when Briggs singles to Rogan, who boots the ball for his second game error. Mendez replaces his leadoff hitter Rogan with Mothell. Next, Briggs goes to third on Warfield's single to right. After Warfield steals second, Drake gives a free pass to the dangerous Mackey to fill the bases. With the bases loaded, Hilldale's most feared hitter, Louis Santop, comes to the plate with an opportunity to redeem himself from yesterday's mishap. But Drake kills the rally by getting Santop to pop up behind the pitcher's mound for the third out.

The Monarchs come back in their half of the eighth with a leadoff single by Heavy Johnson. After Joseph forces Heavy at second, he challenges Briggs's arm to score on Moore's single to short right field. The daring play by Joseph ties the game, 3 all, as McNair goes down on strikes (for the sixth time) and Hawkins flies out.

In the ninth, Drake gives up a double to Judy Johnson. And when Thomas attempts to bunt Judy over to third, Drake hesitates and throws too late to get Judy. Drake's indecision has really put Kansas City in a hole with runners on first and third and no outs. Mendez springs from the dugout and races to the mound — not to manage, but to pitch. A fired-up Mendez strikes out George Johnson and gets Carr to ground out to Hawkins at first. Only Hawkins's throw to second is too tardy to get Thomas, while Judy scores the go-ahead run. The dangerous Winters is walked, bringing Briggs to the plate. Thomas scores run number five when Briggs's grounder is mishandled by Hawkins' second mistake of the inning. Mendez glares at Hawk but leaves him in the game. Realizing the lack of fielding support by his teammates, a frustrated Mendez strikes out Warfield on three pitches to end the bloodshed.

Down by two runs entering the ninth inning, the Monarchs easily go 1–2–3, as Winters picks up his third World Series victory and closes out his performance with a microscopic ERA of 1.16. Winters was able to survive four errors by his teammates. However, Drake is tagged with the loss, as the Monarchs commit a series record five errors. With the series tied at four games apiece, tomorrow's game will decide who will be crowned the champions of black baseball.

9

Sunday, October 19, 1924
Schorling Park, Chicago, Illinois

Hilldale Batting	AB	R	H	2b	3b	HR	RBI	SB	SO	BB	AVG.
Briggs, rf	6	0	3	0	0	0	0	0	0	0	.250
Warfield, 2b	5	1	2	1	0	0	0	1	1	0	.257
Mackey, 3b	4	1	2	0	0	0	1	0	0	1	.243
Santop, c	4	0	2	0	0	0	0	0	0	1	.381
Judy Johnson, ss	5	1	1	1	0	0	0	0	0	0	.390
Thomas, lf	4	1	1	0	0	0	0	0	1	0	.229
George Johnson, cf	5	0	0	0	0	0	0	0	2	0	.257
Carr, 1b	4	0	2	0	0	0	1	0	1	1	.333
Winters, p	3	1	0	0	0	0	0	0	0	2	.250
Totals	39	5	13	2	0	0	2	1	5	5	.333

Monarch Batting	AB	R	H	2b	3b	HR	RBI	SB	SO	BB	AVG.
Rogan, rf	4	0	0	0	0	0	0	0	0	0	.361
Mothell, rf (a)	1	0	0	0	0	0	0	0	0	0	.111
Newt Allen, 2b	4	0	1	1	0	0	0	0	0	0	.278
Oscar Johnson, lf	4	0	2	0	0	0	0	0	1	0	.250
Joseph, 3b	4	1	0	0	0	0	0	0	1	0	.143
Moore, ss	4	1	1	0	0	0	1	0	0	0	.297
McNair, cf	3	0	1	0	0	0	0	0	1	0	.152
Hawkins, 1b	4	1	1	0	0	0	0	0	0	0	.194
Duncan, c	4	0	0	0	0	0	0	0	0	0	.118
William Bell, p	2	0	1	0	0	0	1	0	0	0	.250
Drake, p	1	0	1	0	0	0	0	0	0	0	.500
Mendez, p	1	0	0	0	0	0	0	0	0	0	.000
Totals	35	3	8	1	0	0	2	0	3	0	.229

(a) Mothell replaced Rogan in right field in the 8th inning.

Hilldale	000	020	012	5
Kansas City	020	000	010	3

Hilldale Pitching	IP	H	R	ER	BB	K	HB	WP	SAV	F/G	BF
Winters (W, 3–1)	9	8	3	1	0	3	0	0	0	6–14	37

Monarch Pitching	IP	H	R	ER	BB	K	HB	WP	SAV	F/G	BF
W. Bell	4	8	2	1	2	0	0	0	0	0–12	23
Drake (L, 0–1)	4	5	3	1	2	3	0	0	0	6–2	20
Mendez	1	0	0	0	1	2	0	0	0	0–1	5
Totals	9	13	5	2	5	5	0	0	0	6–15	48

Game-Winning RBI: George Carr
Errors: Hilldale — Mackey, Carr (3); KC — Rogan (2), Moore (2), Hawkins (1)
Left on Base: — Hilldale — 15 Kansas City — 7
Double Plays: none
Sacrifices: Warfield, McNair, Thomas
Passed Balls: Santop
Umpires: McGrew, Costello, Goeckle, Moore
Attendance: 6,271
Time: not available.

SUMMARY

Main man: Nip Winters nails down his third world series win. He gives up one earned run and seven singles and an extra base hit in capturing the victory.

Turning point: After shutting down the heart of Hilldale's lineup in the fifth inning, Drake's mental error for failing to get an out on a bunt attempt allows Hilldale to score the winning run.

Silent stats: The Monarchs commit five errors on the rugged infield, allowing three unearned runs and in the process lose a fine relief performance by Plunk Drake.

Game 9, Out by Out

First Inning

Hilldale
> Briggs beats out hit over second base.
1 — Warfield sacrifices, Bell to Hawkins.
2 — Mackey hits to Bell, who catches Briggs in rundown between second and third.
> Santop walks.
3 — Judy Johnson forces Santop at second.
> H-1, R-0, LOB-2, E-0

Kansas City
1 — Rogan out, Winters to Carr.
2 — N. Allen out, Warfield to Carr.
> O. Johnson singles to right. Goes to second on passed ball.
3 — Joseph flies to Thomas.
> H-1, R-0, LOB-1, E-0

Second Inning

Hilldale
> Thomas singles over second.
1 — G. Johnson forces Thomas out at second.
> Moore overthrows first. G. Johnson goes to second.
> Carr walks.
2 — Winters out, N. Allen to Hawkins.
3 — Briggs out, Bell to Hawkins.
> H-1, R-0, LOB-2, E-0

Kansas City
> Moore safe on Carr's error.
1 — McNair sacrifices, Santop to Carr.
> Hawkins safe on Carr's second error.
> Moore scores. Hawkins to second on throw to the plate.
2 — Duncan out, Warfield to Carr, Hawkins goes to third.

W. Bell singles to center, Hawkins scoring.

3 — W. Bell out stealing second.

H-1, R-2, LOB-0, E-2

Score after Two Innings: Hilldale 0, Monarchs 2

Third Inning

Hilldale

1 — Warfield out, Allen to Hawkins.

Mackey singles.

Santop singles to center.

2 — J. Johnson forces Mackey at third.

3 — Thomas forces Santop at second.

H-2, R-0, LOB-2, E-0

Kansas City

1 — Rogan out, J. Johnson to Carr.

Allen doubles.

2 — Heavy Johnson strikes out.

3 — Joseph out, Mackey to Carr.

H-1, R-0, LOB-1, E-0

Fourth Inning

Hilldale

1 — G. Johnson out, N. Allen to Hawkins.

Carr hits one off of Allen's shin.

2 — Winters out to Hawkins, unassisted.

3 — Briggs out, Moore to Hawkins.

H-1, R-0, LOB-1, E-0

Kansas City

1 — Moore out, Mackey to Carr.

McNair singles to right.

Hawkins sneaks a hit by Warfield.

2 — Duncan out, Mackey to Carr on a great play.

3 — W. Bell flies out to Briggs in foul territory.

H-2, R-0, LOB-2, E-0

Fifth Inning

Hilldale

Warfield doubles to center.

Mackey singles to right, Warfield scoring.

Santop singles to right.

Mackey scoring on Rogan's misplay, Santop to second.

Drake now pitching for Kansas City.

1 — J. Johnson grounds out to Joseph.

2 — Thomas strikes out.

3 — G. Johnson grounds out to Drake.

H-3, R-2, LOB-1, E-1

Kansas City

1 — Rogan flies to center.

　　N. Allen safe on Carr's third error.

2 — Heavy Johnson out, Warfield to Carr.

3 — Joseph called out on strikes.

H-0, R-0, LOB-1, E-1

Score after Five Innings: Hilldale 2, Monarchs 2

Sixth Inning

Hilldale

　　Carr singles to center.

1 — Winters fouls out to Duncan.

　　Briggs singles to left.

2 — Warfield out to Rogan, Carr goes to third.

3 — Briggs is picked off first on pitch out. Duncan to Hawkins to Moore to Allen.

H-2, R-0, LOB-1, E-0

Kansas City

1 — Moore flies to G. Johnson.

2 — McNair out, Warfield to Carr.

3 — Hawkins out, Warfield to Carr.

H-0, R-0, LOB-0, E-0

Seventh Inning

Hilldale

1 — Mackey flies out to O. Johnson.

2 — Santop flies out to Joseph.

　　J. Johnson safe on Moore's error.

3 — Thomas flies out to McNair.

H-0, R-0, LOB-1, E-1

Kansas City

1 — Duncan lines out to Mackey.

　　Drake singles to center.

2 — Rogan pops up to Warfield.

3 — N. Allen forces Drake out at second.

H-1, R-0, LOB-1, E-0

Eighth Inning

Hilldale

1 — G. Johnson called out on strikes.

2 — Carr strikes out.

　　Winters walks.

　　Briggs singles, Winters scoring on Rogan's second error.

　　Mothell in game to replace Rogan.

　　Warfield singles to right, Briggs to third.

　　Warfield steals second.

　　Mackey intentionally walked. Bases loaded.

3 — Santop out on pop up behind pitcher's mound.

H-2, R-1, LOB-3, E-1

Kansas City

Heavy Johnson singles to left.

1 — Joseph forces Johnson out at second.

Moore singles to short right center, taking second, while Joseph is scoring tying run.

2 — McNair strikes out.

3 — Hawkins flies out to Thomas.

H-2, R-1, LOB-1, E-0
Score after Eight Innings: Hilldale 3, Monarchs 3

Ninth Inning

Hilldale

J. Johnson doubles to left.

Thomas attempts sacrifice bunt, Drake's throw too late to get J. Johnson at third.

Mendez, the manager is now pitching.

1 — G. Johnson strikes out.

2 — Carr rolls out to Hawkins unassisted, Hawkins' throw to Moore to get Thomas is late.

J. Johnson scores on the relay.

Winters walks.

Briggs safe on Hawkins' error, Thomas scores.

3 — Warfield strikes out.

H-1, R-2, LOB-2, E-1

Kansas City

1 — Duncan flies out to G. Johnson.

2 — Mendez called out on strikes.

3 — Mothell out, J. Johnson to Carr.

H-0, R-0, LOB-0, E-0
Final Score: Hilldale 5, Kansas City 3

GAME 10

Mendez vs. Lee

Monday, October 20, 1924
Chicago, Illinois

Game Conditions
Temperature: 54 degrees
Humidity: 77 percent
Winds: Northeast 12 miles per hour
Forecast: Partly cloudy

Park
Schorling Park or South Side Park

Jose Mendez, the pitching legend, had not started a game since July 26. He had aced the weak-hitting Cleveland Browns, pitching 6⅔ innings and giving up three hits and three runs for a win. Mendez's season record showed a runs-per-game average of 4.21. As pitcher-manger, Mendez had struck out 25 batters and walked six in 47 innings this season. More importantly, Mendez was battling a viral infection and had pitched an inning in yesterday's game. With game temperature in the fifties and a strong breeze coming in from the north, this was not ideal pitching weather for an ailing man. With the championship on the line, and against doctor's orders, Mendez decides to take the mound.

Going for Hilldale is seasoned veteran Scrip Lee, making his first series start. During the season, another junk-baller named Luis Padrone of the Chicago American Giants had defeated the Monarchs three times. Normally, Hilldale's number two starter, Phil Cockrell, would get the nod to pitch. However Cockrell had not been effective in previous appearances, giving up ten runs over the last 9⅔ innings. Hilldale's hopes for a world title were hang-

Jose Mendez: Despite suffering from illness, he pitches a super game, giving up three stingy hits in pitching a shutout victory (NoirTech Research).

ing on the ability of Lee, a World War I Purple Heart recipient. Lee, having been effective in series relief appearances, gets the nod. With Winters and Currie unavailable for pitching duty, Cockrell not able to solve the Monarch mystery, and Red Ryan's pitching style easily solved by the Monarchs, Lee is poised for another award-winning performance.

To everyone's surprise, the game turns into a pitching duel. Through the first seven innings, true to junkie form, Lee held the Monarchs to a lone single by Duncan in the third inning. Duncan stole second on Santop's wide throw to the bag, but that was as far as any Monarch got until the eighth inning. For seven innings, Lee had the Monarch sluggers confused, retiring the last 14 batters in a row. His junk deliveries were so deceptive that the Monarchs were throwing their bats at his off-speed pitches, trying to connect.

In contrast, starting the eighth inning, Lee peculiarly changes from his submarine delivery to throwing overhanded. After working Lee to a full count,

Moore singles sharply to right center, and moves to second on McNair's sacrifice bunt down the third base line. Moore scores easily on Heavy Johnson's double to center. Taking no chances, Lee issues his first walk to Duncan, setting up the possible double play with Mendez coming to bat. Yet the old gladiator Mendez singles to center, with the runners moving up one base. Now with the bases loaded, Newt Allen bangs the second pitch to right for a single, scoring Johnson and Duncan. Score: Monarchs 3, Hilldale 0. Mendez takes third and Allen goes to second on the late throw to get Duncan at the plate. The next batter, Mothell, who replaced the injured Hawkins (strained ligaments), doubles to left center for two more ribbies. Mothell is thrown out sneaking to third base and Rogan pops out to Judy Johnson at short to end the explosive inning.

Down by five runs going into the top of the ninth, Hilldale is down to its last three hopes. Is the season over for Hilldale? They had scored a total of 11 runs in the ninth innings of previous games (more than any other inning), during the series. Bolden sends in Nip Winters to pinch hit for Lee. Winters had hit four homers during the season, tying Mackey and Judy Johnson for third best on the team. Winters sends a tremendous blast, deep to McNair on the warning track, for the first out. Briggs bounces out to Mothell at first and after Warfield walks, and Mackey pops out to shortstop Moore to end the game. Mendez emerges as the game's hero.

How well did Mendez pitch? Hilldale only got three hits off his delivery. Thomas got the first one in the second frame with two out; Carr opened the sixth with a safe blow to center field, and in the seventh Mackey led off with a single. In all, thirteen Hilldalers flied out and nary a runner got to second base and only four reached first base, with Warfield drawing the only walk in the ninth. Both Warfield and Thomas were left stranded at first, and Carr was forced out at second. The last potential threat was aborted when the veteran Biz Mackey made a rookie mistake and got picked off first, after leading off the seventh inning with a single up the middle.

Rube Foster added after the game, "Mendez pitched with all the years of experience I expected. He had the Hilldale club believing each inning that they would get him in the next inning and their anxiety to do it — instead of waiting him out — beat them. Believe me, I am proud of that bird." With Foster's knowledge of the Hilldale batters' weakness and craftiness by the old veteran Mendez, the Kansas City Monarchs won the first Colored World Series, despite being outplayed, outhit and outpitched by Hilldale.

Umpire Bert Gholston summarized Mendez's feat the best: "Jose Mendez was a World Series superman. It was his wonderful pitching in the last game of the World Series when his pitching staff was apparently shot to pieces that stopped the enemy and turned them back. He was more than a hero. Heroes come in common mold; but supermen are cast from strange clay. He was superman.

"History has known but one Colonel Rounge; the stage has but one Bert Williams; the ring has seen but one Joe Gans; and Baseball has but one Jose Mendez. There will never be another.

"Senor Jose Mendez was a superman, attaining the unattainable, accomplishing the impossible, doing the undoable and making it look easy. Yet you can't class supermen as heroes. Heroes are human, and in the attainments of supermen are something of the immortal. The superman of that World Series was Senor Jose Mendez."

Mendez and the Monarchs were able to win the series despite little production from their big gun, Hurley McNair, coupled with their inability to hit Hilldale's Nip Winters with any consistency. The Monarchs received an unexpected fine pitching performance from their manager Jose Mendez, as he gained two key victories. And Bullet Rogan pitched very well in the series, winning two games and also leading the Monarch batting with a .325 average and seven RBIs. His teammate Newt Allen provided timely clutch hitting early in the series with a record seven doubles. The Hilldale attack was led by Judy Johnson with a .364 average and .591 slugging percentage. His seven ribbies were the most of any batter in the series. He received very little offensive RBI support from his brash brothers Biz and Lou, who hit .244 and .333 respectively.

In summarizing the level of play in the series, umpire Dolan said, "This is far better than anything in the International League. While umpire McDevitt added, "Play is as good as any in the white leagues. One thing I like about these men they are always perfect gentlemen and sportsmen, and we have had no trouble with them."

The following day, a defeated Hilldale team arrived back in Philadelphia at the Broad Street Station to greet a modest crowd of faithful fans. George W. Robinson, former owner of the Washington Potomacs, held an impromptu party at his New Roadside Hotel in Philadelphia. That Friday, a formal banquet was organized by Robinson and held at the Hotel Brotherhood on Bainbridge Street in South Philly to honor the players' gallant but disappointing efforts. Meanwhile, Kansas City nightclub owner Piney Brown sponsored a party at the Sunset Inn, Chicago's "biggest and best amusement place" to celebrate the Monarch victory. The triumphant Monarchs enjoyed food, dancing and a musical revue by Billie Young, Blanche Calloway and Amon Davis, as they are crowned the World's First Colored Champions of Baseball. Back home in Kansas City, the black-owned *Call* newspaper reveled, "Let no hint of how long the party continued, nor the condition of the guests on leaving escape. Just remember that it happened in Chicago—and guess the rest!"

The first Colored World Series was a small success. The *Chicago Defender* reported that the series was the "biggest move in the history of colored baseball" and had done "more to gain the fans' attention to the national pastime as regards to our group than anything that has been done in recent years." The Kansas City *Call* concurred with the editorial, "Negro sport has done what Negro churches, Negro lodges, Negro businesses could not do. The series has shown that a Negro can get attention for a good deed well done, and that publicity is no longer the exclusive mark of our criminals."

10

Monday, October 20, 1924
Schorling Park, Chicago, Illinois

Hilldale Batting	AB	R	H	2b	3b	HR	RBI	SB	SO	BB	AVG.
Briggs, rf	4	0	0	0	0	0	0	0	0	0	.227
Warfield, 2b	3	0	0	0	0	0	0	0	0	1	.237
Mackey, 3b	4	0	1	0	0	0	0	0	0	0	.244
Santop, c	3	0	0	0	0	0	0	0	0	0	.333
Judy Johnson, ss	3	0	0	0	0	0	0	0	1	0	.364
Thomas, lf	3	0	1	0	0	0	0	0	0	0	.237
George Johnson, cf	3	0	0	0	0	0	0	0	1	0	.237
Carr, 1b	3	0	1	0	0	0	0	0	0	0	.333
Lee, p	2	0	0	0	0	0	0	0	0	0	.286
Winters, ph (a)	1	0	0	0	0	0	0	0	0	0	.235
Totals	29	0	3	0	0	0	0	0	2	1	.103

Monarch Batting	AB	R	H	2b	3b	HR	RBI	SB	SO	BB	AVG.
Newt Allen, 2b	4	1	1	0	0	0	2	0	1	0	.275
Mothell, 1b	4	0	1	1	0	0	2	0	0	0	.154
Rogan, cf	4	0	0	0	0	0	0	0	1	0	.325
Joseph, 3b	3	0	0	0	0	0	0	0	0	0	.132
Moore, ss	3	1	1	0	0	0	0	0	0	0	.300
McNair, rf	2	0	0	0	0	0	0	0	1	0	.143
Oscar Johnson, lf	3	1	1	1	0	0	1	0	0	0	.259
Duncan, c	2	1	1	0	0	0	0	1	0	1	.139
Mendez, p	3	1	1	0	0	0	0	0	0	0	.111
Totals	28	5	6	2	0	0	5	1	3	1	.214

(a) Winters flies out for Lee in 9th inning.

Hilldale		000		000		000	0
Kansas City		000		000		05x	5

Hilldale Pitching	IP	H	R	ER	BB	K	HB	WP	SAV	F/G	BF
Lee (L, 0–2)	8	6	5	5	1	3	0	0	0	11–9	30

Monarch Pitching	IP	H	R	ER	BB	K	HB	WP	SAV	F/G	BF
Mendez (W, 2–0)	9	3	0	0	1	2	0	0	0	13–10	30

Game-Winning RBI: Oscar Johnson
Errors: None
Left on Base: Hilldale — 3, Kansas City — 1
Double Plays: none
Sacrifices: McNair
Umpires: Costello, Goeckel, Moore, Conlin
Attendance: 1,549
Time: not available

Summary

Main man: Despite suffering from feverish conditions, Jose Mendez pitches a superb game, giving up three stingy singles in pitching a shutout victory.

Turning point: In an attempt to keep the Monarchs off stride, Scrip Lee changes his submarine delivery in the eighth inning to the conventional overhand style. Big, big mistake! The Monarchs were not fooled and preceded to score five big runs.

Silent stats: The Monarchs left only one runner on base in this most crucial game.

Game 10, Out by Out

First Inning

Hilldale
1— Briggs out to Mothell, unassisted.
2 — Warfield roll out, Moore to Mothell.
3 — Mackey out, Joseph to Mothell.
H-0, R-0, LOB-0, E-0

Kansas City
1— N. Allen out, Warfield to Carr.
2 — Mothell out, Mackey to Carr.
3 — Rogan with a full count, misses bunt attempt.
H-0, R-0, LOB-0, E-0

Second Inning

Hilldale
1 — Santop fouls out to Mothell.
2 — J. Johnson flies to Moore in short center.
Thomas singles to center.
3 — G. Johnson pops to Moore behind third.
H-1, R-0, LOB-1, E-0

Kansas City
1 — Joseph rolls out, Warfield to Carr.
2 — Moore grounds out.
3 — McNair strikes out.
H-0, R-0, LOB-0, E-0

Third Inning

Hilldale
1 — Carr flies out to Rogan in center.
2 — Lee rolls out, N. Allen to Mothell.
3 — Briggs flies out to Rogan in center.
H-0, R-0, LOB-0, E-0

Kansas City
1 — O. Johnson fouls out to Carr near first.

Duncan singles to left.

Duncan steals second. Santop throws wide of bag.

2 — Mendez out, Lee to Carr.

3 — N. Allen strikes out.

H-1, R-0, LOB-1, E-0

Fourth Inning

Hilldale

1 — Warfield flies out to McNair in right.

2 — Mackey out to Mothell unassisted.

3 — Santop out, Joseph to Mothell.

H-0, R-0, LOB-0, E-0

Kansas City

1 — Mothell flies out to G. Johnson.

2 — Rogan sent a long drive to right, Briggs makes great catch.

3 — Joseph sent G. Johnson to the wall for final out.

H-0, R-0, LOB-0, E-0

Fifth Inning

Hilldale

1 — J. Johnson strikes out, Duncan drops ball, throws to first for out.

2 — Thomas flies to Rogan in center.

3 — G. Johnson out, Allen to Mothell.

H-0, R-0, LOB-0, E-0

Kansas City

1 — Moore flies out to Briggs.

2 — McNair out to Carr unassisted.

3 — O. Johnson out, Warfield to Carr.

H-0, R-0, LOB-0, E-0

Sixth Inning

Hilldale

Carr hits a scratch single.

1 — Lee pops up to Duncan.

2 — Briggs, fielders choice, Carr forced out at second.

3 — Warfield sends a drive to right in the swirling winds and McNair makes
a sensational catch.

H-1, R-0, LOB-1, E-0

Kansas City

1 — Duncan flies to Thomas.

2 — Mendez flies to Briggs in right.

3 — N. Allen pops up to J. Johnson.

H-0, R-0, LOB-0, E-0

Seventh Inning

Hilldale

Mackey singles up the middle.

1 — Santop flies to Rogan.

2 — Mackey picked off first (Mendez to Mothell to Allen)

3 — Warfield flies out to McNair.

H-1, R-0, LOB-0, E-0

Kansas City

1 — Mothell flies out to Briggs.

2 — Rogan flies out to Briggs.

3 — Joseph out, Judy Johnson to Carr.

H-0, R-0, LOB-0, E-0

Eighth Inning

Hilldale

1 — Thomas flies out to Allen.

2 — G. Johnson strikes out.

3 — Carr rolls out, N. Allen to Mothell.

H-0, R-0, LOB-0, E-0

Kansas City

Moore singles to right center.

1 — McNair sacrifices, Mackey to Carr.

O. Johnson doubles to center, Moore scores.

Duncan walks.

Mendez singles to center, bases loaded.

N. Allen singles to right, O. Johnson and Duncan scoring.

Mendez took third, Allen took second on the throw to the plate to get Duncan.

Mothell doubles to left center, Mendez and Allen score.

2 — Mothell out trying to stretch double into a triple, Santop to Mackey.

3 — Rogan pops up to J. Johnson.

H-5, R-5, LOB-0, E-0

Ninth Inning

Hilldale

Winters pinch hits for Lee.

1 — Winters flies out to McNair.

2 — Briggs rolls out to Mothell unassisted.

Warfield walks.

3 — Mackey pops up to Moore, for the final out and ending the first Colored World Series.

H-0, R-0, LOB-1, E-0

Final Score: Kansas City 5, Hilldale 0

5

The Series in Summary

MVP OF THE SERIES
Nip Winters
Pitcher, Hilldale Giants

The Most Valuable Player Award should be given to Nip Winters for his exceptionally fine pitching performance.

What he did: He started and completed four games, winning three, with his only loss coming in Game Seven, which went 12 innings. He struck out 21 batters in 38⅔ innings, while compiling a diminutive ERA of 1.16. Primarily, Hilldale would not have been invited to the championship party without Winters.

Other candidates: A case can be made for the all-purpose player Bullet Rogan, as he excelled with the bat, hitting .325 and on the mound (a 2.57 ERA), but his fielding performance was less than Roganesque. Hilldale's Judy Johnson led his team with a .364 average and seven ribbies. He was a clutch performer throughout the ten-game series, getting key hits in Games Three, Five and Six. At the minimum, the ancient warrior, Jose Mendez, who won two games despite subpar health, deserves an honorable mention.

LEAST VALUABLE PLAYER
OF THE SERIES

Hurley "Air" McNair

Had the Monarchs lost the series, their premier power hitter, McNair, would have been partly to blame. His futility at the plate is unprecedented in Negro

League history. Listed below, bat-by-bat, is McNair's failure to deliver in clutch situations during the World Series.

Game	At Bat Action	Pitcher	Men on Base
#1	*Grounds out to second base*	*Cockrell*	*2b*
	Sacrifice	Cockrell	1b
	Intentionally walked	Cockrell	2b, 3b
	Flies to center field	Cockrell	2b
	Strikes out (1)	Cockrell	1b
#2	*Grounds out to pitcher*	*Winters*	*1b, 2b*
	Grounds out to pitcher	Winters	none on
	Force out	Winters	1b
	Flies to center field	Winters	none on
#3	*Grounds out to second*	*Ryan*	*2b*
	Strikes out (2)	Ryan	1b
	Grounds out to third	Lee	3b
	Strikes out (3)	Lee	none on
	Grounds out to second	Lee	1b
	Intentionally walked	Lee	2b
#4	*Grounds out to second*	*Ryan*	*2b*
	Pops up to second	Currie	1b
	Grounds to second	Currie	1b
	Flies out to left field	Currie	1b
#5	*Flies out to left field*	*Winters*	*none on*
	Grounds out to first	Winters	none on
	Strikes outs (4)	Winters	none on
#6	*Singles to shallow right, 1 rbi*	*Cockrell*	*2b, 3b*
	Infield hit to shortstop	Lee	none on
	Flies out to left field	Lee	3b
	Pops up to third	Lee	1b
#7	*Strikes out (5)*	*Winters*	*1b, 2b, 3b*
	Flies out to center	Winters	1b, 2b
	Grounds out to short	Winters	none on
	Oscar Johnson pinch hits for McNair (2 for 26)		
#8	*Flies out to center*	*Currie*	*1b*
	Singles to right	Currie	1b
	Flies out to center	Currie	none on
	Singles to center, 1 rbi	Currie	1b, 2b
#9	*Sacrifices to third*	*Winters*	*1b*
	Singles to right	Winters	none on
	Grounds out to second	Winters	none on
	Strikes out (6)	Winters	2b
#10	*Strikes out (7)*	*Lee*	*none on*
	Grounds to first	Lee	none on
	Sacrifices to third	Lee	1b

In summary, McNair left 32 men on bases, 15 of them in scoring position. His potential threat as a hitter was evident by the two intentional walks, one in first game with runners on second and third, and in game #3 with a runner on second base. However, Hilldale had little to fear, as McNair's batting average (zero-for-10) with runners in scoring position was a woeful .000. Zero was his hero!

COMPOSITE BOX SCORES
Games 1 Through 10

Editor's note:

Hilldale scored more runs, had more hits, more RBIs, and more walks. They hit for a higher average and made fewer errors in the field. Their pitching staff had a lower ERA, gave up fewer hits per inning, struck out more batters, walked fewer hitters, but still lost the series. The deciding factor may have been that Hilldale abandoned 86 men on the bases and the Kansas City Monarchs had the home field advantage in the last six games. Hilldale's only consolation was they won the statistical war and possibly the unofficial Most Valuable Player award.

(Leaders in **Bold**)
Kansas City Batting Summary

	G	AB	R	H	2B	3B	HR	RBI	BB	SB	CS	SO	E	AVG	SLG	OBP
Allen, Newt	10	40	**8**	11	**7**	0	0	2	2	1	0	4	3	.275	.450	.310
Bell, Cliff	2	4	0	0	0	0	0	0	0	0	0	1	0	.000	.000	.000
Bell, William	4	8	1	2	1	0	0	2	0	0	1	1	1	.250	.375	.250
Drake, Plunk	4	4	0	2	0	0	0	1	0	0	0	0	0	.500	.500	.500
Duncan, Frank	10	36	2	5	1	0	0	2	**4**	2	1	3	0	.139	.167	.225
Hawkins, Lem	9	31	4	6	1	0	0	0	3	2	0	2	2	.194	.226	.265
Johnson, Heavy	9	27	2	7	3	0	0	2	2	0	0	4	0	.259	.370	.310
Joseph, Newt	10	38	6	5	1	0	**1**	4	3	3	2	12	4	.132	.237	.195
McCall, Bill	0	0	0	0	0	0	0	0	0	0	0	0	0	.000	.000	.000
McNair, Hurley	10	35	3	5	0	0	0	2	2	0	0	7	2	.143	.143	.189
Mendez, Jose	4	9	1	1	0	0	0	0	0	0	0	2	0	.111	.111	.111
Moore, Dobie	10	40	7	12	0	0	0	4	1	2	1	1	5	.300	.300	.317
Morris, Harold	1	0	0	0	0	0	0	0	0	0	0	0	0	.000	.000	.000
Mothell, Dink	7	13	0	2	1	0	0	2	0	0	0	1	1	.154	.231	.154
Rogan, Bullet	10	40	4	**13**	1	0	0	**7**	3	**3**	**3**	2	5	**.325**	.350	**.372**
Sweatt, George	5	18	0	5	1	**2**	0	3	0	0	0	2	0	.278	**.556**	.278
Totals	10	343	38	76	17	2	1	31	20	13	9	42	23	.222	.292	.264

Hilldale Batting Summary

	G	AB	R	H	2B	3B	HR	RBI	BB	SB	CS	SO	E	AVG	SLG	OBP
Allen, Tom	6	19	3	3	1	0	0	2	0	0	0	3	0	.158	.211	.158
Briggs, Otto	10	44	5	10	3	0	0	2	3	**4**	1	1	0	.227	.296	.277
Campbell, Bill	1	0	1	0	0	0	0	0	0	1	0	0	0	.000	.000	.000
Carr, George	8	18	1	6	0	0	0	3	3	3	0	5	4	.333	.333	**.429**
Cockrell, Phil	4	4	0	0	0	0	0	0	0	0	0	0	3	.000	.000	.000
Currie, Rube	3	7	0	1	0	0	0	1	0	0	0	3	0	.143	.143	.143
Johnson, George	10	38	3	9	2	**2**	0	4	3	0	0	7	0	.237	.395	.293
Johnson, Judy	10	44	7	**16**	**5**	1	**1**	**7**	2	0	0	2	3	**.364**	**.591**	.391
Lee, Script	4	7	1	2	0	0	0	1	2	0	0	2	0	.286	.286	.444
Lewis, Joe	7	17	1	3	1	0	0	3	0	0	0	1	0	.176	.235	.176
Mackey, Biz	10	41	7	10	0	1	0	2	**6**	1	1	1	4	.244	.293	.340
Ryan, Red	2	0	0	0	0	0	0	0	0	0	0	0	0	.000	.000	.000
Santop, Louis	9	24	2	8	0	0	0	2	3	0	0	0	2	.333	.333	.407
Stephens, Jake	1	2	0	0	0	0	0	0	0	0	0	0	0	.000	.000	.000
Thomas, Clint	10	38	6	9	1	0	0	2	3	0	0	3	0	.237	.263	.293
Warfield, Frank	10	38	5	9	2	0	0	4	**6**	2	0	3	2	.237	.289	.326
Winters, Nip	7	17	1	4	0	0	0	2	4	0	0	4	0	.235	.235	.381
Totals	10	358	43	90	15	4	1	35	35	11	2	35	18	.251	.324	.318

Kansas City Pitching Summary

	G	GS	CG	IP	H	R	ER	BB	SO	HB	WP	W	L	ERA
Bell, Cliff	2	2	1	9⅓	6	6	5	3	4	1	2	0	1	4.82
Bell, William	3	3	0	24	9	13	9	13	6	1	0	1	0	3.38
Drake, Plunk	4	0	0	13⅔	14	8	6	5	5	1	0	0	1	3.95
McCall, Bill*	1	1	0	0	1	3	3	1	0	1	0	0	1	—
Mendez, Jose	4	1	1	19	11	4	3	5	6	0	0	2	0	1.42
Morris, Harold	1	0	0	1	2	0	0	0	0	0	0	0	0	0.00
Rogan, Wilber	4	3	3	28	27	9	8	8	14	1	0	2	1	2.57
Totals		10	5	95	90	43	34	35	35	5	2	5	4	3.22

*McCall faced 3 batters in game 3.
Saves— None

Hilldale Pitching Summary

	G	GS	CG	IP	H	R	ER	BB	SO	HB	WP	W	L	ERA
Cockrell, Phil	2	2	1	9⅔	10	10	6	4	5	0	1	0	1	5.58
Currie, Rube	3	1	1	16⅓	12	3	1	2	3	1	0	1	1	0.55
Lee, Script	3	1	1	23⅓	19	9	8	4	10	2	0	0	2	3.09
Ryan, Red	2	2	0	6⅓	8	7	6	2	3	1	0	0	0	8.53
Winters, Nip	4	4	4	38⅔	27	9	5	8	21	0	0	3	1	1.16
Totals		10	7	94⅓	76	38	26	20	42	4	1	4	5	2.48

Saves: Plunk Drake, Game 6
Game-Winning RBIS: (game number)
By Monarchs: Moore (1), Sweatt (6), Rogan (7), Duncan (8), O. Johnson (10)
By Hilldale: Mackey (2), Santop (4), J. Johnson (5), Carr (9)
Double Plays: *Monarchs*— Allen to Moore to Hawkins (1); Moore to Hawkins (3);
  Allen to Moore to Hawkins (3); McNair to Duncan (3); Mothell Unassisted (6)
  Moore to N. Allen to Mothell (6); Drake to Joseph to Moore (7)
Hilldale:— Mackey to Warfield to T. Allen (2); J. Johnson to
  Warfield to T. Allen (2); Warfield to J. Johnson to Carr (4);
  Stephens to Carr (7); Briggs to Warfield (7); Warfield to Carr to
  Thomas (7)

Men Left on Base: Games	1	2	3	4	5	6	7	8	9	10	Total
By Monarchs—	7,	6,	8,	6,	2,	5,	8,	4,	7,	1	54
By Hilldale—	7,	8,	15,	3,	12,	8,	7,	8,	15,	3	86

Sacrifices: by *Kansas City*: McNair-3, N. Allen-1, W.Bell-1, Sweatt-2, Joseph-1.
  by *Hilldale*: Currie-1, T.Allen-1, Carr-1, Mackey-1, Santop-1, Warfield-4, Thomas-3,
  Briggs-1, G.Johnson-1, Ryan-1.
Hit by Pitch: (Game #)
        (1) N. Allen by Cockrell
        (2) Warfield by McCall, Briggs by Drake
        (3) N. Allen by Ryan, Briggs by W. Bell
            Mothell and Joseph by Lee
        (4) Warfield by C. Bell
        (5) Briggs by Rogan
        (8) O. Johnson by Currie
Passed Balls: Santop 2, Duncan, Lewis
Umpires: Anderson, Costell, Doolan, Freeman, Goeckel, McBride, McDevitt, McGrew.

Game-by-Game Summary

Game 1					Wining/Losing Pitcher
Kansas City	000	005	001	6	*Rogan (W)*
Hilldale	000	000	002	2	Cockrell (L)

Game 2					
Kansas City	000	000	000	0	McCall (L)
Hilldale	522	002	00x	11	*Winters (W)*

Game 3						
Kansas City	002	200	001	001	0	6
Hilldale	001	030	001	001	0	6

13 innings — game called because of darkness

Game 4					
Kansas City	201	000	000	3	C. Bell (L)
Hilldale	003	000	001	4	*Currie (W)*

Game 5					
Hilldale	000	100	004	5	*Winters (W)*
Kansas City	200	000	000	2	Rogan (L)

Game 6					
Hilldale	202	001	000	5	Lee (L)
Kansas City	400	100	01x	6	*W. Bell (W)*

Game 7						
Hilldale	020	000	001	000	3	Winters (L)
Kansas City	000	200	010	001	4	*Mendez (W)*

Game 8					
Hilldale	000	001	100	2	Currie (L)
Kansas City	000	000	003	3	*Rogan (W)*

Game 9					
Hilldale	000	20	012	5	*Winters (W)*
Kansas City	020	000	010	3	Drake (L)

Game 10					
Hilldale	000	000	000	0	Lee (L)
Kansas City	000	000	05x	5	*Mendez (W)*

Editor's note:
Four games were decided by one run and five games were decided in the last inning. Meanwhile, the Monarchs' pitcher-manager, Jose Mendez, picked up two victories.

Score by Innings

G#	Team	1	2	3	4	5	6	7	8	9	10	11	12	13	F	W
1	KC	0	0	0	0	0	5	0	0	1					6	KC
	H	0	0	0	0	0	0	0	0	2					2	
2	KC	0	0	0	0	0	0	0	0	0					0	
	H	5	2	2	0	0	2	0	0	x					11	H
3	KC	0	0	2	2	0	0	0	0	1	0	0	1	0	6	
	H	0	0	1	0	3	0	0	0	1	0	0	1	0	6	TIE
4	KC	2	0	1	0	0	0	0	0	0					3	
	H	0	0	3	0	0	0	0	0	1	(a)				4	H
5	H	0	0	0	1	0	0	0	0	4					5	H
	KC	2	0	0	0	0	0	0	0	0					2	
6	H	2	0	2	0	0	1	0	0	0					5	
	KC	4	0	0	1	0	0	0	1	x					6	KC

G#	Team	1	2	3	4	5	6	7	8	9	10	11	12	13	F	W
7	H	0	2	0	0	0	0	0	0	1	0	0	0		3	
	KC	0	0	0	2	0	0	0	1	0	0	0	1	(b)	4	KC
8	H	0	0	0	0	0	1	1	0	0					2	
	KC	0	0	0	0	0	0	0	0	3	(c)				3	KC
9	H	0	0	0	0	2	0	0	1	2					5	H
	KC	0	2	0	0	0	0	0	1	0					3	
10	H	0	0	0	0	0	0	0	0	0					0	
	KC	0	0	0	0	0	0	0	5	x					5	KC
95	H	7	4	8	1	5	4	1	1	11	0	0	1	0	43	
94⅓	KC	8	2	3	5	0	5	0	8	5	0	0	2	0	38	

(a) None out when the winning run scored.
(b) Two were out when the winning run scored.
(c) Two were out when the winning run scored.

Report Card

The 1924 Colored World Series	The Kansas City Monarchs from Kansas City, Missouri	The Hilldale Giants from Darby, Pennsylvania
Batting	C+ The Monarchs were able to drive in many clutch runs with timely hitting. Without some timely hitting from Bullet Rogan and Newt Allen, the Monarchs would have lost the series.	C- The fact is Hilldale left far too many players on the basepaths. Despite a fine hitting performance by Judy Johnson, others like Mackey, Santop, and Thomas failed to meet their batting standards.
Pitching	B- The Monarchs got unexpected help from manager Mendez, with his two wins. Meanwhile, Bullet Rogan turned in a fine performance, picking up two victories in pivotal games.	B+ A stellar effort by Nip Winters kept the Hilldale squad in the running. This superstar showing captured three wins. Performances by Ryan and Cockrell fell very short of their seasonal standards.
Fielding	D- The Monarchs' atrocious fielding kept Hilldale in the series.	D+ Hilldale was not much better committing errors at crucial stages.
Base Running	B The Monarchs were aggressive on the basepaths, gambling at every opportunity. Newt Joseph, not known for his speed, was a vital factor in creating havoc for the Hilldale Club.	B- Hilldale lived up to its image as a team with speed. Speedy Otto Briggs and George Carr were terrors on the bases. However deadly running mistakes by Mackey and other Giants led to losses.
Managing	C+ Except for some questionable pinch-hitting and pitching decisions, the Monarchs played most chess moves by the book.	D Failure by management to start Winters in the first game will always haunt them. In retrospect, realizing Winters' dominance during the series, this decision proved to be fatal.

6

Greenbacks

The fact that I'm not around, now that Negro ballplayers are getting a break, bothers me, no little. Think of the salary I, along with a lot of other colored guys, might have made with the hustle which was typical of our time.

— Raleigh "Biz" Mackey

The economic growth of the twenties was largely due to the Industrial Age. The Great Migration had spurned the birth of manufacturing plants for cars, creating a new mobility for Americans. This economic growth was seen as an opportune time to initiate a World Series involving colored ball players.

This period showed an average per capita income for Americans of approximately $650. Meanwhile, income for baseball games was almost exclusively generated from gate receipts. Radio and advertising revenue had not become marketing instruments. In addition, a small portion of income came from concession sales and an even smaller amount from park rental and parking fees.

Without radio sponsorship and later television, the paying public normally carried the financial burden of a successful franchise. Attendance figures for major leagues teams in 1924 reached almost 10 million fans. The majors maintained that level until 1930 before breaking the 10 million plateau. While in the same year, only one twentieth, or less than 500,000 fans, attended games played in the Negro National Leagues. Attendance figures were not available for the Eastern Colored League games. The attendance in the inaugural year of the Colored World Series averaged a meager 1,825 fans per game.

Following are the gate receipts, expenses and salaries for the 1924 Colored World Series.

Kansas City Monarchs vs. Philadelphia Hilldales

Gate Receipts	**$52,113.90**
Expenses—	
Rental of Parks	$9,384.63
Transportation for Ball Clubs	$5,094.80
War Tax	$4,941.00
Commissions' Fare, Hotel and Salaries	$2,360.27
Umpires Salaries, R.R. Fare, Hotels	$2,277.58
Hotel, Board for Clubs	$1,370.00
Park Personnel, Ticket Sellers, Ushers, etc.	$1,017.25
Advertising and Printing	$775.30
Newspaper Reporters Salaries, Fare, Hotel	$457.08
Newspaper Publicity	$300.00
Baseballs	$208.60
Photo Accounts	$173.75
Music/Entertainment	$150.00
Car Fare and Buses Hired for Clubs	$72.55
Adjustments and Refunds on Tickets, etc.	$67.65
Total Expenses	($28,650.46)
Balance to be Distributed	**$23,463.44**

Distribution	
Amount to be Distributed	23,463.44
35 Percent	
Kansas City Monarchs	$4,927.32
Philadelphia Hilldales	$3,284.88
35 Percent	
Kansas City Club Owners	$4,927.32
Hilldale Club Owners	$3,284.88
10 Percent	
Commission, Western League	$1,173.17
Commission, Eastern League	$1,173.17
12 Percent	
Chicago American Giants (2nd place — West)	$1,407.80
Baltimore Black Sox (2nd place — East)	$1,407.80
8 Percent	
Detroit Stars (3rd place — West)	$938.55
Lincoln Giants (3rd place — East)	$938.55
Total Distribution	**$23,463.44**

Player's Share (35% of Receipts less Expenses)	**$8,212.20**
Winner's Share— 60% Percent	
16 Monarchs received $307.96 each.	$4,927.32
Loser's Share— 40% Percent	
17 Hilldales received $193.23 each.	$3,284.88

Attendance Figures for the Series

Attendance	Receipts
October 3, Friday — Philadelphia	5,366
October 4, Saturday — Philadelphia	8,661
October 5, Sunday — Baltimore	5,503
October 6, Monday — Baltimore	584
October 11, Saturday — Kansas City	3,891
October 12, Sunday — Kansas City	8,885
October 14, Tuesday — Kansas City	2,539
October 18, Saturday — Chicago	2,608

Attendance	Receipts
October 19 — Sunday — Chicago	6,271
October 20 — Monday — Chicago	1,549
Figures based on Totals of 45,857	$52,113.90

Statement from the Commission Office
Andrew (Rube) Foster, Chairman
Charles P. Spedden, Treasurer
Alex Pompez, Treasurer
Dr. Howard M. Smith, Treasurer

Comparison of Greenbacks
White vs. Colored World Series Winners

	Washington Senators	Kansas City Monarchs
Games Played	7	10
Total Attendance	283,665	45,857
Average per game	40,524	4,586
Total Gate Receipts	$1,093,104.00	$52,114.00
Total Players' Share	$331,093.51	$8,212.20
A Winner's Share	$5,959.64	$307.96
A Loser's Share	$3,820.29	$193.23

Although gambling was not legalized in Las Vegas, Nevada, until 1931, the Kansas City Monarchs were installed as 3 to 2 favorites to beat the Hilldale Club. Overall, betting extended from pocket change up to as much as $300 per wager was reported.

Gate Receipts — Negro National League, 1920–24

Year	Teams	Gate Receipts	Percentage
1920			
	Chicago American Giants	$66,100.25	27.4%
	Chicago Giants	did not report receipts	0.0%
	Cuban Stars	$23,110.39	9.6%
	Dayton Marcos	$12,723.28	5.3%
	Detroit Stars	$36,478.86	15.1%
	Indianapolis ABCs	$32,403.70	13.4%
	Kansas City Monarchs	$48,868.20	20.2%
	St. Louis Giants	$21,826.49	9.0%
	19.2%	**$241,511.17**	**100.0%**
1921			
	Bacharach Giants (associate)	$10,268.78	3.7%
	Chicago American Giants	$87,240.00	31.3%
	Chicago Giants	$13,159.51	4.7%
	Cleveland Tate Stars (associate)	$7,731.70	2.8%
	Columbus Buckeyes	$17,152.55	6.1%
	Cuban Stars	$25,006.32	9.0%
	Detroit Stars	$24,829.73	8.9%

Year	Teams	Gate Receipts	Percentage
1921			
	Hilldale	$5,429.23	1.9%
	Indianapolis ABCs	$23,825.95	8.5%
	Kansas City Monarchs	$38,810.63	13.9%
	Pittsburgh Keystones (associate)	$3,990.80	1.4%
	St. Louis Giants	$21,529.63	7.7%
	22.2%	$278,974.83	100.0%
1922			
	Chicago American Giants	$99,072.78	35.9%
	Chicago Giants (associate)	$4,774.70	1.7%
	Cleveland Tate Stars	$24,604.81	8.9%
	Cuban Stars	$19,216.58	7.0%
	Detroit Stars	$27,760.99	10.0%
	Hilldale (associate)	$6,209.15	2.2%
	Indianapolis ABCs	$24,106.27	8.7%
	Kansas City Monarchs	$44,031.05	15.9%
	Nashville Elite Giants (associate)	$414.44	0.2%
	Pittsburgh Keystones	$5,536.31	2.0%
	St. Louis Stars	$20,538.54	7.4%
	22.0%	$276,265.62	100.0%
1923			
	Chicago American Giants	$71,503.76	31.6%
	Chicago Giants (associate)	$2,417.12	1.1%
	Cuban Stars	$18,774.11	8.3%
	Detroit Stars	$26,067.77	11.5%
	Indianapolis ABCs	$22,797.08	10.1%
	Kansas City Monarchs	$40,702.20	18.0%
	Milwaukee Bears	$12,921.80	5.7%
	St. Louis Stars	$25,559.46	11.3%
	Toledo Tigers	$5,429.63	2.4%
	18.0%	$226,172.93	100.0%
1924			
	Birmingham Black Barons	$23,082.14	9.9%
	Chicago American Giants	$96,453.87	41.2%
	Cleveland Browns	$8,088.43	3.5%
	Cuban Stars	$13,096.30	5.6%
	Detroit Stars	$22,328.19	9.5%
	Indianapolis ABCs (associate)	$3,892.01	1.7%
	Kansas City Monarchs	$29,998.09	12.8%
	Memphis Red Sox	$13,840.39	5.9%
	St. Louis Stars	$23,120.23	9.9%
	18.6%	$233,899.65	100.0%
	Grand Total for 1920 through 1924	**$1,256,824.20**	

Note: Each club received 45 percent of the receipts at home, while receiving 35 percent of the gate receipts on the road. The remaining 20 percent went to the league office for administrative and booking cost. These figures do not include money received from rental of the parks or collection of war tax, required by the federal government. Also note that the Chicago American Giants routinely sold more tickets than any other club in the league, with the Kansas City Monarchs coming in a distance second place. During the five-year period, the years 1921 and 1922 generated the most income, with 22.2 percent of the total.

Appendix 1:
Program for the First Colored World Series

EAST *versus* WEST

FOR

World's Colored Championship

1924

THOMPSON 4

GETTING TOGETHER

HILLDALE *vs* KANSAS CITY

CHAMPIONS
EASTERN COLORED LEAGUE

CHAMPIONS
NEGRO NATIONAL LEAGUE

:: *Offical Souvenir Program* ::

PRICE, TWENTY-FIVE CENTS

LEMAITRE, PRINT

LOVERS OF SPORT

TAKE HOME A COPY OF

The Philadelphia Tribune

Turn to the Sport Pages and

READ—

The Witty Sport Comment—
Snappy Sport News—
Clever Sport Cartoons—
Brilliant Sport Opinion—
and Plenty of Pictures

Special Writers will cover the
WORLD SERIES
Between Hilldale and Kansas City

HILLDALE

	1	2	3	4	5	6	7	8	9	R	H	E
Briggs, rf..........												
Stevens, ss.........												
Mackey, 1b........												
Santop, c.........												
Thomas, lf												
J. Johnson, 3b......												
Warfield, 2b........												
G. Johnson, cf......												
Cockrell, p.........												
Winters, p..........												
TOTALS												

KANSAS CITY

	1	2	3	4	5	6	7	8	9	R	H	E
Hawkins, 1b........												
Allen, 2b..........												
O. Johnson, lf.......												
McNair, rf.........												
Moore, ss..........												
Joseph, 3b.........												
Mothel, cf..........												
Duncan, c..........												
Rogan, p..........												
Drake, p..........												
TOTALS												

HILLDALE									
KANSAS CITY									

Official Souvenir Program

For the first time in the history of colored baseball a series is to be played to determine the champion colored club of the world. Although many clubs have laid claim to the signal honors of reigning supreme in the ranks of Negro baseball, the title was self-applied and only through the recent organization has it been possible to eliminate all doubt regarding the logical club or clubs to assume the title of champions.

Strangely enough the present clubs of the East and West that are battling for the world's colored championship, represent the two cities that have the honor of sponsoring the organizations that are now recognized as the "majors" of Negro baseball. In 1920 Kansas City, Mo., was the scene of several clubs, that operate in the Western section of the country, gathering together and out of the conclave grew the present Negro National League. For two consecutive seasons, 1923-24, the Kansas City Monarchs have won the penant in the Western organization. Philadelphia was the meeting place where the colored clubs of the Eastern section gathered in 1922 and formed the Eastern Colored League, like the Kansas City Monarchs. The Hilldale Club has the honor of being two ply champions, having won the championship of the Eastern Colored League the past and present season.

KAY SEE MONARCHS

The Kansas City Monarchs are the outgrowth of the All Nations' Club that operated in Kansas City back in 1916. J. L. Wilkerson, who operates the club, has scoured the country to secure the present pennant winning combination. By looking over a source that managers never gave credence for producing promising material owner Wilkerson has drew such stars from the U. S. Army as Moore, Rogan, Hawkins and "Heavy" Johnson. Following is a detailed account of the baseball career's of the Kansas City players.

WILBUR ROGAN

WILBUR ROGAN, known to the baseball world as "Bullet Rogan," has been said by baseball authority to be the greatest Negro baseball pitcher in the game. Rogan is a native of the State of Kansas, and started out as a catcher. He is often called upon to play every position on the local team with the exception of a catcher. He is in the game more than any other pitcher in baseball. He is one of the most modest men in baseball. Rogan is now 31 years of age and has spent more than 12 years in the U. S. Army. He first started out to play baseball with the Pullman Colts, of Kansas City, Kan., in 1908 to 1911, when he enlisted in the 25th Infantry, U. S. A., becoming a member of their baseball team as a catcher. He later joined the Los Angeles White Socks, then returning to the Army as a pitcher. Rogan joined the Monarchs during the season of 1920 and since that time has been recognized as the star of this league. He is a dangerous hitter, batting right handed.

WALTER MOORE

WALTER MOORE, the greatest negro shortstop of all times, is known by the baseball fans throughout the country as "Dobbie Moore." Shortstops have come and shortstops have gone, but Moore is the peer of all. Moore has been with the local team for the past three seasons, coming to the Monarchs from the 25th Infantry, U. S. A., where he played with Hawkins and Rogan, now members of the Monarchs. Moore can hit, run, field and think, which goes to make him the peer of his position. He was a member of the pennant winning team of the Cuban Winter League during the past season. Moore, it has been stated, would be worth $50,000 to any Major league club if he was a white man. It is a real treat to see Dobie play the short position.

NEWT ALLEN, second sacker for the Monarchs, is now playing his first regular season with the local teams. Allen was with the Monarchs for a part of the season of 1923. Allen is known among the local baseball fans as "Colt Allen" and his actions on the playing field has been said by baseball critics as resembling that of Eddie Collins, of the Chicago White Socks. Allen was born in the State of Texas, a State that has given us more star baseball players than any other state in the Union. Allen is now making his home in this great Missouri City and has a wife and child. He bats both right and left handed. He was a former member of the All-Nations baseball club and the Omaha Federals, a strong Semi-Pro team. Allen has been selected by several fans as the second sacker for the All-Star Team of the Negro National League.

HAROLD "Yellow Horse" MORRISS, another member of the local pitching staff, just joined the local club this season, coming direct from Oakland California, where he has been the mainstay for the Pierce Giants. Morris is one of the most promising youngsters in the league and will be given a chance to show his wares against the strong Hilldale club in the present series.

OSCAR JOHNSON

OSCAR JOHNSON, known to the fans as "Heavy Johnson," is the largest man in Negro baseball. Johnson tips the beam at more than 240 lbs. Johnson is known as the Black Babe Ruth of Negro baseball. He has more than 60 home runs to his credit this season. Johnson is not the most finished fielder in the game, but he is the most terrific hitter. He came to the local club as a catcher, but was put into the outer garden on account of his hitting ability. Watch out for Johnson in this comin— series.

JOSE MENDEZ

JOSE MENDEZ, the Manager of the Monarchs, is one of the greatest pitchers the game has ever known. Mendez is a Cuban and has pitched against all of the big Major league clubs that have journeyed to Cuba. He has engaged in a pitchers battle with the great Christy Mathewson, when he was the ace for the New York Giants, and emerged victor on each occasion. Mendez was a former member of the American Giants and the Detroit Stars, and has been a member of the Monarchs for the past five years. He was the first manager of the Monarchs, for one season, then he gave over the reins to Sam Crawford for two seasons. He again was made manager for the season of 1923, and again for the present season.

CARROL MOTHEL, the Monarchs great utility player, has been with the local club off and on for the past five seasons, but it was the good old season of 1924 that he arrived. Mothel is known by the fans as "Dink Mothel." He was born and raised at Topeka, the capitol of the State of Kansas. Mothel has played every position on the local club with the exception of pitcher, and has the reputation of being one of the best utility players in the league. Mothel has played professional ball only with the Monarchs and the All-Nations Club, which is controlled by the same management. He is a husky youngster and one of the hardest fighters on the team. He subs for Duncan behind the bat and for Allen on second, Moore at short, Joseph on third, Hawkins on first and the entire outfield. Mothel is expected to shine in the coming World Series.

GEORGE SWEATT, the tall lanky outfielder of the Monarchs, is known as the school teacher of baseball. During the winter he has charge of the Negro Schools of Coffyville, Kansas. Sweatt is the greatest all-round athlete in Negro baseball. He is a graduate of the Pittsburg, Kansas, Normal College, where he was a member of the track team, the baseball team, the basketball team and the football team. He has been a member of the Monarchs for the past two seasons and has played in all of the outfield positions, also in the infield.

WILLIAM DRAKE

WILLIAM DRAKE is known by all baseball fans as "Plunk" Drake and is today one of the leading pitchers in the National League. Drake was for several years a member of the St. Louis Giants, then owned by Charles Mills. He first joined St. Louis in 1916, and played there until 1922, when he was sent to Kansas City in a trade. Drake is a native of Missouri, known as the "Show-Me State." He is considered as the most effective Negro pitcher in the game against major league baseball clubs. He has defeated such teams as the St. Louis Cardinals, Indianapolis American Association Club, the Kansas City Blue of the American Association.

JULIUS "JUDY" JOHNSON—Third Baseman

One of the Hilldale champions who acquired his baseball experience close to his present field of endeavors is Judy Johnson, a product of Wilmington, Del. Judy was enticed to Atlantic City in 1917 and played part of the season with Tom Jackson's Bacharach Giants. In the latter part of the season 1918 the draft for the World War struck the Hilldale club and depleted the ranks of Bolden's athletes by quite a few. At that time a manager had the alternative of recruiting players either over or under the draft age and the Hilldale manager, in Judy's case, chose the latter and grabbed the Wilmington youth who had not attained the age to shoulder a musket. Judy finished the season with the Philadelphia team but was considered too light in weight to hold over for the next season. However, during the season of 1921 the Hilldale infield was in a very much crippled condition and once more Ed. Bolden sought the services of Judy Johnson, who in the meantime had been playing with Danny McClellan's Madison Stars. With a couple additional years of age and experience Judy fit into the Hilldale outfit like the missing link and has been holding down the hot corners in an approved manner. Judy has also been shifted to shortstop on several occasions. He throws and bats right handed, hails from Wilmington, Del., and shares the honor with Stevens of being the most youthful member of the team, being 23 years old.

TOUSSAINT "T-A" ALLEN—First Baseman

Allen is another one of Pop Watkins' products. He started out with the Havana Red Sox in 1914 and played with the Watertown Club until 1917. From there he went to the Philadelphia Giants until he entered the service in the World War. In camp and overseas he played with his company team, the 349th Field Artillery. After being mustered out he joined the Hilldale team in 1919 and has since been a member of Ed. Bolden's club. Allen has exceptionally large hands and has no equal in scooping low throws to the initial bag. He throws left handed, but hits from the right side of the plate. 28 years old, he first saw the light of day in Atlanta, Ga.

MERVEN J. "RED" RYAN—Pitcher

A native of Brooklyn, N. Y., the red-topped Ryan started out in 1915 with the Pittsburg Stars, of Buffalo, N. Y. The Brooklyn Royal Giants was the next club that he joined. He then played with in turn the Lincoln Stars, Bacharach Giants, Harrisburg Giants and joined Hilldale in the latter part of the season of 1922. Red, who only weighs in the neighborhood of 158 lbs., throws the fastest ball for any pitcher his size, and for that matter has more speed than many larger men. Ryan is second only to Winters in pitching record of the Hilldale hurlers. Brooklyn, the city of churches, is Red's home town, while 25 years ago he celebrated his first birthday. Ryan pitches and bats right handed.

FRANK DUNCAN, said to be the greatest catcher in the game, is a local boy, and this will be the first time that he has been old enough to vote in a Presidential election. Frank is known to the fans as "Dunk" and he has a record of catching more regular games in this league than any other catcher. Dunk is a tall, thin, kid and full of pep. He was the battery mate for Rube Curry, now a pitcher for the Hilldale team. His first professional ball was when he joined the Monarchs.

FRANK DUNCAN

NEWT JOSEPH, the pepperiest player in baseball, has been a member of the Monarchs for the past three years. Joseph is the only member of the Monarchs that reported to the team at his own expense. Unknown to the club he reported here one day and asked for a uniform and informed the management that he was here to stay. He was given a uniform as a matter of a joke, but today he is regarded as the best third baseman in this league. Joseph had a hard time getting started as a hitter, but the records of the team this year stamps him as one of the most dangerous hitters in the game. Joseph keeps the other members of the team right on their toes with his chatter and is the life of the team. He was born in he State of Alabama, but was reared in the State of Oklahoma. Joseph started out as a catcher and later on made quite a record as a pitcher. When he came to the locals he was placed on the hot corner and has made good. He is the Beau-Brummell of the Monarchs. Joseph bats right handed.

HURLY McNAIR is the grand old man of Negro baseball. He has been a member of the local team since the starting of the league. McNair is today one of the greatest fielders in the game and the greatest sunfielder of all times. He is a small fellow but one of the most dangerous hitters. He has been playing baseball for the past 15 years and has several more years of good baseball in him. Where ever the sun shines that is the place he is going to play.

LEMUEL HAWKINS, the scrappy first sacker for the Monarchs, is better known around the circuit as "Hawk." "Hawk" has developed into the star first sacker of the league. He is a product of Georgia and started his baseball career in the U. S. Army, where he played five years with the 25th Infantry. Later he joined the Los Angeles White Socks, where he played for two seasons. He has been a member of the Monarchs since 1921, when he played a part of that season with Joe Green's Chicago Giants. "Hawk" at this time is the Captain of the team.

TWO BELLS

WM. BELL and CLIFFORD BELL, two of the Monarchs pitching staff, are both from the State of Texas. One is a heavy built Bell, while Cliff is a rather lanky boy. Cliff has been a member of the local team for the past three seasons, while Wm. has been with the boys for the past two years.

The Hilldale Club

Without a doubt the Hilldale Club is the only first class colored club now operating, that started out as a purely amateur organization. In 1910 the club was organized by a group of boys and shortly afterwards was taken in hand by Ed. Bolden, the present manager, who has guided the organization through it's stages of development.

When the Eastern Colored League was formed, in 1922, the Hilldale Club was one of the charter members of the organization. The present array of baseball talent that represents the Philadelphia team, has been recruited from the four points. Many of the players have been with the Hilldale team for a number of consecutive seasons. Bolden also has the distinction of unearthing two of the greatest finds in recent years in "Judy" Johnson and Paul Stevens, both mere youth's, whose work against the veterans in the present series will be watched with interest. Frank Warfield, the clever second baseman who captains the team, is possibly the youngest player among the league clubs that has been elevated to that post. Frank has just attained his 26th birthday and in appreciation of his first year as leader of the Hilldale players he has turned in a winner. Similar to the Kansas City Monarch's, the Hilldale team has won its second straight championship and is one of the logical clubs to figure in the first colored world's series. Following is the professional records and diamond deeds achieved by the present wearers of the Hilldale uniforms.

FRANK "WEASEL" WARFIELD—Second Baseman

Starting out as a shortstop with the St. Louis Giants in 1916 Warfield was picked up by C. I. Taylor and stationed at second base for the Indianapolis A. B. C. Team. From there he moved to Tenny Blunt's Detroit Stars and joined the Hilldale team in 1923. He played out the first season under Johnny Henry Lloyd and when Lloyd moved to Atlantic City the captaincy of the Philadelphia club was handed to quiet Frank. By turning in a winner his first season bids fair for the Indiana youth to stick on the job. Warfield is a wonderful fielder with a unique underhand snap throw that aids materially in making double plays. A fast base runner and a good hitter. Frank throws and bats right handed. Indianapolis, Ind., is his home town and he has just passed his 26th birthday.

JOSEPH "SLEEPY" LEWIS—Catcher

Joe Lewis is one of the original Baltimore Black Sox that started the club in the Monumental City. Joe put in five seasons with the dark-hosed crew for gold and glory and was signed by Ben Taylor for the Washington Potomac's in 1923. However, the same season he finished up with the Homestead Grays in Pittsburg and in the spring of the present season was signed by the Hilldale club. Joe started out as a third baseman, but shifted behind the bat and has been playing that position throughout his professional career. Joe is a competent receiver and a good hitter. Sparrow's Point, Md., is where Joe received his first training from Ma Lewis and 28 years have rolled around since Joe made his bow to the household.

JESSE "NIMP" WINTERS—Pitcher

Winters is the only southpaw on the Hilldale pitching staff and also enjoys the distniction of being the leading pitcher of the Eastern Colored League in 1923. Winters received his first experience on the sand lots of Washington, D. C., with the LeDroit Tigers. Chappie Johnson grabbed him in 1919 as a member of the Norfolk Stars. The following year he went to the Bacharach Giants and to the Philadelphia and Harrisburg Giants in turn. In 1923 he signed with Hilldale. Winters throws and bats left handed and one of his eccentric traits is that he never wears a toe plate, which is customary for all pitchers. Jesse was born in Washington, D. C., and is 25 years old.

HILLDALE, EASTERN COLORED LEAGUE CHAMPIONS—1924

Back Row, Left to Right: Carr, Allen, J. Johnson, G. Johnson Mgr. Bolden, Mackey, Winters, Currie, Santop
Front Row: Lewis, Thomas, Lee, Capt. Warfield, Mascot "Rocky," Stevens, Briggs, Campbell, Ryan

KANSAS CITY MONARCHS, NEGRO NATIONAL LEAGUE CHAMPIONS—1924

Front Row, Left to Right: Sweatt, Drake, Mothel, McCall, Duncan, Hawkins, W. Bell, Morris.
Back Row: Joseph, Allen, Johnson, C. Bell, Sec'y; Gilmore, Rogan, Moore, Manager Mendez

LOUIS "BIG BERTHA" SANTOP
Catcher

"Top" broke into professional ball with the Fort Worth Wonders, of Fort Worth, Texas, in 1909. The following year he played with the Oklahoma Monarchs, of Guthrie, Okla., and came east in the spring of 1911 to join Sol White's Philadelphia Giants. The same year he played with the Lincoln Giants and remained with them until 1915, when he went to the Brooklyn Royal Giants. He then played with the Lincoln Stars and Royal Giants and was one of the first professional stars to play with Hilldale when the Philadelphia team graduated from an amateur organization. After playing the season of 1918 with Hilldale, "Top" was inducted into the naval service of the World War, playing part of a season with the Royal Giants. After being mus-

LOUIS SANTOP

tered out he rejoined Hilldale in 1920 and has been one of the mainstays behind the bat for Ed. Bolden's team during his stay. Santop throws right handed, but bats from the left side of the plate and beside being regarded as a heady catcher has always been rated as one of the most dangerous batters in colored ranks. His present average of .407 leads one to believe that "Top" is not slipping any in the hitting department. A native of Ft. Worth, Texas, Santop began his career as a "pro" at the age of twenty. The big catcher is now rounding out his 35th year.

OTTO "MIRROR" BRIGGS—Right Field

The late C. I. Taylor started Otto on his professional career in the spring of 1914. The famous A. B. C.'s left Palm Beach, Fla., with Briggs in tow. When the club reached West Baden, Ind., he was turned over to the Sprudels of that city. From there he went to the Dayton Marcos, of Dayton, Ohio. In 1917 he joined the Hilldale team and captained the club that season. The same year he entered the World War as a member of the 368th Infantry, Co. E., 92nd Division, and played ball with his outfit in camp and "over there." After being mustered out he joined the newly formed Madison Stars, in Philadelphia, the season of 1919. He finished the season with the Hilldale club and has remained with them since that date. Otto is known as one of the best lead off men playing the game and has batted in first position during his entire stay with Hilldale. He throws right handed and hits from the left side of the plate. Kings Mountain, N. C., is the land of his youth and the official census taker has him listed as 33 years old.

RALEIGH "BIZZ" MACKEY—Catcher and all-around player

From the land of sage brush and alkali dust hails Bizz Mackey. Starting out from his home town, San Antonio, Texas, with the San Antonio Giants, in 1918 Mackey joined the A. B. C.'s in 1920 and immediately proved to be a sensation with C. I. Taylor's team. He has played every position on the ball club and since joining the Hilldale team in 1923 he has been shifted around whereever the club needed strengthening. Mackey, however, excells as a catcher, has a great throwing arm and is reasonably fast for a big man. Bizz throws right handed, but swings a wicked cudgel from either side of the plate. His first year in the East he led the Eastern Circuit at bat with an average of .440. Born in 1897, Mackey is rounding out his 27th year.

PHILIP "FISH" COCKRELL—Pitcher

Phil started attracting attention in the baseball world in 1913 with Pop Watkins' Havana Red Rox, of Watertown, N. Y. In 1917 Cockrell found his way to little old New York and was signed by Jim Keenan's Lincoln Giants. The following season he moved to Philadelphia and since that time has been a member of the Hilldale team. During his stay with Ed. Bolden's team he has pitched three no-hit, no-run games. Cockrell is a very good hitter for a pitcher and also plays the outfield well and is fast on the bases. Phil pitches and bats right-handed, is a native of Augusta, Ga., and 26 years old.

RUBE CURRIE—Pitcher

REUBEN "RUBE" CURRIE—Pitcher

Currie is one of the very few athletes who have the moniker of Rube and did not obtain it from a foreign source. Rube left his home town in Kansas City, Mo., to join the Chicago Unions in quest of fame and fortune. However, the following year he decided to stick around the odor of home coking and play with the Kansas City Monarchs. In the spring of 1924 he came East as a member of the Hilldale Club. Rube throws with his right digit, is 26 years old and hits from the righ side of the platter.

PAUL "UNCLE JAKE" STEVENS—Shortstop

Paul Stevens is one of the few boys who jumped right off the lots to a first-class club. Stevie advised Mr. Ed. Bolden via postman that he was the best short fielder that ever matriculated among the white roses of York, Pa., and Bolden, who in turn was impressed by his confident air, sent for Stevie in the spring of 1921. He had not yet reached the voting age and only weighed 120 pounds, but his nerve and speed in handling ground balls was the means of him sticking around on the bench for three seasons.

In the spring of the present year, Bolden farmed him out to the Philadelphia Giants in order to give him a chance to play every day. He was recalled in July and is now filling a regular berth at shortstop. Stevens uncanny ability to field ground balls has caused him to be nick-named the human jumping jack. Since returning to Hilldale Stevens has been hitting in better form and a few additional pounds picked up has stamped him as an improved ball player. Stevens' home is in York, Pa., and the family records show that he is 23 years old. He throws and hits right handed.

HOLSEY S. "SCRIPT" LEE—Pitcher

Chappie Johnson figured in the development of Script Lee, who came out with the Norfolk Stars in 1920, but Lee had acquired quite a bit of baseball experience with the 1st Separate, N. G., Co. B., from Washington, D. C., when he was a member of that outfit. Script also played with the Philadelphia Stars and joined Hilldale in 1923. The freak underhand delivery adopted by Lee is the secret of his success as a pitcher. Script also is a good hitter and fields his position well. He pitches and bats right handed, is 23 years old and was born in Washington, D. C.

CLINTON "BUCKEYE" THOMAS—Left Fielder

Clint Thomas is one of the fastest men playing the outfield in colored ranks and has developed within a remarkably short time, playing his first professional engagement with the Brooklyn Royal Giants, under John Henry Lloyd, in 1920, as a second baseman. Thomas joined the now defunct Columbus Buckeyes in 1921. In 1922 he moved to the Detroit Stars and was shifted from second base to the outfield. In 1923 he was signed by Hilldale and has been a fixture in the outfield of Bolden's club since his return East. Thomas bats and throws right handed, is a very fast base runner and one of the hardest hitters on the Hilldale team. Clinton first saw the light of day in Columbus, Ohio, and is now 26 years old.

GEORGE "TANK" CARR—Utility

Just a ball player is a very concise manner of describing the baseball ability of George Carr, general all around man of the Hilldale team. George has played six different positions since joining the Hilldale team and filled them all in a manner creditable to a regular. Carr, who is the wonder boy from the Pacific slope, started out grabbing nickels with the Los Angeles White Sox in 1912. He stuck around the land of red wood and oranges until 1920 when he was induced to cast his lot with the Kansas City Monarchs. In 1923 he came East and joined the Hilldale club. George, who tips the beam well over 200 lbs., is without a doubt the fastest big man among the colored players. He throws right handed and hits from both sides of the plate. Father Time will toll off his 29th year when he cuts his next birthday cake.

GEORGE "DIBO" JOHNSON—Center Field

Another member of the Hilldale team from the land of "long horns" is George Johnson, whose home is in San Marcos, Texas. George broke in with the Ft. Worth Wonders in 1909. He left the lone star state in 1912 and played with the Kansas City Giants. From there he went to the Brooklyn Royal Giants and joined the Hilldale team in 1918. George started out as a pitcher but was shifted to the outfield. The ability of George to cover plenty of ground in the middle garden has caused him to be a fixture at that position during his seven year stay with Bolden's team. George broke his left leg sliding into third base the first season that he was with Hilldale, but the injury failed to slow him up in the least. George is 36 years old.

WILLIAM "ZOOP" CAMPBELL—Pitcher

Campbell is the infant member of the Hilldale squad, having joined the team the latter part of the present season. Ben Taylor started Campbell on his professional career with the Washington Potomacs in 1923. In 1924 he started out with the Philadelphia Giants and when that club floundered he secured a berth with the Hilldale champions. Campbell pitches and bats right handed, is 28 years old and hails from Boston, Mass.

THREE INVADERS

Joseph   Hawkins   McNair

CLINT THOMAS

GEORGE JOHNSON

"THE GARDEN PATROL"

The big three of the Hilldale outfield have won their spurs as forming the best combination of fly-chasers in the Eastern circuit. Their ability to cover the pasture has aided materially in piling up the pitcher's records, as it's a hard job to "hit 'em where they ain't." "Buckeye" Clint Thomas has an edge on the others, summing them up in all departments. Thomas is faster on the base paths, hits as often and harder than either of his comrades. Clint is leading the Hilldale sluggers with home runs, he has gathered in 28 round trippers during the present campaign. Arduous Otto Briggs is the real plugger on the roster of the Eastern Champions. The spirit and morale that Briggs injects into the Philadelphia team works wonders toward supplying the old punch that is necessary to win ball games. Otto also is one of the most consistent hitters in baseball and covers a lot of ground in an ungainly fashion in the field. George Johnson has experienced the worst batting slump this season since he became a member of the •Hilldale team, but has apparently regained his eye and is hitting in better form. George's fielding is all that could be desired, but his nonchalant manner of gathering in a fly seems rather risky to the average fan. The Hilldale outfield is sure to play a big part in the title series.

OTTO BRIGGS

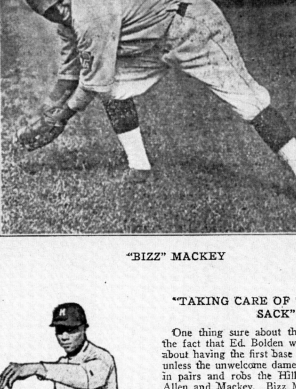

"BIZZ" MACKEY

"TAKING CARE OF THE INITIAL SACK"

One thing sure about the present series is the fact that Ed. Bolden won't have to worry about having the first base well taken care of, unless the unwelcome dame, misfortune, stalks in pairs and robs the Hilldale team of both Allen and Mackey. Bizz Mackey, whose versatility on the diamond is known to the fans everywhere, has horned into the limelight recently as a first baseman. The big boy from Texas shows marked agility for his poundage and takes high, wide and difficult throws with the ease of a regular. It's almost a foregone conclusion that Santop and Spunky Joe Lewis will do the catching during the series unless either one is injured or fails to show regular form. This leaves "Bizz" to break in at another point and the way he is slugging the apples, he's too valuable a man to keep out of the game.

"T-A" ALLEN

However, the mantle may fall on Allen, and if it does, the hitting strength may be weakened a bit, but the defense is improved. Absolutely the best fielding first baseman in the Eastern League, Allen is without a rival fielding low and difficult throws. Injuries may keep Stevens out of the game. This will mean that Mackey will be shifted to third and Allen will hold down first.

THE HOME-TOWN TEAM

(Dedicated to the Hilldale Club—1924)

By THOMPSON

We all are deep dyed
With that old civic pride,
   When a product is stamped as home-grown;
We'll swear by a stack,
We've th' best apple-jack,
   And our soil, it's th' world's richest loam.

But listen here, bo,
And 'tis no tale of woe,
   We've a weakness for imported skates;
For here in Kendrick's domain,
We've got guys grabbing fame;
   A legend I now will relate.

A full-grown gazobo,
Was Phil Cockrell, you know,
   Ere he peeped up at old Billy Penn;
Now, then, at Augusta, Ga.,
Is where Phil first saw th' day,
   But Quaker fans say "he's now one of them."

Allen is another from that Cotton State,
Where Sherman's pilgrimage made rebels abate.
   While Mackey, George Johnson and Louis Santop,
Have all wandered here from Sam Houston's plot;
For Texas produced these three knights of swat.
   That fair Philadelphia's been proud to adopt.

Along with a many thousand more,
Maryland's far-famed Eastern Shore,
   Turned out "Judy" of Johnson fame:
Clint Thomas, Joe Lewis and Merven th' red,
And all of th' others are foreign-bred,
   But they're ours, Philadelphians acclaim.

Sure, he may come from Walla Walla,
Or hail from Possum Hollow,
   And to him League Island is unknown;
But we'll rear up just th' same,
And reverberate his name,
   If he's plugging for th' town we call our own.

WORLD SERIES

For Championship of Colored Baseball Clubs

Hilldale versus Kansas City

Philadelphia . . . . October 3rd, 4th
Baltimore . . . . October 5th
Kansas City . . . . October 11th, 12th and 13th
Chicago . . . . October 15th and 16th

(Series to be the best out of nine games)

Starting time for all of the series games, 2 P. M.

Appendix 2: Series Batting Order

Kansas City Monarchs

Batter	AB	R	H	D	T	HR	RBI	SB	BB	AVG.	SLG.
1	42	4	8	1	0	0	2	3	4	.190	.214
2	38	7	10	8	1	0	2	0	1	.263	.526
3	41	4	14	1	0	0	7	2	4	.341	.366
4	38	5	2	1	0	0	1	3	3	.053	.079
5	40	7	12	0	0	0	4	2	1	.300	.300
6	38	4	11	2	0	0	4	1	0	.289	.342
7	35	4	8	2	1	1	5	0	3	.229	.429
8	36	2	5	0	0	0	3	2	4	.139	.139
9	35	1	6	2	0	0	3	0	0	.171	.229
Totals	343	38	76	17	2	1	31	13	20	.222	.292

Monarchs' 3-4-5 power slots totals:

	AB	R	H	D	T	HR	RBI	SB	BB	AVG.	SLG.
	119	16	28	2	0	0	12	7	8	.235	.252

Hilldale Giants

Batter	AB	R	H	D	T	HR	RBI	SB	BB	AVG.	SLG.
1	44	5	10	3	0	0	2	4	3	.227	.295
2	40	5	7	2	0	0	2	2	5	.175	.225
3	41	7	10	0	1	0	2	1	6	.244	.293
4	42	8	14	1	0	0	6	0	4	.333	.357
5	41	5	13	2	1	1	7	0	3	.317	.488
6	38	5	15	5	1	0	4	0	3	.395	.579
7	40	2	5	1	1	0	4	1	1	.125	.200
8	37	4	9	1	0	0	6	3	3	.243	.270
9	35	2	7	0	0	0	2	0	6	.200	.200
Totals	358	43	90	15	4	1	35	11	34	.251	.324

Giants' 3-4-5 power slots totals:

	AB	R	H	D	T	HR	RBI	SB	BB	AVG.	SLG.
	124	20	37	3	2	1	15	1	13	.298	.379

The Monarchs, the best hitting team in baseball, were powerless in the cleanup spot, hitting a woeful .053 average and slugging only .079. Although the Hilldale Club were no dynamos in the meat of their batting order, their slugging percentage for the 3-4-5 spots were 127 points higher than the Monarchs'.

Appendix 3: Game by Game Log

Kansas City Monarchs — 1924

Date	Game #	Site	Opposing Team	Score	Winning Pitcher	Losing Pitcher	W	L
4/27/24	1	Home	St. Louis Stars	5–2	Plunk Drake	Fred "Lefty" Bell	1	0
4/27/24	2	Home	St. Louis Stars	2–1	Bullet Rogan	William Ross	2	0
5/3/24		Chicago	Chicago American Giants	10–3	Plunk Drake	Luis Padrone	3	0
5/4/24		Chicago	Chicago American Giants	10–5	Bullet Rogan	Richard Whitworth	4	0
5/5/24		Chicago	Chicago American Giants	3–2	Cliff Bell	Tom Williams	5	0
5/6/24		Chicago	Chicago American Giants	14–10	Plunk Drake	Richard Whitworth	6	0
5/10/24		Detroit	Detroit Stars	10–1	Cliff Bell	Buck Alexander	7	0
5/12/24		Detroit	Detroit Stars	9–5	Jose Mendez	Andy "Lefty" Cooper	8	0
5/17/24		Home	Indianapolis ABC's	11–5	Jose Mendez	Dizzy Dismukes	9	0
5/18/24		Home	Indianapolis ABC's	19–4	Yellowhorse Morris	Bill Evans	10	0
5/20/24	1	Home	Indianapolis ABC's	5–1	Bullet Rogan	Harold Treadwell	11	0
5/20/24	2	Home	Indianapolis ABC's	13–1	Plunk Drake	Hop Bartlett	12	0
5/24/24		Home	St. Louis Stars	9–3	William Bell	Fred "Lefty" Bell	13	0
5/25/24		Home	St. Louis Stars	6–4	Bullet Rogan	George Mitchell	14	0
5/27/24		Home	St. Louis Stars	2–5	Fred "Lefty" Bell	Plunk Drake	0	1
5/30/24	1	Chicago	Chicago American Giants	5–1	William Bell	Aubrey Owens	15	0
5/30/24	2	Chicago	Chicago American Giants	2–6	Eddie "Buck" Miller	Plunk Drake	0	2
5/31/24		Chicago	Chicago American Giants	0–7	Luis Padrone	Jack Marshall	0	3
6/1/24		Chicago	Chicago American Giants	5–2	Bullet Rogan	Willie Foster	16	0
6/7/24		Chicago	Detroit Stars	2–6	Jack Combs	Plunk Drake	0	4
6/8/24		Chicago	Detroit Stars	2–3	Andy "Lefty" Cooper	Bullet Rogan	0	5
6/13/24		Home	Birmingham Black Barons	6–3	Plunk Drake	Sam Streeter	17	0
6/14/24		Home	Birmingham Black Barons	14–8	William Bell	Bill Mccall	18	0
6/15/24	1	Home	Birmingham Black Barons	8–0	Yellowhorse Morris	Harry Salmon	19	0
6/15/24	2	Home	Birmingham Black Barons	5–1	Bullet Rogan	Fred Daniels	20	0
6/21/24		Home	Detroit Stars	6–0	Cliff Bell	Buck Alexander	21	0
6/22/24	1	Home	Detroit Stars	12–7	Yellowhorse Morris	Jack Combs	22	0
6/22/24	2	Home	Detroit Stars	4–3	Bullet Rogan	Andy "Lefty" Cooper	23	0
6/23/24		Home	Detroit Stars	20–3	Homer Bartlett	Fred Bell	24	0
6/27/24		Home	Cuban Stars	5–3	Plunk Drake	Pasquel Hartinez	25	0
6/28/24		Home	Cuban Stars	10–3	William Bell	Lazaro Salazar	26	0
6/29/24	1	Home	Cuban Stars	9–5	Cliff Bell	Eustaquio Pedroso	27	0
6/29/24	2	Home	Cuban Stars	4–2	Bullet Rogan	Lucas Boada	28	0
7/3/24		Home	Chicago American Giants	7–5	Bullet Rogan	George Harney	29	0
7/4/24	1	Home	Chicago American Giants	12–6	William Bell	Aubrey Owens	30	0

Date	Game #	Site	Opposing Team	Score	Winning Pitcher	Losing Pitcher	W	L
7/4/24	2	Home	Chicago American Giants	7–9	George Harney	Jose Mendez	0	6
7/5/24		Home	Chicago American Giants	2–1	Plunk Drake	Harold Treadwell	31	0
7/6/24		Home	Chicago American Giants	11–13	George Harney	Bullet Rogan	0	7
7/7/24		Birmingham	Birmingham Black Barons	8–3	Yellowhorse Morris	Sam Streeter	32	0
7/8/24		Birmingham	Birmingham Black Barons	3–1	William Bell	Bill Mccall	33	0
7/9/24		Birmingham	Birmingham Black Barons	15–5	Plunk Drake	Dizzy Dismukes	34	0
7/10/24		Birmingham	Birmingham Black Barons	7–10	Bill Mccall	Bullet Rogan	0	8
7/12/24		St. Louis	St. Louis Stars	6–9	Charles Robinson	Yellowhorse Morris	0	9
7/13/24		St. Louis	St. Louis Stars	5–7	William Ross	Plunk Drake	0	10
7/19/24		Detroit	Detroit Stars	5–2	Plunk Drake	Andy "Lefty" Cooper	35	0
7/20/24		Detroit	Detroit Stars	13–2	Bullet Rogan	Lawrence Terrell	36	0
7/21/24		Detroit	Detroit Stars	6–3	William Bell	Buck Alexander	37	0
7/22/24		Detroit	Detroit Stars	6–8	Jack Combs	Cliff Bell	0	11
7/26/24		Cleveland	Cleveland Browns	15–5	Jose Mendez	John Fields	38	0
7/27/24	1	Cleveland	Cleveland Browns	3–7	Herman Gordon	Plunk Drake	0	12
7/27/24	2	Cleveland	Cleveland Browns	5–3	Bullet Rogan	Albert Clark	39	0
7/28/24		Cleveland	Cleveland Browns	15–3	Deke Mothell	Otto Ray	40	0
8/2/24		Chicago	Chicago American Giants	2–5	George Harney	Plunk Drake	0	13
8/3/24		Chicago	Chicago American Giants	8–7	Bullet Rogan	Tom Williams	41	0
8/4/24		Chicago	Chicago American Giants	9–5	William Bell	Eddie "Buck" Miller	42	0
8/5/24		Chicago	Chicago American Giants	0–1	Luis Padrone	Yellowhorse Morris	0	14
8/9/24		Home	Birmingham Black Barons	6–3	Bullet Rogan	Robert Poindexter	43	0
8/10/24		Home	Birmingham Black Barons	7–6	Plunk Drake	Sam Streeter	44	0
8/11/24		Home	Birmingham Black Barons	6–2	William Bell	Bill Mccall	45	0
8/12/24		Home	Birmingham Black Barons	11–0	Yellowhorse Morris	Dizzy Dismukes	46	0
8/16/24		Home	Memphis Red Sox	5–4	Yellowhorse Morris	Hulan "Lefty" Stamps	47	0
8/17/24	1	Home	Memphis Red Sox	7–0	Bullet Rogan	Carl Glass	48	0
8/17/24	2	Home	Memphis Red Sox	4–1	William Bell	Harry Salmon	49	0
8/18/24		Home	Memphis Red Sox	9–2	Plunk Drake	William Spearman	50	0
8/30/24		Chicago	Chicago American Giants	3–5	Ed Rile	William Bell	0	15
8/31/24		Chicago	Chicago American Giants	9–5	Bullet Rogan	Eddie "Buck" Miller	51	0
9/1/24		Chicago	Chicago American Giants	3–5	Luis Padrone	Yellowhorse Morris	0	16
9/2/24		Chicago	Chicago American Giants	2–9	Ed Rile	Bullet Rogan	0	17
9/6/24		Home	St. Louis Stars	5–6	William Ross	William Bell	0	18
9/7/24	1	Home	St. Louis Stars	19–9	Bill Mccall	Sam Crawford	52	0
9/7/24	2	Home	St. Louis Stars	4–7	Slap Hensley	Yellowhorse Morris	0	19
9/8/24		Home	St. Louis Stars	4–2	Bullet Rogan	Slap Hensley	53	0

Date	Game #	Site	Opposing Team	Score	Winning Pitcher	Losing Pitcher	W	L
9/13/24		Home	Chicago American Giants	2–3	Aubrey Owens	Plunk Drake	0	20
9/14/24	1	Home	Chicago American Giants	3–4	Eddie "Buck" Miller	Bullet Rogan	0	21
9/14/24	2	Home	Chicago American Giants	8–1	Bill Mccall	Ed Rile	54	0
9/27/24		Chicago	Chicago American Giants	6–8	Aubrey Owens	Plunk Drake	0	22
9/28/24		Chicago	Chicago American Giants	11–6	Jose Mendez	George Harney	55	0

77 games
7 runs per game.

Note: The Monarchs started off the season by sweeping series from the St. Louis Stars (2 games), Chicago American Giants (4), Detroit Stars (2) and the Indianapolis ABC's (4).
Later in the season they swept the Birmingham Black Barons (4), Detroit Stars (4), Cuban Stars (4) the Black Barons again in August (4), and finally the Memphis Red Sox (4). A total of nine sweeps.
During the season, the Monarchs lost two series. One series to the Chicago American Giants (1 of 3 games) and another series to the Detroit Stars in Comiskey Park, (0 for 2 games).
The Monarch's longest winning streak was 14 games twice. They were undefeated against the Memphis Red Sox, the Cuban Stars and the Indianapolis ABC's.
Twice, they had three-game losing streaks.
During the season the Monarchs scored 71 percent more runs than their opponents; 551 to 323 runs.
20 games in which they scored in double digits. They shutout out their opponents four times.

Hilldale Giants — 1924

Date	Game #	Location	Opposing Team	Score	Winning Pitcher	Losing Pitcher	W	L
4/26/24		Home	Harrisburg Giants	6–4	Nip Winters	Darltie Cooper	1	0
5/1/24		Home	Royal Giants	7–1	Nip Winters	Dick Redding	2	0
5/3/24		Home	Royal Giants	6–5	Nip Winters	Smokey Joe Williams	3	0
5/4/24	1	New York	Lincoln Giants	4–6	John Taylor	Rube Currie	0	1
5/4/24	2	New York	Lincoln Giants	8–5	Red Ryan	Dave "Lefty" Brown	4	0
5/10/24		Home	Washington Potomacs	1–2	String Bean Williams	Nip Winters	0	2
5/15/24		Home	Cuban Stars	7–4	Phil Cockrell	Isidro Fabre	5	0
5/17/24		Home	Cuban Stars	8–7	Red Ryan	Juanelo Mirabal	6	0
5/24/24		Home	Bacharach Giants	4–3	Nip Winters	John Harper	7	0
5/25/24	1	Baltimore	Baltimore Black Sox	1–2	George "Chippy" Britt	Red Ryan	0	3
5/25/24	2	Baltimore	Baltimore Black Sox	11–9	Nip Winters	Hubert Lockhart	8	0
5/30/24	1	Home	Cuban Stars	1–2	Oscar Levis	Red Ryan	0	4
5/30/24	2	Home	Cuban Stars	6–4	Nip Winters	Juanelo Mirabal	9	0
6/1/24	2	Atlantic City	Bacharach Giants	13–3	Phil Cockrell	Hubert Lockhart	10	0

Date	Game #	Location	Opposing Team	Score	Winning Pitcher	Losing Pitcher	W	L
6/2/24		Atlantic City	Bacharach Giants	2–5	John Harper	Red Ryan	0	5
6/3/24		Atlantic City	Bacharach Giants	10–5	Nip Winters	Hubert Lockhart	11	0
6/5/24		Home	Lincoln Giants	2–4	John Taylor	Scrip Lee	0	6
6/7/24		Home	Lincoln Giants	4–10	Dave "Lefty" Brown	Nip Winters	0	7
6/9/24		Wilmington Del	Washington Potomacs	3–1	Red Ryan	Claude "Red" Grier	12	0
6/14/24		New York	Lincoln Giants	9–0	Red Ryan	Dave "Lefty" Brown	13	0
6/15/24	1	New York	Lincoln Giants	4–6	John Taylor	Phil Cockrell	0	8
6/15/24	2	New York	Lincoln Giants	6–1	Nip Winters	Otis "Lefty" Starks	14	0
6/19/24		Home	Baltimore Black Sox	9–7	Red Ryan	George "Chippy" Britt	15	0
6/21/24		Home	Royal Giants	4–2	Nip Winters	Smokey Joe Williams	16	0
6/22/24	1	Baltimore	Baltimore Black Sox	5–4	Red Ryan	William Force	17	0
6/22/24	2	Baltimore	Baltimore Black Sox	1–4	William Force	Rube Currie	0	9
6/26/24		Home	Cuban Stars	5–4	Phil Cockrell	Oscar Levis	18	0
6/28/24		Home	Cuban Stars	5–4	Red Ryan	Juanelo Mirabal	19	0
7/4/24	1	Home	Lincoln Giants	3–4	Bill Holland	Red Ryan	0	10
7/4/24	2	Home	Lincoln Giants	8–6	Phil Cockrell	Fred Daniels	20	0
7/5/24		Home	Lincoln Giants	3–2	Nip Winters	Dave "Lefty" Brown	21	0
7/7/24		Home	Washington Potomacs	4–7	Lewis Hampton	Nip Winters	0	11
7/10/24		Home	Royal Giants	5–1	Nip Winters	Connie Rector	22	0
7/12/24		Home	Royal Giants	2–8	Pud Flournoy	Red Ryan	0	12
7/17/24		Home	Baltimore Black Sox	7–4	Nip Winters	Bob McClure	23	0
7/19/24		Home	Bacharach Giants	13–9	Rube Currie	Otis "Lefty" Starks	24	0
7/20/24	1	Baltimore	Baltimore Black Sox	11–5	Nip Winters	William Force	25	0
7/20/24	2	Baltimore	Baltimore Black Sox	5–6	Bob Mcclure	Scrip Lee	0	13
7/22/24		Wilmington Del	Harrisburg Giants	5–7	Darltie Cooper	Rube Currie	0	14
7/23/24		Wilmington Del	Harrisburg Giants	7–2	Red Ryan	Charlie Henry	26	0
7/24/24		Home	Baltimore Black Sox	10–3	Nip Winters	Bob McClure	27	0
7/26/24		Home	Baltimore Black Sox	7–6	Phil Cockrell	George "Chippy" Britt	28	0
7/31/24		Home	Royal Giants	3–4	Connie Rector	Nip Winters	0	15
8/2/24		Home	Royal Giants	7–4	Phil Cockrell	Pud Flournoy	29	0
8/3/24		Atlantic City	Bacharach Giants	2–3	Hubert Lockhart	Nip Winters	0	16
8/4/24		Atlantic City	Bacharach Giants	8–1	Red Ryan	John Harper	30	0
8/5/24		Atlantic City	Bacharach Giants	2–3	John Harper	Rube Currie	0	17
8/7/24		Home	Harrisburg Giants	5–4	Phil Cockrell	Charlie Henry	31	0
8/9/24		Home	Cuban Stars	6–1	Red Ryan	Juanelo Mirabal	32	0
8/10/24		Washington Dc	Washington Potomacs	7–2	Nip Winters	Claude "Red" Grier	33	0
8/11/24		Washington Dc	Washington Potomacs	1–8	Lewis Hampton	Rube Currie	0	18

Date	Game #	Location	Opposing Team	Score	Winning Pitcher	Losing Pitcher	W	L
8/15/24		Home	Washington Potomacs	4–3	Red Ryan	Claude "Red" Grier	34	0
8/16/24	1	Home	Washington Potomacs	4–2	Nip Winters	Lewis Hampton	35	0
8/16/24	2	Home	Washington Potomacs	9–2	Phil Cockrell	Daltie Cooper	36	0
8/18/24		Wilmington Del	Harrisburg Giants	4–9	Willie Haynes	Red Ryan	0	19
8/21/24		Home	Cuban Stars	11–2	Red Ryan	Oscar Estrada	37	0
8/23/24		Home	Cuban Stars	3–2	Phil Cockrell	Claude "Red" Grier	38	0
8/24/24	1	New York	Lincoln Giants	14–5	Nip Winters	John Taylor	39	0
8/24/24	2	New York	Lincoln Giants	4–5	Dave "Lefty" Brown	Rube Currie	0	20
8/30/24	1	Home	Royal Giants	5–1	Nip Winters	Pud Flournoy	40	0
8/30/24	2	Home	Royal Giants	7–1	Scrip Lee	Smokey Joe Williams	41	0
9/1/24	1	Home	Harrisburg Giants	9–4	Phil Cockrell	Darltie Cooper	42	0
9/1/24	2	Home	Harrisburg Giants	7–3	Red Ryan	Julian Bell	43	0
9/3/24	1	Home	Harrisburg Giants	2–0	Nip Winters	Charles Corbett	44	0
9/3/24	2	Home	Harrisburg Giants	5–6	Daltie Cooper	Scrip Lee	0	21
9/4/24		Home	Washington Potomacs	4–6	Lewis Hampton	Red Ryan	0	22
9/6/24		Home	Washington Potomacs	5–4	Scrip Lee	Wayne Carr	45	0
9/11/24		Home	Bacharach Giants	5–6	John Harper	Scrip Lee	0	23
9/13/24		Home	Bacharach Giants	3–0	Nip Winters	John Harper	46	0
9/27/24		Home	Harrisburg Giants	2–0	Red Ryan	Charlie Henry	47	0
				390				

70 games

5½ runs per game.

Note: The Hilldale club participated in a dozen doubleheaders this season. Four DHs in a row towards the latter part of the season. Their longest winning streak was five (5) games, and their longest losing streak was two (2) games, thrice.

They scored in double-digits in eight ball games. Three times each against the Bacharach Giants and the Baltimore Black Sox. Hubert Lockhart was the victim in three of the games.

Hilldale pitchers hurled four shutouts; two each by Nip Winters and Red Ryan. The Hilldales scored roughly 42 percent more runs (115) than the opposing teams. They won every series except two; against the Lincoln Giants in June, losing both games, against the Bacharach Giants, in August, losing two of three games. In each series, their ace, Nip Winters was defeated.

Appendix 4: Home and Away Splits, by Player and by Pitcher

Home and Away Splits, by Player

KANSAS CITY MONARCHS

Allen, Newt

		G	AB	R	H	D	T	HR	RBI	W	SAC	SB	E	AVG.	SLG.
1924	Home	41	165	31	51	2	3	1	22	19	6	1	16	.309	.376
1924	Away	32	129	21	29	7	0	1	7	22	6	2	11	.225	.302
1924	Neutral	2	8	0	3	1	0	0	3	0	1	0	2	.375	.500
	1924	75	302	52	83	10	3	2	32	41	13	3	29	.275	.348

Bartlett, Homer

		G	AB	R	H	D	T	HR	RBI	W	SAC	SB	E	AVG.	SLG.
1924	Home	1	2	0	0	0	0	0	0	0	0	0	0	.000	.000
	1924	1	2	0	0	0	0	0	0	0	0	0	0	.000	.000

Bell, Cliff

		G	AB	R	H	D	T	HR	RBI	W	SAC	SB	E	AVG.	SLG.
1924	Home	4	9	0	1	0	0	0	0	0	1	1	0	.111	.111
1924	Away	3	8	1	1	0	0	0	0	2	0	0	1	.125	.125
	1924	7	17	1	2	0	0	0	0	2	1	1	1	.118	.118

Bell, William

		G	AB	R	H	D	T	HR	RBI	W	SAC	SB	E	AVG.	SLG.
1924	Home	10	25	1	3	1	0	0	0	0	0	0	0	.120	.160
1924	Away	12	32	2	6	0	0	0	2	2	0	0	0	.188	.188
	1924	22	57	3	9	1	0	0	2	2	0	0	0	.158	.175

Donaldson, John

		G	AB	R	H	D	T	HR	RBI	W	SAC	SB	E	AVG.	SLG.
1924	Home	2	5	1	1	0	0	0	0	0	1	0	0	.200	.200

Drake, Plunk

		G	AB	R	H	D	T	HR	RBI	W	SAC	SB	E	AVG.	SLG.
1924	Home	16	30	3	6	1	0	1	2	1	0	0	2	.200	.333
1924	Away	10	28	2	10	2	1	0	4	1	1	1	2	.357	.500
1924	Neutral	1	1	0	0	0	0	0	0	0	0	0	1	.000	.000
	1924	27	59	5	16	3	1	1	6	2	1	1	5	.271	.407

Duncan, Frank

		G	AB	R	H	D	T	HR	RBI	W	SAC	SB	E	AVG.	SLG.
1924	Home	36	126	34	37	5	1	0	23	19	4	2	4	.294	.349
1924	Away	32	113	17	28	5	2	0	14	16	7	4	1	.248	.327
1924	Neutral	2	8	0	1	0	0	0	0	0	0	0	0	.125	.125
	1924	**70**	**247**	**51**	**66**	**10**	**3**	**0**	**37**	**35**	**11**	**6**	**5**	**.267**	**.332**

Green, Willie

		G	AB	R	H	D	T	HR	RBI	W	SAC	SB	E	AVG.	SLG.
1924	Away	1	5	0	2	0	0	0	1	0	0	0	1	.400	.400

Hawkins, Lem

		G	AB	R	H	D	T	HR	RBI	W	SAC	SB	E	AVG.	SLG.
1924	Home	41	168	44	53	3	6	0	19	18	2	0	7	.315	.405
1924	Away	20	96	13	22	4	0	0	8	5	0	1	3	.229	.271
1924	Neutral	2	8	1	1	0	0	0	0	2	0	1	1	.125	.125
	1924	**63**	**272**	**58**	**76**	**7**	**6**	**0**	**27**	**25**	**2**	**2**	**11**	**.279**	**.349**

Hill, Fred

		G	AB	R	H	D	T	HR	RBI	W	SAC	SB	E	AVG.	SLG.
1924	Away	2	7	1	1	1	0	0	0	0	0	0	0	.143	.286

Johnson, Heavy

		G	AB	R	H	D	T	HR	RBI	W	SAC	SB	E	AVG.	SLG.
1924	Home	37	126	29	47	7	4	1	29	19	3	0	0	.373	.516
1924	Away	33	140	31	54	12	3	4	33	5	5	2	1	.386	.600
1924	Neutral	2	6	0	0	0	0	0	0	1	0	0	0	.000	.000
	1924	**72**	**272**	**60**	**101**	**19**	**7**	**5**	**62**	**25**	**8**	**2**	**1**	**.371**	**.548**

Joseph, Newt

		G	AB	R	H	D	T	HR	RBI	W	SAC	SB	E	AVG.	SLG.
1924	Home	37	137	26	47	12	4	0	28	9	4	0	7	.343	.489
1924	Away	34	134	32	52	9	1	4	32	12	3	2	7	.388	.560
1924	Neutral	2	8	2	2	0	1	0	0	0	0	0	2	.250	.500
	1924	**73**	**279**	**60**	**101**	**21**	**6**	**4**	**60**	**21**	**7**	**2**	**16**	**.362**	**.523**

Manese, Ed

		G	AB	R	H	D	T	HR	RBI	W	SAC	SB	E	AVG.	SLG.
1924	Away	1	4	2	0	0	0	0	0	0	0	0	0	.000	.000

Marshall, Jack

		G	AB	R	H	D	T	HR	RBI	W	SAC	SB	E	AVG.	SLG.
1924	Home	2	4	0	0	0	0	0	0	0	0	0	0	.000	.000
1924	Away	2	6	0	2	1	0	0	2	2	0	0	0	.333	.500
	1924	**4**	**10**	**0**	**2**	**1**	**0**	**0**	**2**	**2**	**0**	**0**	**0**	**.200**	**.300**

McCall, "Bill"

		G	AB	R	H	D	T	HR	RBI	W	SAC	SB	E	AVG.	SLG.
1924	Home	2	4	2	1	0	0	0	0	0	0	0	0	.250	.250
1924	Away	1	2	1	1	0	0	0	0	0	0	0	0	.500	.500
	1924	**3**	**6**	**3**	**2**	**0**	**0**	**0**	**0**	**0**	**0**	**0**	**0**	**.333**	**.333**

McNair, Hurley

		G	AB	R	H	D	T	HR	RBI	W	SAC	SB	E	AVG.	SLG.
1924	Home	41	144	37	53	3	4	1	28	17	4	4	1	.368	.465
1924	Away	29	123	28	44	7	2	7	27	8	2	1	1	.358	.618
1924	Neutral	2	8	0	0	0	0	0	0	0	0	0	0	.000	.000
	1924	**72**	**275**	**65**	**97**	**10**	**6**	**8**	**55**	**25**	**6**	**5**	**2**	**.353**	**.520**

Mendez, Jose

		G	AB	R	H	D	T	HR	RBI	W	SAC	SB	E	AVG.	SLG.
1924	Home	7	12	4	2	1	0	1	1	3	0	0	0	.167	.500
1924	Away	7	9	2	3	1	0	0	0	0	0	0	1	.333	.444
1924	Neutral	1	2	0	0	0	0	0	0	0	0	0	0	.000	.000
	1924	15	23	6	5	2	0	1	1	3	0	0	1	.217	.435

Moore, Dobie

		G	AB	R	H	D	T	HR	RBI	W	SAC	SB	E	AVG.	SLG.
1924	Home	41	157	40	59	11	8	2	31	10	5	1	22	.376	.586
1924	Away	34	144	28	51	11	3	3	22	13	2	2	5	.354	.535
1924	Neutral	2	8	0	1	0	0	0	0	0	0	0	0	.125	.125
	1924	77	309	68	111	22	11	5	53	23	7	3	27	.359	.550

Morris, Yellowhorse

		G	AB	R	H	D	T	HR	RBI	W	SAC	SB	E	AVG.	SLG.
1924	Home	10	22	6	6	0	1	0	2	3	1	0	2	.273	.364
1924	Away	8	17	2	2	0	1	0	1	1	1	0	2	.118	.235
	1924	18	39	8	8	0	2	0	3	4	2	0	4	.205	.308

Mothell, Deke

		G	AB	R	H	D	T	HR	RBI	W	SAC	SB	E	AVG.	SLG.
1924	Home	38	130	35	46	7	6	0	27	15	4	1	3	.354	.500
1924	Away	30	106	15	23	4	1	0	10	18	6	1	2	.217	.274
1924	Neutral	2	7	0	0	0	0	0	0	1	0	0	0	.000	.000
	1924	70	243	50	69	11	7	0	37	34	10	2	5	.284	.387

Rogan, Bullet

		G	AB	R	H	D	T	HR	RBI	W	SAC	SB	E	AVG.	SLG.
1924	Home	26	72	17	29	3	4	1	20	6	0	1	2	.403	.597
1924	Away	22	78	14	33	7	2	4	23	7	2	3	1	.423	.718
1924	Neutral	2	5	1	2	0	0	0	1	0	0	0	0	.400	.400
	1924	50	155	32	64	10	6	5	44	13	2	4	3	.413	.652

Sweatt, George

		G	AB	R	H	D	T	HR	RBI	W	SAC	SB	E	AVG.	SLG.
1924	Home	14	35	4	5	1	0	0	2	3	1	0	0	.143	.171
1924	Away	19	81	21	27	4	2	3	14	6	1	1	0	.333	.543
1924	Neutral	1	2	0	0	0	0	0	0	0	0	0	0	.000	.000
	1924	34	118	25	32	5	2	3	16	9	2	1	0	.271	.424

Williams, Henry

		G	AB	R	H	D	T	HR	RBI	W	SAC	SB	E	AVG.	SLG.
1924	Away	1	4	0	0	0	0	0	0	0	0	0	0	.000	.000

HILLDALE GIANTS

Allen, Tom

		G	AB	R	H	D	T	HR	RBI	W	SAC	SB	E	AVG.	SLG.
1924	Home	19	46	4	8	1	1	0	1	3	3	1	0	.174	.239
1924	Away	7	15	1	4	1	0	0	2	0	3	0	3	.267	.333
1924	Neutral	2	5	0	1	0	0	0	0	0	0	0	0	.200	.200
	1924	28	66	5	13	2	1	0	3	3	6	1	3	.197	.258

Briggs, Otto

		G	AB	R	H	D	T	HR	RBI	W	SAC	SB	E	AVG.	SLG.
1924	Home	35	138	21	44	11	0	0	10	15	7	8	3	.319	.399
1924	Away	21	82	15	20	1	2	0	3	15	4	3	1	.244	.305
1924	Neutral	2	8	2	1	0	0	0	1	1	0	0	1	.125	.125
	1924	58	228	38	65	12	2	0	14	31	11	11	5	.285	.355

Campbell, Zip

		G	AB	R	H	D	T	HR	RBI	W	SAC	SB	E	AVG.	SLG.
1924	Away	1	1	0	0	0	0	0	0	0	0	0	2	.000	.000

Carr, George

		G	AB	R	H	D	T	HR	RBI	W	SAC	SB	E	AVG.	SLG.
1924	Home	31	100	23	33	11	3	1	15	3	3	9	7	.330	.530
1924	Away	20	69	13	19	2	1	0	10	5	2	4	5	.275	.333
1924	Neutral	3	11	0	1	0	0	0	1	0	0	0	0	.091	.091
1924		**54**	**180**	**36**	**53**	**13**	**4**	**1**	**26**	**8**	**5**	**13**	**12**	**.294**	**.428**

Cockrell, Phil

		G	AB	R	H	D	T	HR	RBI	W	SAC	SB	E	AVG.	SLG.
1924	Home	14	36	6	8	0	1	0	4	1	2	3	0	.222	.278
1924	Away	6	11	2	3	0	0	0	1	1	3	0	2	.273	.273
1924		**20**	**47**	**8**	**11**	**0**	**1**	**0**	**5**	**2**	**5**	**3**	**2**	**.234**	**.277**

Currie, Rube

		G	AB	R	H	D	T	HR	RBI	W	SAC	SB	E	AVG.	SLG.
1924	Home	3	6	0	3	0	0	0	3	0	0	0	1	.500	.500
1924	Away	6	10	1	1	0	0	0	0	1	0	0	1	.100	.100
1924	Neutral	1	3	0	1	0	0	0	0	0	0	0	0	.333	.333
1924		**10**	**19**	**1**	**5**	**0**	**0**	**0**	**3**	**1**	**0**	**0**	**2**	**.263**	**.263**

Johnson, George

		G	AB	R	H	D	T	HR	RBI	W	SAC	SB	E	AVG.	SLG.
1924	Home	39	128	24	31	6	2	2	13	11	11	3	3	.242	.367
1924	Away	23	89	8	25	7	0	1	15	12	2	1	1	.281	.393
1924	Neutral	2	7	0	0	0	0	0	0	0	0	0	0	.000	.000
1924		**64**	**224**	**32**	**56**	**13**	**2**	**3**	**28**	**23**	**13**	**4**	**4**	**.250**	**.366**

Johnson, Judy

		G	AB	R	H	D	T	HR	RBI	W	SAC	SB	E	AVG.	SLG.
1924	Home	42	151	29	51	15	2	4	33	10	7	4	7	.338	.543
1924	Away	25	102	21	34	6	3	0	12	10	2	6	7	.333	.451
1924	Neutral	3	10	1	5	1	0	0	3	0	0	0	0	.500	.600
1924		**70**	**263**	**51**	**90**	**22**	**5**	**4**	**48**	**20**	**9**	**10**	**14**	**.342**	**.510**

Lee, Scrip

		G	AB	R	H	D	T	HR	RBI	W	SAC	SB	E	AVG.	SLG.
1924	Home	5	11	0	5	0	0	0	3	0	1	0	2	.455	.455
1924	Away	2	5	0	1	0	0	0	0	0	0	0	0	.200	.200
1924	Neutral	1	1	0	0	0	0	0	0	0	0	0	0	.000	.000
1924		**8**	**17**	**0**	**6**	**0**	**0**	**0**	**3**	**0**	**1**	**0**	**2**	**.353**	**.353**

Lewis, Joe

		G	AB	R	H	D	T	HR	RBI	W	SAC	SB	E	AVG.	SLG.
1924	Home	13	40	7	12	5	1	0	5	4	0	3	3	.300	.475
1924	Away	11	39	8	15	6	0	0	4	2	2	0	2	.385	.538
1924	Neutral	3	5	0	1	0	0	0	0	1	0	0	0	.200	.200
1924		**27**	**84**	**15**	**28**	**11**	**1**	**0**	**9**	**7**	**2**	**3**	**5**	**.333**	**.488**

Mackey, Biz

		G	AB	R	H	D	T	HR	RBI	W	SAC	SB	E	AVG.	SLG.
1924	Home	42	164	27	56	11	1	2	21	8	4	4	19	.341	.457
1924	Away	25	107	23	35	8	2	2	19	6	3	4	7	.327	.495
1924	Neutral	3	9	0	2	0	0	0	1	0	0	0	0	.222	.222
1924		**70**	**280**	**50**	**93**	**19**	**3**	**4**	**41**	**14**	**7**	**8**	**26**	**.332**	**.464**

Ryan, Red

		G	AB	R	H	D	T	HR	RBI	W	SAC	SB	E	AVG.	SLG.
1924	Home	16	42	4	7	0	0	0	0	2	1	2	2	.167	.167
1924	Away	10	30	1	5	1	0	0	3	0	3	1	1	.167	.200
1924	Neutral	2	5	1	0	0	0	0	0	1	0	0	0	.000	.000
	1924	28	77	6	12	1	0	0	3	3	4	3	3	.156	.169

Santop, Louis

		G	AB	R	H	D	T	HR	RBI	W	SAC	SB	E	AVG.	SLG.
1924	Home	32	114	16	34	6	2	2	16	6	3	4	6	.298	.439
1924	Away	16	64	12	27	4	0	3	12	3	1	0	2	.422	.625
1924	Neutral	1	3	0	1	0	0	0	1	0	0	0	0	.333	.333
	1924	49	181	28	62	10	2	5	29	9	4	4	8	.343	.503

Stephens, Paul

		G	AB	R	H	D	T	HR	RBI	W	SAC	SB	E	AVG.	SLG.
1924	Home	14	51	7	9	1	1	0	1	3	3	1	6	.176	.235
1924	Away	12	46	3	9	3	0	1	5	3	3	3	2	.196	.326
1924	Neutral	2	7	1	1	0	0	0	0	0	0	0	2	.143	.143
	1924	28	104	11	19	4	1	1	6	6	6	4	10	.183	.269

Thomas, Clint

		G	AB	R	H	D	T	HR	RBI	W	SAC	SB	E	AVG.	SLG.
1924	Home	42	160	23	44	10	5	4	29	4	9	9	3	.275	.475
1924	Away	25	102	22	33	5	2	4	19	14	0	5	9	.324	.529
1924	Neutral	3	11	1	0	0	0	0	0	0	0	0	0	.000	.000
	1924	70	273	46	77	15	7	8	48	18	9	14	12	.282	.476

Warfield, Frank

		G	AB	R	H	D	T	HR	RBI	W	SAC	SB	E	AVG.	SLG.
1924	Home	42	158	29	49	11	1	1	21	10	10	17	4	.310	.411
1924	Away	25	104	19	34	3	0	1	15	8	8	5	4	.327	.385
1924	Neutral	3	10	1	2	0	0	0	0	0	0	0	1	.200	.200
	1924	70	272	49	85	14	1	2	36	18	18	22	9	.313	.393

Winters, Nip

		G	AB	R	H	D	T	HR	RBI	W	SAC	SB	E	AVG.	SLG.
1924	Home	23	55	8	16	4	0	3	7	0	2	3	0	.291	.527
1924	Away	11	32	3	9	0	1	1	5	2	1	0	3	.281	.438
	1924	34	87	11	25	4	1	4	12	2	3	3	3	.287	.494

Home and Away Splits, by Pitcher

KANSAS CITY MONARCHS

Bartlett, Homer

	G	GS	CG	IP	HA	RS	ER	RPG	ERA	K	BB	WP	HB	SO	SV	W	L	PCT
Home	1	0	0	5.0	4	1	1	1.80	1.80	0	3	0	0	0	0	1	0	1.000

Bell, Cliff

	G	GS	CG	IP	HA	RS	ER	RPG	ERA	K	BB	WP	HB	SO	SV	W	L	PCT
Home	4	2	1	22.0	17	6	6	2.45	2.45	5	7	0	0	1	1	2	0	1.000
Away	4	4	2	21.0	18	10	8	4.29	3.43	2	4	0	2	0	0	2	1	.667
	8	6	3	43.0	35	16	14	3.35	2.93	7	11	0	2	1	1	4	1	.800

Bell, William

	G	GS	CG	IP	HA	RS	ER	RPG	ERA	K	BB	WP	HB	SO	SV	W	L	PCT
Home	8	7	5	58.3	62	28	23	4.32	3.55	26	14	0	0	0	0	6	1	.857
Away	9	7	3	60.3	55	27	18	4.03	2.69	15	14	0	0	0	0	4	1	.800
	17	14	8	118.7	117	55	41	4.17	3.11	41	28	0	0	0	0	10	2	.833

Drake, Plunk

	G	GS	CG	IP	HA	RS	ER	RPG	ERA	K	BB	WP	HB	SO	SV	W	L	PCT
Home	15	10	5	79.3	73	34	26	3.86	2.95	24	25	0	2	0	0	7	2	.778
Away	10	8	5	65.7	70	42	33	5.76	4.52	32	30	2	4	0	0	4	5	.444
Neutral	1	1	0	3.0	3	5	2	15.00	6.00	3	2	0	0	0	0	0	1	.000
	26	19	10	148.0	146	81	61	4.93	3.71	59	57	2	6	0	0	11	8	.579

Marshall, Jack

	G	GS	CG	IP	HA	RS	ER	RPG	ERA	K	BB	WP	HB	SO	SV	W	L	PCT
Home	2	2	0	8.7	8	4	4	4.15	4.15	1	3	0	0	0	0	0	0	.000
Away	1	1	0	7.0	7	7	2	9.00	2.57	4	5	0	0	0	0	0	1	.000
	3	3	0	15.7	15	11	6	6.32	3.45	5	8	0	0	0	0	0	1	.000

McCall, Bill

	G	GS	CG	IP	HA	RS	ER	RPG	ERA	K	BB	WP	HB	SO	SV	W	L	PCT
Home	2	1	1	10.7	9	2	2	1.69	1.69	6	3	1	0	0	0	2	0	1.000
Away	1	0	0	5.0	4	4	4	7.20	7.20	2	3	0	0	0	0	0	0	.000
	3	1	1	15.7	13	6	6	3.45	3.45	8	6	1	0	0	0	2	0	1.000

McNair, Hurley

	G	GS	CG	IP	HA	RS	ER	RPG	ERA	K	BB	WP	HB	SO	SV	W	L	PCT
Away	1	0	0	2.0	1	0	0	0.00	0.00	2	0	0	0	0	0	0	0	.000

Mendez, Jose

	G	GS	CG	IP	HA	RS	ER	RPG	ERA	K	BB	WP	HB	SO	SV	W	L	PCT
Home	6	1	0	23.0	23	12	10	4.70	3.91	20	1	0	0	0	2	1	1	.500
Away	6	1	0	16.0	12	6	4	3.37	2.25	8	4	0	0	0	0	3	0	1.000
Neutral	1	0	0	5.0	3	1	1	1.80	1.80	3	0	0	0	0	0	0	0	.000
	13	2	0	44.0	38	19	15	3.89	3.07	31	5	0	0	0	2	4	1	.800

Morris, Yellowhorse

	G	GS	CG	IP	HA	RS	ER	RPG	ERA	K	BB	WP	HB	SO	SV	W	L	PCT
Home	9	6	3	52.0	40	20	17	3.46	2.94	10	13	0	2	2	0	5	1	.833
Away	9	3	1	35.3	32	26	19	6.62	4.84	14	15	0	1	0	1	1	3	.250
	18	9	4	87.3	72	46	36	4.74	3.71	24	28	0	3	2	1	6	4	.600

Mothell, Deke

	G	GS	CG	IP	HA	RS	ER	RPG	ERA	K	BB	WP	HB	SO	SV	W	L	PCT
Away	1	1	1	9.0	10	3	3	3.00	3.00	0	0	0	0	0	0	1	0	1.000

Rogan, Bullet

	G	GS	CG	IP	HA	RS	ER	RPG	ERA	K	BB	WP	HB	SO	SV	W	L	PCT
Home	13	12	10	94.0	78	41	25	3.93	2.39	56	23	2	1	1	0	10	2	.833
Away	9	9	7	73.0	68	41	25	5.05	3.08	40	33	0	0	0	0	6	2	.750
Neutral	1	1	1	9.0	8	3	3	3.00	3.00	5	1	0	0	0	0	0	1	.000
	23	22	18	176.0	154	85	53	4.35	2.71	101	57	2	1	1	0	16	5	.762

HILLDALE GIANTS

Campbell, Zip

	G	GS	CG	IP	HA	RS	ER	RPG	ERA	K	BB	WP	HB	SO	SV	W	L	PCT
Away	1	1	0	3.0	5	4	2	12.00	6.00	2	1	0	0	0	0	0	0	.000

Cockrell, Phil

	G	GS	CG	IP	HA	RS	ER	RPG	ERA	K	BB	WP	HB	SO	SV	W	L	PCT
Home	12	12	8	93.7	78	46	39	4.42	3.75	39	23	1	2	0	0	9	0	1.000
Away	4	3	1	22.0	22	13	12	5.32	4.91	10	9	0	0	0	0	1	1	.500
	16	15	9	115.7	100	59	51	4.59	3.97	49	32	1	2	0	0	10	1	0.909

Currie, Rube

	G	GS	CG	IP	HA	RS	ER	RPG	ERA	K	BB	WP	HB	SO	SV	W	L	PCT
Home	4	2	0	16.3	18	11	6	6.06	3.31	8	2	0	0	0	0	1	0	1.000
Away	5	3	2	29.3	39	18	8	5.52	2.45	8	8	1	0	0	0	0	5	.000
Neutral	2	1	1	10.7	14	10	8	8.44	6.75	3	2	0	0	0	0	0	1	.000
	11	6	3	56.3	71	39	22	6.23	3.51	19	12	1	0	0	0	1	6	0.143

Lee, Scrip

	G	GS	CG	IP	HA	RS	ER	RPG	ERA	K	BB	WP	HB	SO	SV	W	L	PCT
Home	4	2	2	26.0	24	11	9	3.81	3.12	9	4	0	0	0	0	2	2	0.500
Away	3	0	0	11.0	9	5	5	4.09	4.09	3	1	0	1	0	0	0	2	.000
Neutral	1	0	0	1.7	2	2	0	10.80	0.00	0	0	0	0	0	0	0	0	.000
	8	2	2	38.7	35	18	14	4.19	3.26	12	5	0	1	0	0	2	4	0.333

Pritchett, Wilbur

	G	GS	CG	IP	HA	RS	ER	RPG	ERA	K	BB	WP	HB	SO	SV	W	L	PCT
Home	1	0	0	1.0	1	0	0	0.00	0.00	0	1	0	0	0	0	0	0	.000

Ryan, Red

	G	GS	CG	IP	HA	RS	ER	RPG	ERA	K	BB	WP	HB	SO	SV	W	L	PCT
Home	15	12	9	118.7	117	45	38	3.41	2.88	52	14	1	1	2	1	9	4	.692
Away	9	8	6	68.0	68	28	12	3.71	1.59	29	14	0	0	0	0	4	2	.667
Neutral	2	2	1	12.3	16	6	4	4.38	2.92	6	1	0	0	0	0	1	1	.500
	26	22	16	199.0	201	79	54	3.57	2.44	87	29	1	1	2	1	14	7	.667

Winters, Nip

	G	GS	CG	IP	HA	RS	ER	RPG	ERA	K	BB	WP	HB	SO	SV	W	L	PCT
Home	20	16	14	144.0	118	49	32	3.06	2.00	76	33	2	1	1	2	13	4	.765
Away	9	8	7	64.0	52	27	18	3.80	2.53	38	22	1	0	1	0	7	1	.875
	29	24	21	208.0	170	76	50	3.29	2.16	114	55	3	1	2	2	20	5	.800

Appendix 5: Player Performance Against League Competition, by Team

Position Players

Kansas City Monarchs

ABC — Indianapolis ABC's; BBB — Birmingham Black Barons; CAG — Chicago American Giants; CBN — Cleveland Browns; DTS — Detroit Stars; MRS — Memphis Red Sox; SLS — St. Louis Stars.

Allen, Newt

	G	AB	R	H	D	T	HR	RBI	W	SAC	SB	E	AVG.	SLG.
ABC	4	17	3	5	0	1	0	3	2	1	0	0	.294	.412
BBB	12	51	13	17	4	1	1	9	5	2	0	7	.333	.510
CAG	24	93	9	19	2	0	0	3	16	4	2	10	.204	.226
CBN	4	18	5	6	3	0	0	3	4	2	1	1	.333	.500
CSW	4	14	5	7	0	0	0	4	4	0	0	0	.500	.500
DTS	12	52	8	11	1	0	1	5	6	2	0	5	.212	.288
MRS	4	17	2	5	0	0	0	2	1	0	0	1	.294	.294
SLS	11	40	7	13	0	1	0	3	3	2	0	5	.325	.375
	75	302	52	83	10	3	2	32	41	13	3	29	.275	.348

Bartlett, Homer

	G	AB	R	H	D	T	HR	RBI	W	SAC	SB	E	AVG.	SLG.
DTS	1	2	0	0	0	0	0	0	0	0	0	0	.000	.000

Bell, Cliff

	G	AB	R	H	D	T	HR	RBI	W	SAC	SB	E	AVG.	SLG.
ABC	1	2	0	0	0	0	0	0	0	0	0	0	.000	.000
CAG	2	4	1	1	0	0	0	0	1	1	0	1	.250	.250
CSW	1	2	0	0	0	0	0	0	0	0	0	0	.000	.000
DTS	3	9	0	1	0	0	0	0	1	0	1	0	.111	.111
	7	17	1	2	0	0	0	0	2	1	1	1	.118	.118

Bell, William

	G	AB	R	H	D	T	HR	RBI	W	SAC	SB	E	AVG.	SLG.
BBB	5	10	0	1	0	0	0	0	0	0	0	0	.100	.100
CAG	8	21	1	4	0	0	0	1	2	0	0	0	.190	.190
CSW	1	4	0	0	0	0	0	0	0	0	0	0	.000	.000
DTS	2	7	0	0	0	0	0	0	0	0	0	0	.000	.000
MRS	1	3	0	1	0	0	0	0	0	0	0	0	.333	.333
SLS	5	12	2	3	1	0	0	1	0	0	0	0	.250	.333
	22	57	3	9	1	0	0	2	2	0	0	0	.158	.175

Donaldson, John

	G	AB	R	H	D	T	HR	RBI	W	SAC	SB	E	AVG.	SLG.
SLS	2	5	1	1	0	0	0	0	0	1	0	0	.200	.200

Drake, Plunk

	G	AB	R	H	D	T	HR	RBI	W	SAC	SB	E	AVG.	SLG.
ABC	1	4	1	2	1	0	0	1	0	0	0	0	.500	.750
BBB	4	12	1	3	0	1	0	1	0	0	0	0	.250	.417
CAG	9	19	0	7	2	0	0	3	1	1	0	4	.368	.474
CBN	1	3	0	1	0	0	0	0	0	0	1	0	.333	.333
CSW	1	3	1	0	0	0	0	0	1	0	0	0	.000	.000
DTS	3	7	1	1	0	0	0	0	0	0	0	1	.143	.143
MRS	2	5	0	0	0	0	0	0	0	0	0	0	.000	.000
SLS	6	6	1	2	0	0	1	1	0	0	0	0	.333	.833
	27	59	5	16	3	1	1	6	2	1	1	5	.271	.407

Duncan, Frank

	G	AB	R	H	D	T	HR	RBI	W	SAC	SB	E	AVG.	SLG.
ABC	4	16	5	5	1	0	0	3	2	1	0	1	.313	.375
BBB	12	46	13	14	2	0	0	8	5	0	3	1	.304	.348
CAG	24	81	18	24	3	3	0	13	14	5	1	2	.296	.407
CBN	4	15	2	4	1	0	0	1	3	1	1	0	.267	.333
CSW	4	14	2	3	0	0	0	2	1	0	0	1	.214	.214
DTS	12	38	5	8	2	0	0	4	6	4	0	0	.211	.263
MRS	3	9	2	2	0	0	0	1	2	0	0	0	.222	.222
SLS	7	28	4	6	1	0	0	5	2	0	1	0	.214	.250
	70	247	51	66	10	3	0	37	35	11	6	5	.267	.332

Green, Willie

	G	AB	R	H	D	T	HR	RBI	W	SAC	SB	E	AVG.	SLG.
CAG	1	5	0	2	0	0	0	1	0	0	0	1	.400	.400

Hawkins, Lem

	G	AB	R	H	D	T	HR	RBI	W	SAC	SB	E	AVG.	SLG.
ABC	4	15	5	7	1	0	0	3	3	1	0	0	.467	.533
BBB	8	35	8	10	0	1	0	3	1	0	0	0	.286	.343
CAG	21	94	17	20	1	1	0	7	9	0	0	6	.213	.245
CBN	3	13	3	4	1	0	0	2	1	0	1	0	.308	.385
CSW	4	17	3	5	1	0	0	2	1	0	0	2	.294	.353
DTS	8	37	8	9	1	2	0	3	5	0	1	2	.243	.378
MRS	4	18	4	8	1	2	0	4	1	0	0	0	.444	.722
SLS	11	43	10	13	1	0	0	3	4	1	0	1	.302	.326
	63	272	58	76	7	6	0	27	25	2	2	11	.279	.349

Hill, Fred

	G	AB	R	H	D	T	HR	RBI	W	SAC	SB	E	AVG.	SLG.
CAG	2	7	1	1	1	0	0	0	0	0	0	0	.143	.286

Johnson, Heavy

	G	AB	R	H	D	T	HR	RBI	W	SAC	SB	E	AVG.	SLG.
ABC	4	17	7	10	4	0	0	6	1	1	0	0	.588	.824
BBB	9	33	12	14	2	3	1	6	4	1	0	0	.424	.758
CAG	25	101	18	33	9	2	0	19	5	2	1	1	.327	.455
CBN	4	18	4	8	1	0	0	5	1	0	1	0	.444	.500
CSW	4	13	3	5	0	0	0	4	2	0	0	0	.385	.385
DTS	12	42	10	16	2	1	4	14	7	3	0	0	.381	.762
MRS	4	15	2	6	1	0	0	4	1	1	0	0	.400	.467
SLS	10	33	4	9	0	1	0	4	4	0	0	0	.273	.333
	72	272	60	101	19	7	5	62	25	8	2	1	.371	.548

Joseph, Newt

	G	AB	R	H	D	T	HR	RBI	W	SAC	SB	E	AVG.	SLG.
ABC	4	17	6	10	5	2	0	6	0	0	0	2	.588	1.118
BBB	8	30	7	13	0	0	3	11	2	2	0	1	.433	.733
CAG	26	101	19	30	8	2	0	20	8	4	1	4	.297	.416
CBN	4	20	4	9	1	0	0	4	1	0	0	2	.450	.500
CSW	4	14	1	2	0	1	0	1	1	0	0	0	.143	.286
DTS	12	49	12	22	5	1	1	12	1	1	1	3	.449	.653
MRS	4	14	3	6	0	0	0	3	1	0	0	0	.429	.429
SLS	11	34	8	9	2	0	0	3	7	0	0	4	.265	.324
	73	279	60	101	21	6	4	60	21	7	2	16	.362	.523

Manese, Ed

	G	AB	R	H	D	T	HR	RBI	W	SAC	SB	E	AVG.	SLG.
CAG	1	4	2	0	0	0	0	0	0	0	0	0	.000	.000

Marshall, Jack

	G	AB	R	H	D	T	HR	RBI	W	SAC	SB	E	AVG.	SLG.
BBB	1	3	0	0	0	0	0	0	0	0	0	0	.000	.000
CAG	2	6	0	2	1	0	0	2	2	0	0	0	.333	.500
SLS	1	1	0	0	0	0	0	0	0	0	0	0	.000	.000
	4	10	0	2	1	0	0	2	2	0	0	0	.200	.300

McCall, Bill

	G	AB	R	H	D	T	HR	RBI	W	SAC	SB	E	AVG.	SLG.
CAG	2	4	1	2	0	0	0	0	0	0	0	0	.500	.500
SLS	1	2	2	0	0	0	0	0	0	0	0	0	.000	.000
	3	6	3	2	0	0	0	0	0	0	0	0	.333	.333

McNair, Hurley

	G	AB	R	H	D	T	HR	RBI	W	SAC	SB	E	AVG.	SLG.
ABC	4	14	6	4	0	0	0	0	3	1	0	0	.286	.286
BBB	12	45	11	16	1	1	3	12	3	1	1	0	.356	.622
CAG	26	100	21	39	6	2	2	23	12	3	3	1	.390	.550
CSW	4	14	4	6	0	1	0	4	1	0	0	0	.429	.571
DTS	11	47	12	12	0	1	3	7	2	0	0	1	.255	.489
MRS	4	14	2	3	1	1	0	1	1	1	0	0	.214	.429
SLS	11	41	9	17	2	0	0	8	3	0	1	0	.415	.463
	72	275	65	97	10	6	8	55	25	6	5	2	.353	.520

Mendez, Jose

	G	AB	R	H	D	T	HR	RBI	W	SAC	SB	E	AVG.	SLG.
ABC	1	3	2	2	1	0	1	1	0	0	0	0	.667	2.000
BBB	1	1	0	0	0	0	0	0	0	0	0	0	.000	.000
CAG	4	4	1	0	0	0	0	0	0	0	0	0	.000	.000
CBN	2	3	1	1	1	0	0	0	0	0	0	1	.333	.667
DTS	3	5	1	2	0	0	0	0	0	0	0	0	.400	.400
SLS	4	7	1	0	0	0	0	0	3	0	0	0	.000	.000
	15	23	6	5	2	0	1	1	3	0	0	1	.217	.435

Moore, Dobie

	G	AB	R	H	D	T	HR	RBI	W	SAC	SB	E	AVG.	SLG.
ABC	4	16	3	7	3	0	0	3	1	1	0	4	.438	.625
BBB	12	48	11	16	2	2	1	9	3	2	0	5	.333	.521
CAG	26	101	17	32	2	5	0	13	12	1	2	10	.317	.436
CBN	4	19	4	8	3	1	0	5	2	0	1	1	.421	.684
CSW	4	16	6	6	2	0	1	2	1	0	0	2	.375	.688
DTS	12	54	17	22	8	0	3	13	1	1	0	1	.407	.722
MRS	4	15	4	7	1	0	0	3	1	0	0	1	.467	.533
SLS	11	40	6	13	1	3	0	5	2	2	0	3	.325	.500
	77	309	68	111	22	11	5	53	23	7	3	27	.359	.550

Morris, Yellowhorse

	G	AB	R	H	D	T	HR	RBI	W	SAC	SB	E	AVG.	SLG.
ABC	1	4	2	1	0	0	0	0	1	0	0	0	.250	.250
BBB	3	10	1	3	0	1	0	1	1	0	0	0	.300	.500
CAG	6	10	1	0	0	0	0	0	2	0	0	3	.000	.000
CBN	1	2	0	0	0	0	0	0	0	1	0	0	.000	.000
CSW	1	2	0	0	0	0	0	0	0	0	0	0	.000	.000
DTS	3	7	3	3	0	1	0	2	0	0	0	0	.429	.714
MRS	1	2	0	0	0	0	0	0	0	1	0	1	.000	.000
SLS	2	2	1	1	0	0	0	0	0	0	0	0	.500	.500
	18	39	8	8	0	2	0	3	4	2	0	4	.205	.308

Mothell, Deke

	G	AB	R	H	D	T	HR	RBI	W	SAC	SB	E	AVG.	SLG.
ABC	4	16	7	7	1	1	0	4	1	1	0	0	.438	.625
BBB	12	44	12	15	3	1	0	7	5	2	0	1	.341	.455
CAG	21	70	11	12	2	2	0	8	11	1	0	1	.171	.257
CBN	4	16	3	6	2	0	0	2	3	0	0	0	.375	.500
CSW	4	14	3	4	1	0	0	3	1	0	0	0	.286	.357
DTS	12	42	8	13	1	1	0	6	8	2	2	0	.310	.381
MRS	3	10	2	3	1	0	0	2	0	1	0	1	.300	.400
SLS	10	31	4	9	0	2	0	5	5	3	0	2	.290	.419
	70	243	50	69	11	7	0	37	34	10	2	5	.284	.387

Rogan, Bullet

	G	AB	R	H	D	T	HR	RBI	W	SAC	SB	E	AVG.	SLG.
ABC	1	3	1	1	1	0	0	1	0	0	0	0	.333	.667
BBB	7	25	3	8	1	1	1	7	1	0	0	0	.320	.560
CAG	18	52	8	23	5	3	0	12	7	0	1	0	.442	.654
CBN	4	17	4	9	1	1	1	7	1	1	2	1	.529	.882
CSW	1	2	0	0	0	0	0	0	1	0	0	0	.000	.000
DTS	8	23	6	9	0	1	3	10	2	1	0	0	.391	.870
MRS	3	12	4	5	1	0	0	2	0	0	0	1	.417	.500
SLS	8	21	6	9	1	0	0	5	1	0	1	1	.429	.476
	50	155	32	64	10	6	5	44	13	2	4	3	.413	.652

Sweatt, George

	G	AB	R	H	D	T	HR	RBI	W	SAC	SB	E	AVG.	SLG.
BBB	10	39	4	5	0	1	0	2	1	1	0	0	.128	.179
CAG	10	29	8	13	2	1	0	6	3	0	0	0	.448	.586
CBN	4	20	8	6	2	0	1	3	3	0	1	0	.300	.550
DTS	6	24	4	6	1	0	2	4	1	0	0	0	.250	.542
SLS	4	6	1	2	0	0	0	1	1	1	0	0	.333	.333
	34	118	25	32	5	2	3	16	9	2	1	0	.271	.424

Williams, Henry

	G	AB	R	H	D	T	HR	RBI	W	SAC	SB	E	AVG.	SLG.
CAG	1	4	0	0	0	0	0	0	0	0	0	0	.000	.000

Hilldale Giants

BAG — Bacharach Giants; BBS — Baltimore Black Sox; BRG — Brooklyn Royal Giants; CSE — Cuban Stars East; HBG — Harrisburg Giants; LIN — Lincoln Giants; WHP — Washington Potomacs.

Allen, Tom

	G	AB	R	H	D	T	HR	RBI	W	SAC	SB	E	AVG.	SLG.
BAG	2	3	0	0	0	0	0	0	0	1	0	1	.000	.000
BBS	4	11	0	3	1	0	0	1	1	2	0	2	.273	.364
BRG	3	11	3	4	1	1	0	1	1	0	1	0	.364	.636
CSE	3	6	0	0	0	0	0	0	0	1	0	0	.000	.000
HBG	4	8	1	2	0	0	0	0	0	0	0	0	.250	.250
LIN	6	12	0	2	0	0	0	1	0	0	0	0	.167	.167
WHP	6	15	1	2	0	0	0	0	1	2	0	0	.133	.133
	28	66	5	13	2	1	0	3	3	6	1	3	.197	.258

Briggs, Otto

	G	AB	R	H	D	T	HR	RBI	W	SAC	SB	E	AVG.	SLG.
BAG	7	26	4	8	1	0	0	0	4	2	1	1	.308	.346
BBS	9	38	8	13	2	1	0	4	6	2	2	1	.342	.447
BRG	7	29	2	8	2	0	0	1	2	0	1	1	.276	.345
CSE	8	28	7	10	3	0	0	2	5	2	6	0	.357	.464
HBG	9	33	5	6	1	0	0	2	6	2	0	1	.182	.212
LIN	10	43	7	10	2	1	0	2	4	2	1	0	.233	.326
WHP	8	31	5	10	1	0	0	3	4	1	0	1	.323	.355
	58	228	38	65	12	2	0	14	31	11	11	5	.285	.355

Campbell, Zip

	G	AB	R	H	D	T	HR	RBI	W	SAC	SB	E	AVG.	SLG.
HBG	1	1	0	0	0	0	0	0	0	0	0	2	.000	.000

Carr, George

	G	AB	R	H	D	T	HR	RBI	W	SAC	SB	E	AVG.	SLG.
BAG	7	30	8	9	1	0	0	2	2	0	2	1	.300	.333
BBS	7	22	4	4	1	1	0	1	0	2	3	2	.182	.318
BRG	6	20	2	6	1	0	0	3	0	0	1	1	.300	.350
CSE	7	22	7	10	4	1	0	6	1	2	3	2	.455	.727
HBG	7	22	4	9	3	1	1	8	0	1	0	0	.409	.773
LIN	11	34	6	12	2	1	0	5	4	0	3	5	.353	.471
WHP	9	30	5	3	1	0	0	1	1	0	1	1	.100	.133
	54	180	36	53	13	4	1	26	8	5	13	12	.294	.428

Cockrell, Phil

	G	AB	R	H	D	T	HR	RBI	W	SAC	SB	E	AVG.	SLG.
BAG	1	3	2	1	0	0	0	0	1	1	0	1	.333	.333
BBS	2	6	0	0	0	0	0	0	0	0	0	0	.000	.000
BRG	3	8	1	2	0	1	0	1	0	0	1	0	.250	.500
CSE	3	9	2	2	0	0	0	1	1	1	1	0	.222	.222
HBG	3	7	1	2	0	0	0	1	0	1	0	0	.286	.286
LIN	6	10	1	4	0	0	0	2	0	2	1	1	.400	.400
WHP	2	4	1	0	0	0	0	0	0	0	0	0	.000	.000
	20	47	8	11	0	1	0	5	2	5	3	2	.234	.277

Currie, Rube

	G	AB	R	H	D	T	HR	RBI	W	SAC	SB	E	AVG.	SLG.
BAG	2	7	0	3	0	0	0	3	0	0	0	2	.429	.429
BBS	2	3	1	0	0	0	0	0	0	0	0	0	.000	.000
CSE	1	1	0	0	0	0	0	0	0	0	0	0	.000	.000
HBG	1	1	0	1	0	0	0	0	1	0	0	0	1.000	1.000
LIN	2	3	0	0	0	0	0	0	0	0	0	0	.000	.000
WHP	2	4	0	1	0	0	0	0	0	0	0	0	.250	.250
	10	19	1	5	0	0	0	3	1	0	0	2	.263	.263

Johnson, George

	G	AB	R	H	D	T	HR	RBI	W	SAC	SB	E	AVG.	SLG.
BAG	10	34	8	13	5	0	0	6	8	1	1	0	.382	.529
BBS	10	38	6	10	3	0	0	6	3	3	1	0	.263	.342
BRG	8	30	3	7	1	1	1	3	0	1	0	1	.233	.433
CSE	9	26	7	5	0	1	1	3	2	4	0	1	.192	.385
HBG	7	29	2	4	1	0	1	1	2	0	0	0	.138	.276
LIN	12	44	5	12	3	0	0	6	5	1	1	2	.273	.341
WHP	8	23	1	5	0	0	0	3	3	3	1	0	.217	.217
	64	224	32	56	13	2	3	28	23	13	4	4	.250	.366

Johnson, Judy

	G	AB	R	H	D	T	HR	RBI	W	SAC	SB	E	AVG.	SLG.
BAG	10	36	7	11	0	1	1	7	4	1	0	0	.306	.444
BBS	10	38	8	16	6	1	1	8	6	1	0	3	.421	.711
BRG	9	33	6	8	2	1	1	6	1	2	1	1	.242	.455
CSE	9	35	10	13	3	0	1	7	1	0	1	1	.371	.543
HBG	10	37	5	14	2	2	0	4	1	2	7	5	.378	.541
LIN	12	46	9	16	4	0	0	10	6	3	0	4	.348	.435
WHP	10	38	6	12	5	0	0	6	1	0	1	0	.316	.447
	70	263	51	90	22	5	4	48	20	9	10	14	.342	.510

Lee, Scrip

	G	AB	R	H	D	T	HR	RBI	W	SAC	SB	E	AVG.	SLG.
BAG	1	4	0	2	0	0	0	0	0	0	0	2	.500	.500
BRG	1	4	0	2	0	0	0	2	0	0	0	0	.500	.500
HBG	2	5	0	1	0	0	0	0	0	0	0	0	.200	.200
LIN	2	2	0	0	0	0	0	0	0	0	0	0	.000	.000
WHP	2	2	0	1	0	0	0	1	0	1	0	0	.500	.500
	8	17	0	6	0	0	0	3	0	1	0	2	.353	.353

Lewis, Joe

	G	AB	R	H	D	T	HR	RBI	W	SAC	SB	E	AVG.	SLG.
BAG	1	5	1	2	1	0	0	0	0	0	1	1	.400	.600
BBS	4	16	1	5	4	0	0	0	2	0	0	2	.313	.563
BRG	3	10	3	4	2	1	0	1	1	0	0	0	.400	.800
CSE	3	11	2	3	2	0	0	2	0	0	2	0	.273	.455
HBG	6	15	3	8	1	0	0	3	0	2	0	0	.533	.600
LIN	4	14	4	3	1	0	0	1	1	0	0	0	.214	.286
WHP	6	13	1	3	0	0	0	2	3	0	0	2	.231	.231
	27	84	15	28	11	1	0	9	7	2	3	5	.333	.488

Mackey, Biz

	G	AB	R	H	D	T	HR	RBI	W	SAC	SB	E	AVG.	SLG.
BAG	10	45	9	19	3	2	0	8	0	0	0	2	.422	.578
BBS	10	41	12	17	3	0	1	11	4	0	1	6	.415	.561
BRG	9	37	4	8	3	0	1	5	2	0	0	2	.216	.378
CSE	9	30	2	12	2	0	0	5	2	4	1	5	.400	.467
HBG	10	36	9	16	5	0	1	5	1	0	1	0	.444	.667
LIN	12	50	8	11	2	1	0	3	3	3	4	8	.220	.300
WHP	10	41	6	10	1	0	1	4	2	0	1	3	.244	.341
	70	280	50	93	19	3	4	41	14	7	8	26	.332	.464

Ryan, Red

	G	AB	R	H	D	T	HR	RBI	W	SAC	SB	E	AVG.	SLG.
BAG	2	7	0	1	0	0	0	0	0	0	0	0	.143	.143
BBS	5	13	2	1	0	0	0	1	1	1	1	1	.077	.077
BRG	1	2	0	0	0	0	0	0	0	0	0	0	.000	.000
CSE	5	16	0	3	0	0	0	0	0	1	1	1	.188	.188
HBG	6	13	2	3	1	0	0	2	0	1	0	0	.231	.308
LIN	6	15	1	3	0	0	0	0	1	1	1	0	.200	.200
WHP	3	11	1	1	0	0	0	0	1	0	0	1	.091	.091
	28	77	6	12	1	0	0	3	3	4	3	3	.156	.169

Santop, Louis

	G	AB	R	H	D	T	HR	RBI	W	SAC	SB	E	AVG.	SLG.
BAG	10	36	7	13	2	1	2	7	3	1	0	1	.361	.639
BBS	7	27	5	12	0	0	0	3	0	1	2	0	.444	.444
BRG	6	24	4	10	1	0	1	5	2	0	2	1	.417	.583
CSE	5	20	2	4	1	0	0	2	0	0	0	1	.200	.250
HBG	7	24	3	10	4	0	2	6	3	0	0	2	.417	.833
LIN	8	32	5	10	2	0	0	4	1	1	0	1	.313	.375
WHP	6	18	2	3	0	1	0	2	0	1	0	2	.167	.278
	49	181	28	62	10	2	5	29	9	4	4	8	.343	.503

Stephens, Jake

	G	AB	R	H	D	T	HR	RBI	W	SAC	SB	E	AVG.	SLG.
BAG	5	19	2	1	0	0	0	0	2	0	0	1	.053	.053
BBS	2	8	0	2	0	0	0	0	0	0	0	0	.250	.250
BRG	4	16	2	3	1	0	0	0	0	0	0	0	.188	.250
CSE	3	8	2	2	0	0	0	1	2	3	1	4	.250	.250
HBG	8	29	2	3	1	0	1	2	1	2	3	0	.103	.241
LIN	2	9	1	5	2	0	0	3	1	1	0	2	.556	.778
WHP	4	15	2	3	0	1	0	0	0	0	0	3	.200	.333
	28	104	11	19	4	1	1	6	6	6	4	10	.183	.269

Thomas, Clint

	G	AB	R	H	D	T	HR	RBI	W	SAC	SB	E	AVG.	SLG.
BAG	10	37	6	12	2	0	1	5	6	1	1	3	.324	.459
BBS	10	40	10	14	4	3	2	13	6	0	0	1	.350	.750
BRG	9	33	7	13	5	1	2	8	0	4	4	0	.394	.788
CSE	9	34	3	9	1	1	1	5	0	2	1	1	.265	.441
HBG	10	38	5	6	0	0	1	5	3	1	3	0	.158	.237
LIN	12	50	11	16	3	2	1	9	2	1	3	7	.320	.520
WHP	10	41	4	7	0	0	0	3	1	0	2	0	.171	.171
	70	273	46	77	15	7	8	48	18	9	14	12	.282	.476

Warfield, Frank

	G	AB	R	H	D	T	HR	RBI	W	SAC	SB	E	AVG.	SLG.
BAG	10	38	5	7	0	0	0	2	5	2	1	2	.184	.184
BBS	10	40	7	11	2	0	0	5	4	4	3	2	.275	.325
BRG	9	34	6	12	3	0	1	6	1	4	5	0	.353	.529
CSE	9	32	6	10	1	1	0	5	4	3	6	1	.313	.406
HBG	10	41	8	11	1	0	0	3	0	1	2	1	.268	.293
LIN	12	50	10	19	3	0	1	8	3	4	4	3	.380	.500
WHP	10	37	7	15	4	0	0	7	1	0	1	0	.405	.514
	70	272	49	85	14	1	2	36	18	18	22	9	.313	.393

Winters, Nip

	G	AB	R	H	D	T	HR	RBI	W	SAC	SB	E	AVG.	SLG.
BAG	5	14	3	5	0	0	2	3	0	0	0	1	.357	.786
BBS	5	13	2	4	2	0	0	1	1	0	0	0	.308	.462
BRG	6	17	3	4	0	0	1	1	0	0	2	0	.235	.412
CSE	2	4	1	1	1	0	0	0	0	0	1	0	.250	.500
HBG	4	7	1	1	0	1	0	1	0	0	0	0	.143	.429
LIN	6	17	1	6	1	0	1	4	1	2	0	1	.353	.588
WHP	6	15	0	4	0	0	0	2	0	1	0	1	.267	.267
	34	87	11	25	4	1	4	12	2	3	3	3	.287	.494

Pitchers

Kansas City Monarchs

Bartlett, Homer

	G	GS	CG	IP	HA	RS	ER	RPG	ERA	K	BB	WP	HB	SO	SV	W	L	PCT
DTS	1	0	0	5.0	4	1	1	1.80	1.80	0	3	0	0	0	0	1	0	1.000

Bell, Cliff

	G	GS	CG	IP	HA	RS	ER	RPG	ERA	K	BB	WP	HB	SO	SV	W	L	PCT
ABC	1	0	0	3.3	2	0	0	0.00	0.00	0	0	0	0	0	1	0	0	.000
BBB	1	1	0	1.0	3	3	2	27.00	18.00	0	1	0	1	0	0	0	0	.000
CAG	2	1	1	12.0	9	5	4	3.75	3.00	1	4	0	0	0	0	1	0	1.000
CSW	1	1	0	6.7	4	3	3	4.05	4.05	2	2	0	0	0	0	1	0	1.000
DTS	3	3	2	20.0	17	5	5	2.25	2.25	4	4	0	1	1	0	2	1	0.667
	8	6	3	43.0	35	16	14	3.35	2.93	7	11	0	2	1	1	4	1	0.800

Bell, William

	G	GS	CG	IP	HA	RS	ER	RPG	ERA	K	BB	WP	HB	SO	SV	W	L	PCT
BBB	4	3	1	23.7	28	9	9	3.42	3.42	8	7	0	0	0	0	3	0	1.000
CAG	6	5	3	38.7	46	24	15	5.59	3.49	14	8	0	0	0	0	3	1	0.750
CSW	1	1	1	9.0	6	3	1	3.00	1.00	4	2	0	0	0	0	1	0	1.000
DTS	2	2	1	16.7	15	7	7	3.78	3.78	2	1	0	0	0	0	1	0	1.000
MRS	1	1	1	7.0	6	1	1	1.29	1.29	5	1	0	0	0	0	1	0	1.000
SLS	3	2	1	23.7	16	11	8	4.18	3.04	8	9	0	0	0	0	1	1	0.500
	17	14	8	118.7	117	55	41	4.17	3.11	41	28	0	0	0	0	10	2	0.833

Drake, Plunk

	G	GS	CG	IP	HA	RS	ER	RPG	ERA	K	BB	WP	HB	SO	SV	W	L	PCT
ABC	1	1	1	7.0	4	1	1	1.29	1.29	2	2	0	0	0	0	1	0	1.000
BBB	3	2	1	23.0	25	11	6	4.30	2.35	6	4	0	0	0	0	3	0	1.000
CAG	9	6	4	53.3	45	26	20	4.39	3.38	21	26	2	3	0	0	3	4	0.429
CBN	1	1	1	8.0	12	7	5	7.88	5.63	7	3	0	0	0	0	0	1	.000
CSW	1	1	1	9.0	11	3	2	3.00	2.00	4	2	0	0	0	0	1	0	1.000
DTS	3	3	1	17.3	17	12	9	6.23	4.67	7	7	0	1	0	0	1	1	0.500
MRS	2	2	1	12.0	12	4	4	3.00	3.00	7	5	0	1	0	0	1	0	1.000
SLS	6	3	0	18.3	20	17	14	8.35	6.87	5	8	0	1	0	0	1	2	0.333
	26	19	10	148.0	146	81	61	4.93	3.71	59	57	2	6	0	0	11	8	0.579

Marshall, Jack

	G	GS	CG	IP	HA	RS	ER	RPG	ERA	K	BB	WP	HB	SO	SV	W	L	PCT
BBB	1	1	0	4.7	4	4	4	7.71	7.71	1	2	0	0	0	0	0	0	.000
CAG	1	1	0	7.0	7	7	2	9.00	2.57	4	5	0	0	0	0	0	1	.000
SLS	1	1	0	4.0	4	0	0	0.00	0.00	0	1	0	0	0	0	0	0	.000
	3	3	0	15.7	15	11	6	6.32	3.45	5	8	0	0	0	0	0	1	.000

McCall, Bill

	G	GS	CG	IP	HA	RS	ER	RPG	ERA	K	BB	WP	HB	SO	SV	W	L	PCT
CAG	2	1	1	12.0	9	5	5	3.75	3.75	8	5	0	0	0	0	1	0	1.000
SLS	1	0	0	3.7	4	1	1	2.45	2.45	0	1	1	0	0	0	1	0	1.000
	3	1	1	15.7	13	6	6	3.45	3.45	8	6	1	0	0	0	2	0	1.000

McNair, Hurley

	G	GS	CG	IP	HA	RS	ER	RPG	ERA	K	BB	WP	HB	SO	SV	W	L	PCT
CAG	1	0	0	2.0	1	0	0	0.00	0.00	2	0	0	0	0	0	0	0	.000

Mendez, Jose

	G	GS	CG	IP	HA	RS	ER	RPG	ERA	K	BB	WP	HB	SO	SV	W	L	PCT
ABC	1	1	0	5.7	8	5	4	7.94	6.35	5	1	0	0	0	0	1	0	1.000
BBB	2	0	0	3.7	2	1	1	2.45	2.45	1	0	0	0	0	1	0	0	.000
CAG	3	0	0	8.0	8	5	4	5.63	4.50	5	3	0	0	0	0	1	1	0.500
CBN	1	1	0	5.7	3	3	2	4.76	3.18	4	1	0	0	0	0	1	0	1.000
DTS	3	0	0	9.0	10	4	4	4.00	4.00	5	0	0	0	0	0	1	0	1.000
SLS	3	0	0	12.0	7	1	0	0.75	0.00	11	0	0	0	0	1	0	0	.000
	13	2	0	44.0	38	19	15	3.89	3.07	31	5	0	0	0	2	4	1	0.800

Morris, Yellowhorse

	G	GS	CG	IP	HA	RS	ER	RPG	ERA	K	BB	WP	HB	SO	SV	W	L	PCT
ABC	1	1	1	9.0	8	4	4	4.00	4.00	0	4	0	2	0	0	1	0	1.000
BBB	3	2	2	26.0	12	0	0	0.00	0.00	7	2	0	0	2	0	3	0	1.000
CAG	6	3	1	22.3	22	18	9	7.25	3.63	6	12	0	0	0	0	0	2	.000
CBN	1	0	0	3.3	2	2	2	5.40	5.40	3	4	0	1	0	1	0	0	.000
CSW	1	0	0	2.3	2	2	2	7.71	7.71	1	1	0	0	0	0	0	0	.000
DTS	3	1	0	12.0	9	6	6	4.50	4.50	3	3	0	0	0	0	1	0	1.000
MRS	1	0	0	6.0	5	2	1	3.00	1.50	2	0	0	0	0	0	1	0	1.000
SLS	2	2	0	6.3	12	12	12	17.05	17.05	2	2	0	0	0	0	0	2	.000
	18	9	4	87.3	72	46	36	4.74	3.71	24	28	0	3	2	1	6	4	0.600

Mothell, Deke

	G	GS	CG	IP	HA	RS	ER	RPG	ERA	K	BB	WP	HB	SO	SV	W	L	PCT
CBN	1	1	1	9.0	10	3	3	3.00	3.00	0	0	0	0	0	0	1	0	1.000

Rogan, Bullet

	G	GS	CG	IP	HA	RS	ER	RPG	ERA	K	BB	WP	HB	SO	SV	W	L	PCT
ABC	1	1	1	7.0	3	1	1	1.29	1.29	10	2	2	0	0	0	1	0	1.000
BBB	3	3	3	26.0	27	14	9	4.85	3.12	14	5	0	0	0	0	2	1	0.667
CAG	9	9	6	69.0	59	44	26	5.74	3.39	32	36	0	1	0	0	5	3	0.625
CBN	1	1	1	9.0	10	3	3	3.00	3.00	5	1	0	0	0	0	1	0	1.000
CSW	1	1	1	7.0	6	2	2	2.57	2.57	4	2	0	0	0	0	1	0	1.000
DTS	3	3	3	25.0	21	8	7	2.88	2.52	14	4	0	0	0	0	2	1	0.667
MRS	1	1	1	9.0	6	0	0	0.00	0.00	8	0	0	0	1	0	1	0	1.000
SLS	4	3	2	24.0	22	13	5	4.88	1.88	14	7	0	0	0	0	3	0	1.000
	23	22	18	176.0	154	85	53	4.35	2.71	101	57	2	1	1	0	16	5	0.762

Hilldale Giants

Campbell, Zip

	G	GS	CG	IP	HA	RS	ER	RPG	ERA	K	BB	WP	HB	SO	SV	W	L	PCT
HBG	1	1	0	3.0	5	4	2	12.00	6.00	2	1	0	0	0	0	0	0	.000

Cockrell, Phil

	G	GS	CG	IP	HA	RS	ER	RPG	ERA	K	BB	WP	HB	SO	SV	W	L	PCT
BAG	2	2	1	10.7	14	8	8	6.75	6.75	4	5	0	0	0	0	1	0	1.000
BBS	2	2	0	13.0	12	11	7	7.62	4.85	9	4	0	1	0	0	1	0	1.000
BRG	2	2	1	17.3	20	9	8	4.67	4.15	6	1	1	0	0	0	1	0	1.000
CSE	3	3	3	27.0	19	10	8	3.33	2.67	15	4	0	1	0	0	3	0	1.000
HBG	2	2	2	18.0	13	8	8	4.00	4.00	6	6	0	0	0	0	2	0	1.000
LIN	4	3	1	20.7	17	11	10	4.79	4.35	8	7	0	0	0	0	1	1	0.500
WHP	1	1	1	9.0	5	2	2	2.00	2.00	1	5	0	0	0	0	1	0	1.000
	16	15	9	115.7	100	59	51	4.59	3.97	49	32	1	2	0	0	10	1	0.909

Currie, Rube

	G	GS	CG	IP	HA	RS	ER	RPG	ERA	K	BB	WP	HB	SO	SV	W	L	PCT
BAG	2	1	1	15.0	15	7	1	4.20	0.60	7	2	1	0	0	0	1	1	0.500
BBS	1	1	1	8.0	7	4	4	4.50	4.50	1	1	0	0	0	0	0	1	.000
CSE	1	1	0	3.3	8	5	5	13.50	13.50	2	2	0	0	0	0	0	0	.000
HBG	3	1	0	12.7	16	7	5	4.97	3.55	2	2	0	0	0	0	0	1	.000
LIN	2	1	0	6.3	12	6	1	8.53	1.42	3	3	0	0	0	0	0	2	.000
WHP	2	1	1	11.0	13	10	6	8.18	4.91	4	2	0	0	0	0	0	1	.000
	11	6	3	56.3	71	39	22	6.23	3.51	19	12	1	0	0	0	1	6	0.143

Lee, Scrip

	G	GS	CG	IP	HA	RS	ER	RPG	ERA	K	BB	WP	HB	SO	SV	W	L	PCT
BAG	1	1	1	10.0	12	6	4	5.40	3.60	3	1	0	0	0	0	0	1	.000
BBS	1	0	0	1.0	3	2	2	18.00	18.00	1	0	0	1	0	0	0	1	.000
BRG	1	1	1	9.0	5	1	1	1.00	1.00	2	3	0	0	0	0	1	0	1.000
HBG	2	0	0	7.7	6	4	2	4.70	2.35	0	0	0	0	0	0	0	1	.000
LIN	2	0	0	7.3	9	5	5	6.14	6.14	2	1	0	0	0	0	0	1	.000
WHP	1	0	0	3.7	0	0	0	0.00	0.00	4	0	0	0	0	0	1	0	1.000
	8	2	2	38.7	35	18	14	4.19	3.26	12	5	0	1	0	0	2	4	0.333

Pritchett, Wilbur

	G	GS	CG	IP	HA	RS	ER	RPG	ERA	K	BB	WP	HB	SO	SV	W	L	PCT
BRG	1	0	0	1.0	1	0	0	0.00	0.00	0	1	0	0	0	0	0	0	.000

Ryan, Red

	G	GS	CG	IP	HA	RS	ER	RPG	ERA	K	BB	WP	HB	SO	SV	W	L	PCT
BAG	2	2	2	17.0	14	6	2	3.18	1.06	7	5	0	0	0	0	1	1	0.500
BBS	6	5	3	44.3	46	21	13	4.26	2.64	17	6	0	0	0	1	3	1	0.750
BRG	1	1	0	8.0	15	8	7	9.00	7.88	3	0	0	0	0	0	0	1	.000
CSE	4	3	3	32.3	26	7	5	1.95	1.39	16	9	0	0	0	0	3	1	0.750
HBG	5	4	3	33.3	34	13	12	3.51	3.24	15	2	1	1	1	0	3	1	0.750
LIN	5	4	3	35.0	33	14	8	3.60	2.06	13	5	0	0	1	0	2	1	0.667
WHP	3	3	2	29.0	33	10	7	3.10	2.17	16	2	0	0	0	0	2	1	0.667
	26	22	16	199.0	201	79	54	3.57	2.44	87	29	1	1	2	1	14	7	0.667

Winters, Nip

	G	GS	CG	IP	HA	RS	ER	RPG	ERA	K	BB	WP	HB	SO	SV	W	L	PCT
BAG	4	4	4	31.0	23	11	9	3.19	2.61	13	7	0	0	1	0	3	1	0.750
BBS	5	3	3	29.7	31	16	11	4.85	3.34	10	5	0	0	0	1	4	0	1.000
BRG	6	5	5	46.7	38	9	9	1.74	1.74	25	11	1	1	0	0	5	1	0.833
CSE	2	1	1	9.3	7	4	2	3.86	1.93	7	1	0	0	0	1	1	0	1.000
HBG	3	2	1	16.0	6	3	3	1.69	1.69	14	6	1	0	1	0	2	0	1.000
LIN	4	4	4	37.0	35	18	9	4.38	2.19	22	13	0	0	0	0	3	1	0.750
WHP	5	5	3	38.3	30	15	7	3.52	1.64	23	12	1	0	0	0	2	2	0.500
	29	24	21	208.0	170	76	50	3.29	2.16	114	55	3	1	2	2	20	5	0.800

Appendix 6: Batter versus Pitcher Match-Ups During the World Series

Monarchs' Cliff Bell, rhp

Batter	AVG	AB	R	H	2b	3b	HR	BI	SO	BB	SLG	OBP
Joe Lewis	1.000	1	0	1	0	0	0	0	0	0	1.000	1.000
George Johnson	.750	4	1	3	0	1	0	1	0	1	1.250	.800
Judy Johnson	.250	4	2	1	0	0	0	0	1	1	.250	.400
Otto Briggs	.200	5	1	1	1	0	0	1	1	0	.400	.200
Bill Campbell	.000	0	1	0	0	0	0	0	0	0	.000	.000
George Carr	.000	2	1	0	0	0	0	0	1	1	.000	.333
Rube Currie	.000	3	0	0	0	0	0	0	1	0	.000	.000
Biz Mackey	.000	5	0	0	0	0	0	0	0	0	.000	.000
Red Ryan	.000	0	0	0	0	0	0	0	0	0	.000	.000
Lou Santop	.000	3	0	0	0	0	0	2	0	0	.000	.000
Jake Stephens	.000	1	0	0	0	0	0	0	0	0	.000	.000
Clint Thomas	.000	4	0	0	0	0	0	0	0	0	.000	.000
Frank Warfield	.000	3	0	0	0	0	0	0	0	0	.000	.000
Total	.171	35	6	6	1	1	0	4	4	3	.257	.237

Monarchs' William Bell, rhp

Batter	AVG	AB	R	H	2b	3b	HR	BI	SO	BB	SLG	OBP
George Carr	1.000	2	0	2	0	0	0	1	0	2	1.000	1.000
Lou Santop	.667	6	1	4	0	0	0	0	0	2	.667	.750
Judy Johnson	.417	12	0	5	2	1	0	3	0	0	.750	.417
Frank Warfield	.400	10	3	4	2	0	0	0	0	1	.600	.455
Scrip Lee	.400	5	1	2	0	0	0	1	2	2	.400	.571
Clint Thomas	.300	10	2	3	1	0	0	0	0	2	.400	.417
Biz Mackey	.300	10	3	3	0	0	0	1	0	3	.300	.462
Otto Briggs	.250	12	1	3	0	0	0	0	0	0	.250	.250
Joe Lewis	.200	5	0	1	1	0	0	2	1	0	.400	.200
Tom Allen	.111	9	2	1	0	0	0	0	1	0	.111	.111
George Johnson	.091	11	0	1	1	0	0	0	2	0	.182	.091
Phil Cockrell	.000	0	0	0	0	0	0	0	0	0	.000	.000

Monarchs' William Bell, rhp (cont.)

Batter	AVG	AB	R	H	2b	3b	HR	BI	SO	BB	SLG	OBP
Nip Winters	.000	2	0	0	0	0	0	0	0	1	.000	.333
Red Ryan	.000	0	0	0	0	0	0	0	0	0	.000	.000
Rube Currie	.000	0	0	0	0	0	0	0	0	0	.000	.000
Totals	.309	94	13	29	7	1	0	8	6	13	.404	.393

Monarchs' Plunk Drake, rhp

Batter	AVG	AB	R	H	2b	3b	HR	BI	SO	BB	SLG	OBP
Tom Allen	1.000	1	0	1	0	0	0	1	0	0	1.000	1.000
George Johnson	.500	4	1	2	1	0	0	2	1	0	.750	.500
Frank Warfield	.429	7	0	3	0	0	0	2	0	0	.429	.429
Otto Briggs	.400	5	0	2	0	0	0	0	0	1	.400	.500
Judy Johnson	.375	8	2	3	1	0	0	1	0	0	.500	.375
Clint Thomas	.333	6	3	2	0	0	0	0	1	0	.333	.333
George Carr	.200	5	0	1	0	0	0	1	2	0	.200	.200
Biz Mackey	.000	5	1	0	0	0	0	0	0	2	.000	.286
Joe Lewis	.000	4	0	0	0	0	0	0	0	0	.000	.000
Jake Stephens	.000	1	0	0	0	0	0	0	0	0	.000	.000
Lou Santop	.000	2	0	0	0	0	0	0	0	1	.000	.333
Scrip Lee	.000	0	0	0	0	0	0	0	0	0	.000	.000
Nip Winters	.000	4	1	0	0	0	0	0	1	1	.000	.200
Totals	.269	52	8	14	2	0	0	7	5	5	.308	.333

Monarchs' Bill McCall, lhp

Batter	AVG	AB	R	H	2b	3b	HR	BI	SO	BB	OBP	SLG
Biz Mackey	1.000	1	1	1	0	0	0	1	0	0	1.000	1.000
Otto Briggs	.000	0	1	0	0	0	0	0	0	1	1.000	.000
Frank Warfield	.000	0	1	0	0	0	0	0	0	0	.000	.000
Totals	1.000	1	3	1	0	0	0	1	0	1	1.000	1.000

Monarchs' Jose Mendez, rhp

Batter	AVG	AB	R	H	2b	3b	HR	BI	SO	BB	OBP	SLG
Nip Winters	.400	5	1	2	0	0	0	0	1	3	.625	.400
George Johnson	.333	6	0	2	0	0	0	1	2	1	.429	.333
Biz Mackey	.286	7	1	2	0	1	0	0	0	0	.286	.571
Clint Thomas	.250	4	0	1	0	0	0	1	0	0	.250	.250
Tom Allen	.250	4	0	1	1	0	0	0	0	0	.250	.500
George Carr	.200	5	0	1	0	0	0	0	1	0	.200	.200
Judy Johnson	.167	6	1	1	1	0	0	0	1	0	.167	.333
Otto Briggs	.100	10	1	1	1	0	0	1	0	0	.100	.200
Frank Warfield	.000	7	0	0	0	0	0	1	1	1	.125	.000
Joe Lewis	.000	4	0	0	0	0	0	0	0	0	.000	.000
Lou Santop	.000	3	0	0	0	0	0	0	0	0	.000	.000
Scrip Lee	.000	2	0	0	0	0	0	0	0	0	.000	.000
Phil Cockrell	.000	1	0	0	0	0	0	0	0	0	.000	.000
Totals	.172	64	4	11	3	1	0	4	6	5	.232	.250

Monarchs' Harold Morris, rhp

Batter	AVG	AB	R	H	2b	3b	HR	BI	SO	BB	OBP	SLG
Clint Thomas	1.000	1	0	1	0	0	0	0	0	0	1.000	1.000
Judy Johnson	1.000	1	0	1	0	0	0	0	0	0	1.000	1.000
Frank Warfield	.000	1	0	0	0	0	0	0	0	0	.000	.000
Biz Mackey	.000	1	0	0	0	0	0	0	0	0	.000	.000
George Johnson	.000	1	0	0	0	0	0	0	0	0	.000	.000
Totals	**.400**	**5**	**0**	**2**	**0**	**0**	**0**	**0**	**0**	**0**	**.400**	**.400**

Monarchs' Bullet Rogan, rhp

Batter	AVG	AB	R	H	2b	3b	HR	BI	SO	BB	OBP	SLG
George Carr	.500	4	0	2	0	0	0	1	1	0	.500	.500
Lou Santop	.400	10	1	4	0	0	0	1	0	1	.455	.400
Nip Winters	.400	5	0	2	0	0	0	2	2	0	.400	.400
Judy Johnson	.385	13	2	5	1	0	1	3	0	1	.429	.692
Biz Mackey	.333	12	1	4	0	0	0	0	1	1	.385	.333
Joe Lewis	.333	3	1	1	0	0	0	1	0	0	.333	.333
Otto Briggs	.250	12	1	3	1	0	0	0	0	1	.308	.333
Rube Currie	.250	4	0	1	0	0	0	0	2	0	.250	.250
Frank Warfield	.167	12	1	2	0	0	0	0	2	3	.333	.167
Clint Thomas	.167	12	1	2	0	0	0	0	2	0	.167	.167
George Johnson	.083	12	1	1	0	1	0	0	2	1	.154	.250
Tom Allen	.000	5	0	0	0	0	0	1	2	0	.000	.000
Phil Cockrell	.000	3	0	0	0	0	0	0	0	0	.000	.000
Total	**.252**	**107**	**9**	**27**	**2**	**1**	**1**	**9**	**14**	**8**	**.304**	**.318**
Monarch Pitching Totals	**.251**	**358**	**43**	**90**	**15**	**4**	**1**	**33**	**35**	**35**	**.318**	**.324**

Hilldale's Phil Cockrell, rhp

Batter	AVG	AB	R	H	2b	3b	HR	BI	SO	BB	OBP	SLG
Bullet Rogan	.600	5	1	3	0	0	0	1	0	0	.600	.600
Lem Hawkins	.333	6	1	2	1	0	0	0	0	0	.333	.500
Newt Allen	.250	4	2	1	1	0	0	0	1	1	.400	.500
Hurley McNair	.250	4	2	1	0	0	0	1	1	1	.400	.250
George Sweatt	.250	4	0	1	0	0	0	1	0	0	.250	.250
Newt Joseph	.200	5	2	1	0	0	0	1	1	1	.333	.200
Dobie Moore	.200	5	2	1	0	0	0	1	0	0	.200	.200
Frank Duncan	.000	4	0	0	0	0	0	0	1	0	.000	.000
Heavy Johnson	.000	3	0	0	0	0	0	0	1	1	.250	.000
Totals	**.250**	**40**	**10**	**10**	**2**	**0**	**0**	**5**	**5**	**4**	**.318**	**.300**

Hilldale's Rube Currie, rhp

Batter	AVG	AB	R	H	2b	3b	HR	BI	SO	BB	OBP	SLG
Dobie Moore	.429	7	1	3	0	0	0	0	0	0	.429	.429
Heavy Johnson	.400	5	0	2	1	0	0	0	0	1	.500	.600
Newt Allen	.333	6	0	2	0	0	0	0	0	0	.333	.333
Hurley McNair	.286	7	1	2	0	0	0	1	0	0	.286	.286
Bullet Rogan	.167	6	1	1	0	0	0	0	0	0	.167	.167
Newt Joseph	.143	7	0	1	1	0	0	0	3	1	.250	.286
Frank Duncan	.125	8	0	1	0	0	0	2	0	0	.125	.125
Lem Hawkins	.000	5	0	0	0	0	0	0	0	0	.000	.000
Cliff Bell	.000	3	0	0	0	0	0	0	0	0	.000	.000
Dink Mothell	.000	3	0	0	0	0	0	0	0	0	.000	.000
George Sweatt	.000	1	0	0	0	0	0	0	0	0	.000	.000
Totals	**.207**	**58**	**3**	**12**	**2**	**0**	**0**	**3**	**3**	**2**	**.233**	**.241**

Hilldale's Scrip Lee, rhp

Batter	AVG	AB	R	H	2b	3b	HR	BI	SO	BB	OBP	SLG
George Sweatt	.400	5	0	2	0	1	0	3	0	0	.400	.800
Jose Mendez	.333	3	1	1	0	0	0	0	0	0	.333	.333
Dobie Moore	.300	10	2	3	0	0	0	0	0	0	.300	.300
Bullet Rogan	.300	10	0	3	0	0	0	1	1	1	.364	.300
Newt Allen	.273	11	2	3	2	0	0	2	1	0	.273	.455
Frank Duncan	.250	8	2	2	0	0	0	0	1	2	.400	.250
Heavy Johnson	.250	4	1	1	1	0	0	1	1	0	.250	.500
William Bell	.250	4	0	1	1	0	0	0	1	0	.250	.500
Lem Hawkins	.200	5	0	1	0	0	0	0	1	0	.200	.200
Dink Mothell	.167	6	0	1	1	0	0	2	0	0	.167	.333
Hurley McNair	.125	8	0	1	0	0	0	0	2	1	.222	.125
Newt Joseph	.000	8	1	0	0	0	0	0	2	0	.000	.000
Plunk Drake	.000	0	0	0	0	0	0	0	0	0	.000	.000
Total	.232	82	9	19	5	1	0	9	10	4	.267	.317

Hilldale's Red Ryan, rhp

Batter	AVG	AB	R	H	2b	3b	HR	BI	SO	BB	OBP	SLG
Newt Allen	1.000	2	3	2	2	0	0	0	0	0	1.000	2.000
Bullet Rogan	.750	4	1	3	1	0	0	4	0	0	.750	1.000
Dobie Moore	.333	3	0	1	0	0	0	1	0	0	.333	.333
Heavy Johnson	.333	3	1	1	1	0	0	0	0	0	.333	.667
Newt Joseph	.333	3	1	1	0	0	1	2	1	0	.333	1.333
Hurley McNair	.000	3	0	0	0	0	0	0	1	0	.000	.000
Frank Duncan	.000	3	0	0	0	0	0	0	0	0	.000	.000
Lem Hawkins	.000	2	1	0	0	0	0	0	0	2	.500	.000
William Bell	.000	2	0	0	0	0	0	0	0	0	.000	.000
Cliff Bell	.000	1	0	0	0	0	0	0	1	0	.000	.000
Totals	.308	26	7	8	4	0	1	7	3	2	.357	.577

Hilldale's Nip Winters, lhp

Batter	AVG	AB	R	H	2b	3b	HR	BI	SO	BB	OBP	SLG
Plunk Drake	.500	4	0	2	0	0	0	1	0	0	.500	.500
William Bell	.500	2	1	1	0	0	0	1	0	0	.500	.500
Dobie Moore	.267	15	2	4	0	0	0	2	1	1	.313	.267
Heavy Johnson	.250	12	0	3	0	0	0	1	2	0	.250	.250
George Sweatt	.250	8	0	2	1	1	0	0	2	0	.250	.625
Dink Mothell	.250	4	0	1	0	0	0	0	1	0	.250	.250
Lem Hawkins	.231	13	2	3	0	0	0	0	1	1	.286	.231
Bullet Rogan	.200	15	1	3	0	0	0	1	1	2	.294	.200
Newt Allen	.176	17	1	3	2	0	0	0	2	1	.222	.294
Frank Duncan	.154	13	0	2	1	0	0	0	1	2	.267	.231
Newt Joseph	.133	15	2	2	0	0	0	1	5	1	.188	.133
Hurley McNair	.077	13	0	1	0	0	0	0	3	0	.077	.077
Jose Mendez	.000	6	0	0	0	0	0	0	2	0	.000	.000
Yellowhorse Morris	.000	0	0	0	0	0	0	0	0	0	.000	.000
Cliff Bell	.000	0	0	0	0	0	0	0	0	0	.000	.000
Totals	.197	137	9	27	4	1	0	7	21	8	.241	.241
Hilldale Pitching Totals	.222	343	38	76	17	2	1	31	42	20	.264	.292

Index

245